ISRAEL'S PROPHETIC HERITAGE

Photograph by John H. Popper

JAMES MUILENBURG

ISRAEL'S PROPHETIC HERITAGE

Essays in honor of James Muilenburg

Edited by

Bernhard W. Anderson

and

Walter Harrelson

WIPF & STOCK · Eugene, Oregon

Wipf and Stock Publishers
199 W 8th Ave, Suite 3
Eugene, OR 97401

Israel's Prophetic Heritage
Essays in Honor of James Muilenburg, Edited by
Bernhard W. Anderson and Walter Harrelson
By Anderson, Bernhard W. and Harrelson, Walter
Copyright©1962 by Anderson, Bernhard W.
ISBN 13: 978-1-60899-687-2
Publication date 5/26/2010
Previously published by Harper, 1962

CONTENTS

CONTRIBUTORS vii

ABBREVIATIONS ix

PREFACE xi

I IN THE BEGINNING, *by Walther Eichrodt* 1

II THE PROPHETS AND THE PROBLEM OF CONTINUITY, *by Norman W. Porteous* 11

III THE LAWSUIT OF GOD: A FORM-CRITICAL STUDY OF DEUTERONOMY 32, *by G. Ernest Wright* 26

IV THE BACKGROUND OF JUDGES 17-18, *by Martin Noth* 68

V THE PROPHETIC CALL OF SAMUEL, *by Murray Newman* 86

VI THE PROPHET AS YAHWEH'S MESSENGER, *by James F. Ross* 98

VII AMOS AND WISDOM, *by Samuel Terrien* 108

VIII "REJOICE NOT, O ISRAEL!" *by Dorothea Ward Harvey* 116

IX ESSENTIALS OF THE THEOLOGY OF ISAIAH, *by Th. C. Vriezen* 128

X NONROYAL MOTIFS IN THE ROYAL ESCHATOLOGY, *by Walter Harrelson* 147

XI   THE KING IN THE GARDEN OF EDEN: A
     STUDY OF EZEKIEL 28:12-19, *by Herbert
     G. May*   166

XII EXODUS TYPOLOGY IN SECOND ISAIAH,
     by Bernhard W. Anderson   177

XIII THE PROMISES OF GRACE TO DAVID IN
     ISAIAH 55:1-5, *by Otto Eissfeldt*   196

XIV THE SAMARITAN SCHISM IN LEGEND
     AND HISTORY, *by H. H. Rowley*   208

XV   PROPHECY AND THE PROPHETS AT QUM-
     RÂN, *by Millar Burrows*   223
     A BIBLIOGRAPHY OF JAMES MUILEN-
     BURG'S WRITINGS, *by R. Lansing Hicks*   233

CONTRIBUTORS

Bernhard W. Anderson, B.D., M.A., Ph.D., D.D., S.T.D., Dean and Henry Anson Buttz Professor of Biblical Theology, The Theological School, Drew University, Madison, New Jersey.

Millar Burrows, B.D., Ph.D., D.D., Winkley Professor of Biblical Theology, Emeritus, and former Chairman of the Department of Near Eastern Languages and Literatures, Yale University, New Haven, Conn.

Walther Eichrodt, D. Theol., D.D., Professor of Old Testament and History of Religion, University of Basle, Basle, Switzerland.

Otto Eissfeldt, D. Phil., D.D., Professor of Old Testament and History of Semitic Religions, Emeritus, Martin Luther University, Halle-Wittenberg, Halle (Saale), Germany.

Walter Harrelson, B.D., Th.D., Professor of Old Testament, The Vanderbilt University Divinity School, Nashville, Tennessee.

Dorothea Ward Harvey, B.D., Ph.D., Assistant Professor of Religion and Philosophy, Milwaukee-Downer College, Milwaukee, Wisconsin.

Robert Lansing Hicks, B.D., Th.D., Professor of Literature and Interpretation of the Old Testament, Berkeley Divinity School, New Haven, Connecticut.

Herbert Gordon May, M.A., B.D., Ph.D., D.D., Professor of Old Testament Language and Literature, Finney Professorship, The Graduate School of Theology, Oberlin College, Oberlin, Ohio.

Murray L. Newman, B.D., M.A., Th.D., Associate Professor of Old Testament, The Virginia Theological Seminary, Alexandria, Virginia.

Martin Noth, D.Theol., Teol. D:r, Professor of Old Testament, University of Bonn, Bonn, Germany.

Norman Walker Porteous, M.A., B.D., D.D., Professor of Hebrew and Semitic Languages, University of Edinburgh, Edinburgh, Scotland.

James F. Ross, B.D., Th.D., Assistant Professor of Old Testament, The Theological School, Drew University, Madison, New Jersey.

Harold Henry Rowley, M.A., D.D., D. Th., LL.D., F.B.A., Emeritus Professor of Hebrew Language and Literature, University of Manchester, Manchester, England.

Samuel Lucien Terrien, Th.D., Auburn Professor of Old Testament, Union Theological Seminary, New York, New York

Theodorus Christiaan Vriezen, D.Theol., Professor of Old Testament, University Utrecht, Utrecht, The Netherlands

G. Ernest Wright, B.D., Ph.D., D.D., Parkman Professor of Divinity, The Harvard University Divinity School, Cambridge, Massachusetts. Curator, The Semitic Museum, Harvard University.

ABBREVIATIONS

AJT	American Journal of Theology
ANET	Ancient Near Eastern Texts relating to the Old Testament, ed. J. B. Pritchard
ARW	Archiv für Religionswissenschaft
ATD	Das Alte Testament Deutsch
BA	Biblical Archaeologist
BASOR	Bulletin of the American Schools of Oriental Research
BJRL	Bulletin of the John Rylands Library
BWANT	Beiträge zur Wissenschaft vom Alten und Neuen Testament
BZAW	Beiheft zur Zeitschrift für die alttestamentliche Wissenschaft
CBQ	Catholic Biblical Quarterly
CC	Christian Century
DB	Dictionary of the Bible, ed. Hastings
EHAT	Exegetisches Handbuch zum Alten Testament
ET	Expository Times
EVT	Evangelische Theologie
FRLANT	Forschungen zur Religion und Literatur des Alten und Neuen Testaments
HAT	Handbuch zum Alten Testament
HKAT	Handkommentar zum Alten Testament
HSAT	Die Heilige Schrift des Alten Testaments
HUCA	Hebrew Union College Annual
IB	Interpreter's Bible
ICC	International Critical Commentaries

IEJ	Israel Exploration Journal
JBL	Journal of Biblical Literature
JBR	Journal of Bible and Religion
JNABI	Journal of the National Association of Biblical Instructors (later Journal of Bible and Religion)
JNES	Journal of Near Eastern Studies
JSS	Journal of Semitic Studies
JTS	Journal of Theological Studies
KHC	Kurzer Handcommentar zum Alten Testament
PEQ	Palestine Exploration Quarterly
PJB	Palästinajahrbuch
PSBA	Proceedings of the Society of Biblical Archaeology
RB	Revue biblique
RGG²	Die Religion in Geschichte und Gegenwart, 2nd ed.
RHPR	Revue d'histoire de et philosophie religieuses
RL	Religion in Life
RR	Review of Religion
SBT	Studies in Biblical Theology
ST	Studia Theologica
TLZ	Theologische Literaturzeitung
TQ	Theologische Quartalschrift
TS	Theological Studies
TWNT	Theologisches Wörterbuch zum Neuen Testament, ed. Kittel
USQR	Union Theological Seminary Quarterly Review
VT	Vetus Testamentum
ZAW	Zeitschrift für die alttestamentliche Wissenschaft
ZTK	Zeitschrift für Theologie und Kirche

Preface

This volume is a tribute to Professor James Muilenburg, whose influence as a scholar, teacher, and churchman has been felt in ever widening circles through the years.

The title of the *Festschrift* is not to be understood in narrow terms. *Israel's Prophetic Heritage* is not represented solely in the portion of the Old Testament canon usually denominated as "the prophets." The prophetic dimension of Israel's faith finds expression throughout the Old Testament, from its beginning to its end, as one can see from the range of writings included in this volume. It is true that Israel's prophecy, in the special sense, has been one of Dr. Muilenburg's central interests in his teaching and in his writings. Those who are acquainted with his masterful introduction to and exegesis of the Second Isaiah in the *Interpreter's Bible* (Vol. V) know that he is indeed a specialist on the prophets who has few peers; and those who know him as a teacher have sensed his deep affinity with Israel's great prophets, for example, Jeremiah. But the scope of his interest and competence is enormously wider than the prophetic literature. No one knows better than he that the study of Israel's prophetic tradition brings to focus the whole field of Old Testament studies.

From the beginning of his professional career Professor Muilenburg has devoted himself to problems of literary criticism. This was evident in his graduate dissertation on "The Literary Relations of the Epistle of Barnabas and the Teaching of the Twelve Apostles." He began his teaching career in the field of English literature, where his literary and aesthetic interests and sensitivities were developed and sharpened. His chief task, however, has been that of Old Testament scholarship, especially since he began teaching in the field of theological education a quarter of a century ago. In this country he has been a forerunner of developments which today lie at the center of scholarly and theological discussion. If one were to trace his scholarly ancestry, it would probably lead back through Hermann Gunkel, the great pioneer of form-criticism, to such figures as Herder and Lowth, who first awakened a poetic appreciation of Old Testament literature. When form criticism was, in this country, only a cloud on the horizon no bigger than a man's hand, Dr. Muilenburg was developing the method of *Gattungskritik*. Those who studied under him when he began his career as a member of a theological faculty in 1936 will remember his rigorous insistence upon the analysis of literary forms and his sensitivity to the literary qualities of Scripture.

While there is in Dr. Muilenburg a Gunkel-like poetic appreciation of Israel's literature, he has departed from the *Religionsgeschichtlicheschule* at the crucial point, namely, his profound sensitivity to the authentic and unique dimensions of Israel's faith. Scholarship of the most meticulous kind has been the servant of Biblical interpretation. The literary-critical labors, the work of a translator, the analyses of form and style, and all the other contributions to Old Testament scholarship by a man of letters have been designed to accomplish one purpose: the elucidation of the faith of Israel which Professor Muilenburg knows so well and with which he is so closely identified personally. Only those who have sat at his feet as students can testify to the power, somewhat charismatic, with which he has opened the Scriptures. Against the background of a stormy international period he has sensed with prophetic insight the radically historical meaning and relevance of the Biblical message. Always his teaching and his research have been infused with a response of reverence: "The place whereon thou standest is holy ground."

Professor Muilenburg has lived through the rise of what is called "Biblical Theology" or the revival of a "theological" approach to the Bible. Indeed, he has contributed significantly to this revival and has approved its general results. Even so, he has been one of the strongest champions in this country of the view that "Biblical Theology" and the other areas of Old Testament scholarship cannot be played off against one another.

All areas of Old Testament study depend upon one another and must not be separated. Proponents of a "Biblical Theology" who inveigh against a "merely" literary-critical approach to the Old Testament find no comfort in Dr. Muilenburg's words or deeds; nor do the proponents of "objective" scholarship who castigate the Biblical theologian for having brought "dogmatism" and slipshod scholarship into Biblical studies. Dr. Muilenburg has maintained his own stand in the middle of these perilous extremes. His students have been required to develop linguistic skills ranging far beyond those which are often considered adequate for the Old Testament student. Theological students at the outset of their program of ministerial studies have been confronted with the necessity of learning the Biblical languages if they expect to be responsible preachers and teachers in the Church. Graduate students have been encouraged to spend long periods of time in linguistic and archaeological work, prior to taking up the writing of dissertations. Old Testament theologians often have been urged to engage in strictly theological assignments, but they have been urged at the same time, by word and by example, to come to terms with the knowledge and skills without which their Biblical Theology would not be worthy of the name.

Rarely have objective, critical scholarship and passionate involvement in the theological meanings of Israel's faith found such a creative embodiment in a single person as they have found in James Muilenburg. Although a man of profound Christian faith, he has insisted upon hearing the testimony of Old Testament faith and upon letting that faith stand for what it is in itself. His conviction that the faith of Israel and the Christian faith stand side by side, each requiring the other for its fuller elucidation, has prevented him from claiming too little or too much for the faith expressed by either community. His insistence upon letting the evidence of open, critical scholarship guide him throughout his career has meant that seldom, if at all, has he succumbed to the temptation to find what one looks for in an ancient text. Without clinging dogmatically to scholarly opinions, he has turned to the scriptural record again and again, convinced that each fresh examination will

bring about a new appropriation and a deeper understanding
of the Biblical message. He has stoutly refused to short-circuit
the exegetical process at any point by ignoring textual, literary,
formal, historical, or archaeological evidence. He typifies the
Biblical Theologian in the best sense of the term: the theologian
whose interpretation rests upon careful, devout exegesis.

It is within this context of Professor Muilenburg's life and
thought that we can understand his wide-ranging interests,
symbolized by the diversity of essays included in this volume.
Those who are in the Old Testament field realize that an almost
academic omniscience is required; for the Old Testament, to be
properly understood, requires the contributions of many disciplines: philology, archaeology, the history and culture of the
ancient Near East, literary and form criticism, theology, to say
nothing of intertestamental literature, the New Testament, and
Judaica. In such a wide field, the co-operation of experts is required. Yet it is astounding how Professor Muilenburg has been
able to move in this vast field of studies with discriminating
judgment, entering into conversation with scholars of all
branches of studies and grasping the interrelationship of the
disciplines. The catholicity of his interests is represented by
these essays, which, generally speaking, follow the pilgrimage of
Israel—a pilgrimage which is set within the far horizon of "the
beginning" and the dawning of the Christian era. The
pilgrimage, as we follow it in these pages, begins with the times
before David, when Israel was constituted as the people of the
Covenant, and it extends through the tumultuous years of
Israel's history to the very threshold of the New Testament.
In this historical context specific essays treat important aspects
of Israel's prophetic heritage.

It is with esteem and affection that we present these studies
to a scholar whom some of us are privileged to honor as a
teacher, others as a professional colleague, and all of us as a
creative interpreter of Israel's faith.

THE EDITORS

I

In the Beginning

A Contribution to the Interpretation of the First Word of the Bible

WALTHER EICHRODT

Every reader of the Bible is familiar with the lapidary sentence with which its first chapter begins: "In the beginning God created the heavens and the earth." This opening of the creation story seems so appropriate that the consideration as to whether it misrepresents the original would appear offhand irrelevant. And yet this consideration goes back to the early Middle Ages, when the Jewish scholars Ibn Ezra (1167) and Rashi (1105) in their commentaries expressed the view that this sentence constitutes a relative indication of time, which either introduces the following verse ("In the beginning, when God created the heavens and the earth, then the earth was . . . ," as in Ibn Ezra) or reaches across the parenthetical vs. 2 to vs. 3 ("In the beginning, when God created the heavens and the earth . . . then God spoke . . . ," as in Rashi). The principal reason for reducing vs. 1 to a secondary stipulation of the following verse lay in the difficulty of harmonizing the assertion of vs. 2 concerning the chaotic primitive condition of the earth with a comprehensive statement concerning the creation of the universe. Thus many Christian exegetes have followed one or the other proposed translation, usually that of Rashi.[1]

At the same time others, dealing with the exegetical difficulties in vs. 2 in a variety of ways, held to the view that the first

[1] Cf., among others, the commentaries of Budde, Dillmann, Holzinger, and Skinner.

sentence of the Bible constitutes a fundamental statement of the activity of God the Creator who called all things into being[2]— an interpretation already attested in the Greek translation. It was acknowledged on all sides that the one translation was as defensible philologically and grammatically as the other. Reasons for the preference of one or the other interpretation of the text stemmed more from the history of religions or from theology, depending upon whether or not one wished to consider the priestly narrator capable of transcending, in principle, the level of Old Testament statements concerning creation.

This line was first crossed by P. Humbert, who maintained that the understanding of Gen. 1:1 as a relative clause might well be established on linguistic historical grounds. He believed it possible to say: *"La seule traduction correcte est donc: 'Lorsque Dieu commença de créer l'Univers, le monde était alors en état chaotique, etc.'"*[3] This rendering of the result of his investigation is so keenly formulated that no exegete can ignore it. Were it sound, an age-old exegetical difference of opinion would have been solved. Thus it would be in the interests of all to examine it carefully. In so doing, we are certain to be acting in accordance with the wishes of this scholar, who is well known for his sagacious Old Testament research.

Of the approximately fifty references to *rē'šit* in the Old Testament only twelve, according to Humbert, are to be understood in the sense of a temporal beginning, while three tend to express principle rather than time. At this point one might ask whether Gen. 10:10, Hos. 9:10, and Mic. 1:13 should not be reckoned with the twelve passages mentioned, Pr. 8:22 and Job 40:19 belonging to those passages where meaning is ambiguous. Nevertheless, since the question before us does not involve these passages, we do not wish to place particular emphasis upon them.

Of the passages which use *rē'šit* in a temporal sense, only two display an absolute construction at first glance, namely Isa. 46:10 and Gen. 1:1. If it can be shown that in even the Isaiah

---

[2] Cf. H. Strack, H. Gunkel, O. Procksch, W. Zimmerli, G. von Rad, among others.

[3] P. Humbert, "Trois notes sur Genèse 1," *Interpretationes ad Vetus Testamentum pertinentes Sigmundo Mowinckel Septuagenario missae* (1955), pp. 85 ff.

passage no absolute statement of time is intended, then the evidence would seem complete that, on the basis of the use of *rē'šît* in the entire Old Testament, one can speak only of a relative beginning in Gen. 1:1 as well.

We must admit, of course, that we are not totally convinced of the cogency of this demonstration. In such an employment of Old Testament passages, is not too little consideration given to the limited extent of the Old Testament literature which has been preserved for us? And is it so irrefutably certain that a passage having as its author a thinker singular in many respects and unique in the Old Testament may be understood only in terms of the twelve or fifteen passages—or, as the case may be, the only passage—from the prophet? In view of the available evidence, may one speak here of more than a high degree of probability? Yet even this would give the translator something to go on.

But it seems to us that in the evidence put before us certain important passages are lacking which ought not to be left out of consideration. Here must be mentioned above all the time-indication *mērō'š* "from the beginning," which derives from the same root as *rē'šît*. It occurs four times in Second Isaiah: 40:21; 41:4; 41:26; 48:16. Of these, the last two passages are to be understood in a relative sense according to the context. In 41:26 the term stands in parallelism with *millᵉpānîm*, "long since," and refers to the beginning of Cyrus' intervention in the history of the Near Eastern states: that is, from the beginning he was accompanied by the prophetic witness to the role assigned him by Yahweh in the destiny of this people. Isa. 48:16 must also be understood in this sense; the allusion to the prophetic witness that Yahweh alone directs the course of history is quite clear, despite the questionable text in vs. 16c.

The situation is nevertheless different in the case of the first two passages mentioned. In 40:21 the parallel time-designation *mîsudôt hā'āreṣ*, "from the foundation of the earth,"[4] is a clear reference to an absolute beginning. "From the beginning of the world" (Duhm) Yahweh, by virtue of his creative act, has proved himself the exalted one before whom all human great-

---

[4] So most commentators read today. The article before *'ereṣ* may perhaps be omitted with the Qumrân MS Isa. 1.

ness sinks into nothingness. And if, in 41:4, the amazing triumphal procession of Cyrus is referred to the God who called the generations "from the beginning," then an absolute beginning of history is meant, in which Yahweh allotted the peoples their task. The continuation in vs. 4b, "I, Yahweh, the first, and with the last, I am the same," points toward the idea of the eternity of God and thereby derives from the act of creation in the beginning an inference of greatest significance for the understanding of the divine being.

That Second Isaiah's allusion to an absolute beginning of the world is not an isolated one can be seen from Pr. 8:23, where *mērō'š* is unequivocally determined by the preceding *mēʿôlām*, "from eternity on," and by the following *miqqadmê 'éreṣ*, "from the primeval times of the earth." If this primordially created wisdom is given in the preceding verse the dignity of *rēʾšit darkô* and *qédem mipʿālāw*, then the second designation may be translated with Köhler in a temporal sense as "the earliest of his works"; as for the first designation, one may waver between the translations "first-born" (cf. Sir. 1:4) and "unique evidence of His might,"[5] detecting also in this passage the transition mentioned by Humbert from the temporal to the material (*sachlich*) meaning of *rēʾšit*. Accordingly, the temporal expressions in Sir. 24:9, *pro tou aiōnos ap'archēs ektisen me*, will be considered a translation of the Hebrew *mēʿôlām* and *mērō'š*.[6]

It is worth noting that the words used here as adverbs of time may be used in an absolute as well as in a relative sense; for *mērō'š* cf. page 3 above; for *lᵉmîmê qédem* in the sense of *lᵉmērāḥôq* cf. II Kg. 19:25; without *l*, Isa. 23:7; Mic. 7:20; and so on. In the strict sense of primeval time Isa. 51:9, *kîmê qédem*, is parallel to *dōrôt ʿôlāmîm*; Pr. 8:23, *miqqadmê 'éreṣ*, cf. paragraph above; *mēʿôlām* absolute in Pr. 8:23, relative in Isa. 42:14; 47:7; and so on. It should be no cause for wonder, then, if something similar were the case with *rēʾšit*.

[5] Cf. J. Savignac, "Note sur le sense du verset Prov. VIII.22," VT, IV (1954), p. 429. J. B. Bauer, "Encore une fois Proverbes VIII.22," VT, VIII (1958), pp. 91 f.

[6] So Ryssel in Kautzsch's *Apokryphen und Pseudepigraphen*, I (1900), p. 353. See also Sir. 16:26; 34:27; 39:25 and the comments on these passages in R. Smend, *Die Weisheit des Jesus Sirach hebr. u. deutsch* (1906).

The use of *mērē'šît* in Isa. 46:10 appears to be determined by its correlation with *'aḥᵃrît*. Does not here (as in Job 8:7; 42:12; Ec. 7:8) a *terminus a quo* stand over against a *terminus ad quem* in order to denote a definite period of time? If so, the correlation would mean relation even in the case of a formally absolute construction of *rē'šît*.[7] Nevertheless, the passage in Isaiah is completely dissimilar to the cited parallel passages, where a period within the earthly passage of time is clearly intended; one can claim the same for Isa. 46:10 only by disregarding the context. On the basis of vs. 9 it is clear that the prophet thinks of something existent from primeval times, the *ri'šōnôt mē'ôlām*. What is to be understood by this, as vs. 9b states plainly enough, is the unique and eternal deity of Yahweh; and it is with this idea—already encountered in other passages[8]—that the prophet combines God's disposition over beginning and end. But one cannot refer this pair of words just to Cyrus' rise and ultimate success, of which vs. 11 speaks. The power to summon Cyrus is deduced here, as in 44:24 ff.; 48:12-15, from the primordial majesty of Yahweh the Creator, who can make known from the beginning (*miqqédem*) that which has not yet been created (vs. 10a) and who therefore causes the end to be proclaimed from the very beginning. Who or what proclaims, whether the works of creation themselves (Ps. 19:2 f.) or wisdom (Pr. 8:30 f.) or the morning stars (Job 38:4)—on this the prophet reflects little, just as in 40:21 he says little of who or what, from the foundation of the earth, is supposed to have brought men to the understanding of God's sublime majesty. It is enough that the transcendent God has determined the end together with the beginning, and therefore commands the entire development of the world. Here then is meant that broad perspective over earthly time which is possible for the Creator alone, and which allows him to declare his counsel irrefutable and his plans certain (vs. 10b). The recognition of God's sovereignty through the force of his unique deity achieves particular significance for the historical moment in which the prophet and his followers live. Under the absolute power of disposal of the Almighty Creator the summons to the

---

[7] Cf. Humbert, *op. cit.*, p. 87.
[8] Cf. p. 4.

bird of prey has been issued, and the revolutionary event thus introduced will be carried through to the end (vs. 11).

Here beginning and end do not comprise a specific period of time within history, but rather historical time as such. For it is the fundamental conviction of Second Isaiah, determining all his prophetic utterances, that this historical time is *now;* arrived at the threshold of a new aeon, it realizes its *'aḥᵃrît* in the fulfillment of the divine decision, through which the peoples —indeed, the whole cosmos—will be laid at the feet of God who alone rules the world (45:14-25; 51:6-8). Set in this larger context, the absolute use of *mērē'šît* might well be assured.

For that matter, neither is the absolute use of *bᵉrē'šît* in Gen. 1:1 so isolated and without analogy as one would like to pretend. Granted its complete independence, it nevertheless represents only one witness among several from the Exilic and post-Exilic period—a period during which a common spiritual concern, not previously evident, became active. One must simply accept, along with his pronounced peculiarity of thought and expression, the fact that the priestly narrator here makes use of the absolute form of *rē'šît* with the preposition *b*—a form which is no longer found elsewhere. In this case, linguistic history obviously cannot be the appropriate means of critical examination. In addition the question as to whether a reciprocal influence exists among the witnesses established in Second Isaiah, in Proverbs, and in P, in which group Ps. 90:2 must also very probably be reckoned, scarcely permits an answer. Von Rad has rightly rejected the attempt to affix a precise date to the Priestly Document of the Hexateuch, a work strongly rooted in the priestly tradition which was preserved and handed down through the centuries.[9] It appears more important to seek out that place where, in such dissimilar documents, the idea of an absolute beginning of the earthly world finds expression with a kind of inner compulsion, thus adding to the linguistic-historical defense of the meaning of this controversial expression an intellectual-historical (*geistesgeschichtlich*) one.

This is probably easiest to do in the case of the prophet of the Exile, who at several points returns to this thought in his message. The indispensable help which he found here in his con-

[9] G. von Rad, *Die Priesterschrift im Hexateuch* (1934), p. 189.

troversy with the pagan world view is evident. Rendtorff has demonstrated clearly how, in Second Isaiah, the action of Yahweh the Creator is closely linked with his redemptive action toward Israel in the present and in the future; and how, through the focusing of the statements about creation upon Israel's existence, actual meaning for the present is won.[10] It is repeatedly emphasized that Yahweh alone, without help, stretched out the heavens and founded the earth (44:24; 45:12, 18); indeed, that the utmost opposites in nature and history—light and darkness, weal and woe—are comprehended in his creative will, revealing him as the only God and Lord (45:6-8). When in these connections the prophet beholds the beginning of creation and the God who stands apart from it in sovereign freedom, he experiences in this vision the supreme moment of divine majesty in the universe: it is the eternal God who, unlike the pagan deities woven into their cosmogony, truly possesses transcendental majesty and therefore justly claims absolute power over the created world (40:21-24, 28;[11] 41:4; 45:6 f., 21; 46:9 f.; 48:12 f.). No wonder that, in the face of the uncontradictable creative act of this eternal God, chaos vanishes. In 44:27 and 50:2 f. one may find perhaps traces of particular features of the chaos image. Yet even when this image emerges once again in the form of the mythical struggle against chaos (51:9 f.), it no longer possesses any intrinsic reality, but rather precludes the reference to the conquest of all historical forces which could challenge the salvation of Israel. From this God who stands above time, whose goodness and righteousness endure eternally (51:8; 54:8), come then in addition gifts of salvation which cannot be challenged by time: an eternal world (40:8), an eternal salvation (45:17; 51:6), an eternal covenant (54:10; 55:3). The prophet's assurance concerning the eternal God soars highest, however, where he describes the salvation also bestowed by God as superior to all the majesty of his creation (51:6-8). God's salvation will endure beyond the fall of this creation; it participates in the eternity of the Creator. Herewith the message of salvation for

[10] R. Rendtorff, "Die theologische Stellung des Schöpferglaubens bei Deuterojesaja," ZTK 51 (1954), pp. 3 ff.

[11] On 'aelōhê 'ôlām cf. E. Jenni, Das Wort 'ôlām im Alten Testament (1953), p. 68.

this God-despairing people first becomes secure against all apparent contradiction, because it is established in the being of God himself. The disciples of the prophet have drawn the conclusion to this message in their proclamation of a new heaven and a new earth (Isa. 65:17; 66:22). Thus it is an immediate concern of faith and no philosophical construction which points to an absolute beginning of this world and correspondingly to its end.

Apart from this aspect of his representation of the beginning of the created world—one governed by the idea of the divine act of salvation—the priestly writer seems inclined to a static interpretation of the creation as an event of the past, to be distinguished from the preservation of the world through divine providence. And yet on closer scrutiny it becomes clear that even Gen. 1 is not meant to make an independent statement concerning the origin of the world, but that it reflects a comprehensive view of God's action toward Israel. The dominant theme of the priestly narrative is preparation of the salvation realized in God's people as a divine gift of fundamental importance to the world, one which takes form little by little in ever new divine ordinances and constitutes the deepest meaning of the course of history. The significance of Israel's salvation for the world finds reflection even in the choice of decisive manifestations in which P sees the divine revelation unveiled: creation, covenant with Noah, covenant with Abraham, revelation on Sinai. Whether the number 4 as the number for world and totality alludes already to the all-inclusive character of the history which here unfolds[12] must probably remain undecided. But in any case God's act of creation, by virtue of its position in this scheme, takes on the characteristic of an initial act in the working out of salvation, opening the way to man for fellowship with his God. The primordial action of God, through which he has determined the basic order of the earthly world, becomes in this way a permanent guarantee for the inevitability and eternal continuance of the salvation granted to Israel. The sanctification of the Sabbath as marking the completion of the miracles of creation clearly indicates the inner connection between the creation of the world and the open offer of divine grace to

[12] Cf. W. Zimmerli, *I Mose I-II. Die Urgeschichte I* (1943), pp. 108 ff.

Israel. Though the source of grace here uncovered remains veiled to human perception, it nevertheless proclaims at the very beginning God's desire for fellowship with his creation, and especially with its appointed lord, mankind. From the beginning on, this creation appears to rest upon the rhythmic pattern of work and festive rest, with which it renounces all claim to self-value and lays down its strengths and achievements at the feet of the God who designed it for his praise and his adoration.

Here the priestly narrator manifests a view of world events which no longer acknowledges the cosmos to be significant in itself but subjects it at every moment to the omnipotent will of God the Sovereign, who wields it according to his purpose. In this context time, as the space within which all life is enacted, plays a significant role. At the time of the creation—indeed, based upon and insured by it—the seven-day week is established with the Sabbath as its conclusion. The stars, not created until the fourth day, have, in contrast to their worship in heathen practice, no other task than to confirm time as created and disposed by God along with the week of creation—to regulate the days, count the ages, determine years and holidays—and in addition to this task of clear delineation to assist in the functioning of civic and cultic life. Thus the evaluation of time as the principle of order designed for God's creation establishes the total dependence of the created world upon the Lord, who stands apart from it in absolute freedom.

The idea of the absolute beginning of the created world thus proves to be a logical expression of the total outlook of the priestly narrator, an indispensable link in the working out of salvation on behalf of Israel in God's world order. What Second Isaiah, in regarding the imminent consummation of history, grasps as a firm basis of faith makes it possible for the priestly writer to emphasize in concise form the divine transcendence over against the world of appearance. This transcendence makes all of the earthly world a mere reflection of its otherworldly glory, only in order to make known in the revelation to Israel the fullness of her redemption.

The wisdom teachers are already in an entirely different situation when they consider the absolute beginning of the world of creation. The broadening of the concept of *ḥokmâ* to a cosmic principle, to which the functional order of the earth is traced, and its elevation to a hypostasis which, at the creation of the universe, is used by God the Creator as the mediator of his will, necessarily led to the reflection on the first beginnings of divine creativity—where, of course, the idea of the world's proceeding from God appears as the effective force in question.[13] Not only is justice done to the transcendence of the divine being without denying his direct intervention in the internal events of the world, but also the authority of wisdom for human life is strengthened by its role as mediator in the formation of the universe, and so is made to coincide with the Word and the Spirit of God. Thus it is hardly surprising that expressions for the absolute beginning appear more and more frequently.

It should now be clear that each reflection on the beginning of creation exercises in its place an important function in the total view of the respective writer. If we understand *bᵉrē'šît* in Gen. 1:1 as absolute, this is not an arbitrary judgment but is closely connected with the most important concern of the priestly conception of history. A relative interpretation of the expression would place an emphasis on the autonomy of the chaotic matter at the beginning of creation contrary to the whole concern of this creation story. The narrator is moved to reflection not by that which preceded the divine creation but by the fact that nothing but the autonomous decree of the transcendent God determined the form of creation. That the *creatio ex nihilo* thereby enters the picture is incontestable; indeed, other concepts in the priestly creation story, which we cannot examine in this connection,[14] point in this same direction. It is enough that the translation of the first sentence of the Bible, "In the beginning God created the heavens and the earth," proves to be the truly pertinent one, not only from the aesthetic-stylistic point of view but also from that of linguistic and intellectual history.

[13] Pr. 8:22 f.; Job 28:25-27; Sir. 1:4; 24:3, 9; Wisdom of Sol. 7:12, 15-22, 25 f.; 9:9.
[14] On this point see my *Theologie des Alten Testaments*, Band 2-3 (1961), Par. 15.II.1.e. S. 63 ff.

II

The Prophets and the Problem of Continuity

NORMAN W. PORTEOUS

Ever since Mowinckel published his epoch-making *Psalmen-studien* there has developed among Old Testament scholars an increasing interest in the Hebrew cult as a medium which gives substance and continuity to the forms of religious thought. It has come to be widely held that in a society such as that of ancient Israel the secret of the survival of religious ideas must be found in cultic institutions rather than in written documents, though, of course, it could not be denied that books played a certain part too, as witnessed by the undoubted discovery in the Jerusalem temple of a book of the Law in the reign of Josiah. It was felt that a cultic explanation accounted most readily for the stylization of form observable in so many of the relevant parts of the Old Testament, in the covenant formulas, in the Psalms, and in the prophetic oracles. Indeed, the problem of the composition of the Psalms, to which Mowinckel and Gunkel before him had devoted so much study, attracted particular attention. It was recognized that the psalmists had to conform more or less closely to prescribed themes and stereotyped forms of expression and that in this way their freedom to innovate had been severely limited.

Even before Mowinckel's time, but with a new eagerness of inquiry since he offered his explanation of the presence of prophetic elements in the Psalter, the conviction has forced itself upon scholars that there was a much closer connection between the prophetic movement and the cult than was pre-

11

viously believed. Today the expression "cultic prophet" is almost taken for granted. There is no doubt at all that, whatever qualifications and reservations have to be made, this line of investigation has proved most fruitful and has illumined a whole range of Hebrew life.

All this is very familiar to present-day students of the Old Testament. It is understandable, however, if at times a certain bewilderment results from the variety of hypotheses and the violent conflicts of opinion within this field of study. Indeed, the eager concentration of scholars upon tracing cultic patterns of thought and the inferences they draw from them seem to this writer to result in some cases in a failure to take account of the whole range of evidence. The phenomena which have to be explained point, to some extent at least, in different directions. Moreover, the problem is complicated by the ever present difficulty of dating the literary evidence or of being sure that something essential to our understanding has not been obliterated by a well-meaning editor.

The particular problem to which this essay would draw attention is that of the relation of the pre-Exilic prophets to the so-called amphicytonic historical and legal traditions. When these traditions are subjected to a form-critical examination it is difficult to resist the conclusion that they have a cultic *Sitz im Leben,* and it is a natural further step to argue that it was in the cult that they were handed down from generation to generation. These very traditions, however—and this has been the theme of much recent work—seem to be presupposed by the eighth- and seventh-century prophets. How was it that the prophets, for whom these traditions were important, were so violent in their condemnation of a cult one of the functions of which was *ex hypothesi* to preserve them. If it be argued that the cult had become corrupt and thoroughly deserved the criticisms it received, then at once we have on our hands the problem of continuity. For how could one and the same cult preserve in its purity a knowledge of the covenantal ritual and of the social morality which the God of Israel had made binding on his people and also exhibit the appalling marks of degeneration which merited the denunciations of the prophets? Are we to

suppose that at least the words which enshrined the pure Israelite faith continued to be spoken faithfully by men who, according to the evidence we have, had gone over to a baalized form
of religion? There are signs in present-day discussion that this
difficulty is not ignored and now and again suggestions toward
a solution are hazarded. This essay will perhaps have served a
useful purpose if it focuses attention upon the problem and
makes one or two tentative moves in the critical debate.

That the question at issue is relevant to the interests of the
distinguished scholar, Dr. James Muilenburg, to whom this
volume of essays is presented as a tribute from his friends, is
shown by a recent article from his pen entitled "The Form and
Structure of the Covenantal Formulations."[1] It illustrates once
more his enviable gift of analyzing literary form, a gift which
was so notably exhibited in his commentary on Isa. 40-66 in the
Interpreter's Bible. In the article referred to, he traces the covenantal pattern from the covenant at Sinai (Ex. 19:3-6) through
the covenant at Shechem (Jos. 24) to the covenant at Gilgal
(I Sam. 12). His special concern is to suggest that this covenantal pattern can be traced back behind the Deuteronomic
reform into the northern kingdom of Israel, where the Elohistic
traditions form a link with the premonarchic amphictyony.
"Many scholars," he writes,[2] "believe that the Elohistic covenant
traditions preserve to some extent an authentic memory of
Mosaic religion and that these traditions lie behind the work
of the prophets." He goes on: "If the origins of the Deuteronomic language, style, and literary structure are to be traced to
the latter part of the eighth century and before that period to
the Shechemite amphictyony in the period of the settlement,
then it is clear that the history of Israel's religious faith requires restatement. This applies *a fortiori* to the covenant formulations of the Elohist and the Deuteronomist, the royal
covenant pericopes, and the covenant contexts in the prophets,
above all Hosea and Jeremiah."

If Dr. Muilenburg is right, this means that we shall have to
give a great deal of attention to the problem of the origin and

---

[1] VT, IX (1959), pp. 347-365.
[2] *Ibid.,* p. 350.

history of the amphictyonic tradition. In particular we shall have to ask by what agencies it continued to be known in the northern kingdom through all the period of cultic corruption and what precisely happened to it in the south when it passed under the aegis of the house of David and assumed a distinctive form in the royal psalms. We shall also have to review once more the question of the origin of Deuteronomy and the problem of its relation to the Psalms. Finally there is the problem of the relation of the prophets to the amphictyonic tradition, which is our particular concern in this essay. In such a closely knit complex of interrelated problems it is extremely difficult to know where to start and, having once started, to avoid going round in circles.

Perhaps it will be most convenient to take a look first at the double change which affected the amphictyonic tradition at the beginning and at the end of the united monarchy of David and Solomon. David installed the Ark on Mount Zion and by that gesture indicated that he had assumed the old amphictyonic authority. No doubt during the troubled years of the Philistine wars there had been a good deal of disruption of cultic practice; but David now realized the importance of centralizing, under his own control and as a support for his newly established monarchy, the great autumn festival which during the premonarchic period had served to give the Hebrew tribes a measure of cohesion. That a major effort was made by some individual or group of individuals to enable the Davidic monarchy to make itself heir to the great traditions which lay behind it in Israel's history seems clear from the evidence of the remarkable group of the so-called royal psalms and from other psalms which probably belong to the pre-Exilic temple cult. When the secession of the northern tribes took place at the beginning of Rehoboam's reign it seems to have been recognized very definitely by the prophet Ahijah, who was behind the revolt, that the Davidic throne had now, and would continue to have, a very definite place in the purpose of God, even though only a rump state would be left under southern control. The evidence of the royal psalms seems to suggest that the authorities in Jerusalem never gave up their claim that Jerusalem was the true center of

Israel and that the king enthroned there was the heir to Israel's covenant traditions.[3] We know that the seceding kingdom was provided with two chief cult centers, at Bethel and Dan, the former being the one most closely associated with the king.[4] It may be presumed that Jeroboam arrogated to himself a religious status analogous to that claimed by the Davidic king. Whether Jeroboam and his successors attempted to surround themselves with the mystique which was associated with the Davidic monarchy we have no certain means of knowing, unless we are to regard Psalm 45 as the one surviving example of a North Israelite royal psalm which has come down to us. If that were indeed so, then it would be necessary to recognize that the northern kings, like their opposite numbers in Jerusalem, were reminded in cultic song that they were guarantors of justice within their realm.[5] The story of Ahab[6] would at least suggest that he was not unaware of the obligation resting upon an Israelite king to refrain from social injustice and that he had even something of a conscience about it as compared with his foreign consort. The story of Ahab and Naboth corresponds to that of David and Uriah.

What we do not know and what we should like to know is how far the amphicytonic tradition continued to attach itself to any of the other northern sanctuaries apart from the two established by Jeroboam as centers of the royal cult. From the Book of Amos[7] we know that pilgrimages were made not only to Bethel but also to Gilgal, which latter sanctuary seems to have been particularly associated with the traditions of the Conquest,[8] and to Beersheba, which, owing to the circumstance that it was situated in the kingdom of Judah, may have seemed to religious circles in the north, who regretted the disruption of the monarchy, peculiarly suitable for a place of pilgrimage. Amos, however, does not regard such pilgrimages as in any way insuring a true relation to the God who alone could confer life on his people. In his message there is no suggestion of an am-

[3] I Kg. 11:29 ff.
[4] I. Kg. 12:33; 13:1; Am. 7:13.
[5] Ps. 45:7-8.
[6] I. Kg. 21.
[7] Am. 5:5.
[8] See E. Nielsen, *Shechem: A Traditio-Historical Investigation* (1954), pp. 295 ff.

phictyonic center at which the worshiper would obtain the blessing of God's favor. When we turn to Hosea's prophecies we find disapproval of pilgrimages to Gilgal and Bethel (Beth-aven), expressed in virtually the same words as in Amos;[9] there is no virtue in swearing by the life of Yahweh at the royal sanctuary. As for going to the old amphictyonic center of Shechem, before ever a man got there he would probably be murdered by the very priests who ought to have been waiting to instruct him.[10]

All this is familiar. What, however, has to be accounted for somehow—and much recent research is forcing this problem to the forefront of interest—is the undoubted fact that, through all the period of apostasy and corruption to which the denuncia-tory oracles of the prophets bear only too clear witness, the tradition of the Sinaitic covenant and all moral obligation that was associated with it not only survived but was preserved in a curiously tenacious pattern of thought. In an important article entitled "Covenant Forms in Israelite Tradition," published some years ago,[11] G. E. Mendenhall writes of the way in which "the tradition of the covenant with Abraham became the pat-tern of a covenant between Yahweh and David, whereby Yahweh promised to maintain the Davidic line on the throne"; he goes on to point out that this seems to have met with acceptance in Judah but not in northern Israel, and then says: "The original center of the old Federation, understandably enough, evidently preserved far more of the old Mosaic covenant traditions. It is for that reason that so much of the evidence for these traditions is dependent upon Deuteronomy and related works." In speak-ing of "the original center of the old Federation" Mendenhall is presumably referring to Shechem.[12] Muilenburg has shown that the same covenant pattern of thought appears in Samuel's speech in I Sam. 12 in connection with the sanctuary at Gilgal, which had also amphictyonic associations.[13]

[9] Hos. 4:15. [10] Hos. 6:9.
[11] George E. Mendenhall, *Law and Covenant in Israel and the Ancient Near East* (Biblical Colloquium, Pittsburgh). Reprinted from BA, XVII, 2 (May, 1954), pp. 26-46, and 3 (Sept., 1954), pp. 49-76.
[12] See Jos. 8:30 ff., ch. 24, and, by implication, Dt. 11:29, and especially ch. 27.
[13] See also Nielsen, *op. cit.*

Now, it is possible that, from the days of Samuel through the early monarchic period and even for some time after the disruption of the monarchy, a center like Shechem may have continued to keep the old traditions alive. Today there seems to be a disposition to follow A. C. Welch in his contention that the Code of Deuteronomy was of northern origin so far as its content was concerned[14] and that the covenantal tradition associated with it was in the direct line of descent from the original covenant at Sinai-Horeb. What remains difficult to account for is the continuity of this tradition as a cultic reality through the period about which we learn from the Book of Hosea[15] that there was no knowledge of God in the land, that the prohibitions of the Decalogue were disregarded, and that the responsibility for this state of affairs lay with the priests. Hosea could scarcely have been more specific than he is in this passage. It is not merely that the people have been disobedient. The guardians of the covenant law have not even troubled to remind them of it. It was an evil time, but even in these days there must have been faithful souls who cherished the old tradition of the covenant and somehow saw to it that the memory of it was not lost, while in their own humble way they put its precepts into practice. If it be said that Hosea denies the existence of such people, it can at least be replied that Hosea is himself an exception to his own sweeping generalization. He at least knew and cherished the amphictyonic tradition. He was familiar with the story of Yahweh's gracious acts toward Israel in the past[16] and with the details of the amphictyonic law,[17] and he makes use of the covenant language.[18] It is, moreover, a familiar fact that there is a close connection of thought between Hosea and Deuteronomy. It looks as though we might not be far wrong in supposing that it was through Hosea, and perhaps others like him of whom we have no direct record, that the covenantal tradition was kept alive, enhanced, and passed on. That Hosea had disciples is probable, for we have to account for the fact that his book was put together and transmitted and also for the fact that Jeremiah

---

[14] See Muilenburg, *op. cit.*, p. 13, for references.
[15] Hos. 4:1-6.
[16] Especially Hos. 11:1 ff.

[17] Especially Hos. 4:2.
[18] Hos. 1:9-10; 2:19, 23.

one hundred years later seems to be familiar with what his great predecessor had said. Jeremiah was Hosea's spiritual successor.

So far as the northern kingdom is concerned, then, we seem to be faced with a break of continuity in the cultic transmission, and the probability suggests itself that we should look to prophetic circles for the bridge to span the gap. Of course, it need not be supposed that the Hebrew cult had been completely Canaanized. But the situation was grim enough for it to be necessary for us to look elsewhere than to the cult as practiced for an explanation of the survival of the tradition. It can scarcely be accidental that the Law book which makes its appearance in the Jerusalem Temple in Josiah's time bears so clearly the traces of Hosea's thought and phraseology and that in Jeremiah we have the living proof that Hosea's influence lived on during the years of apostasy in Judah, when the preparations were being made in secret for the revival of the covenant traditions in Josiah's time.

To get a balanced picture of what took place in Josiah's reformation, however, it is necessary to look back through the history of the kingdom of Judah and ask ourselves how the amphictyonic tradition had fared there. Jerusalem had had no connection at all with the original amphictyonic league and after the disruption of the monarchy there was no other sanctuary within the rump kingdom of Judah which was likely to constitute itself a rival amphictyonic center. Clearly David intended to concentrate the amphictyonic authority in his own hands; after Solomon's time it is likely that, so far as Judah was concerned, the ancient covenant tradition would be preserved cultically to any great extent only in Jerusalem itself, though echoes of it may have been heard at local shrines in the Judean countryside. What is certain, however, is that Amos, a prophet from one of the more desolate parts of that countryside, is familiar with the tradition, even though, unlike Hosea,[19] he never actually mentions the covenant explicitly in any oracle that has come down to us. He knows about the mighty acts of Yahweh on behalf of Israel,[20] and the whole tenor of his pro-

---

[19] Hos. 8:1.   [20] Am. 1:10; 3:1-2; 9:7.

phecies shows that the covenant law is presupposed in his denunciations in Yahweh's name of the sins of Israel. He refers to the covenantal blessing in the injunctions: "Seek me and live," "Seek Yahweh and live" and "Seek good, and not evil, that you may live."[21] That the curse is about to be fulfilled unless the unlikely happens and the people repent is indicated by the oracles of judgment. We have to ask ourselves how Amos was so familiar with the amphictyonic tradition. It seems not impossible that in his case the answer may be in part that he had participated in festivals at the Jerusalem Temple. Certainly the very first oracle that we have in the Book of Amos indicates a theophany upon Mount Zion: "The Lord roars from Zion and utters his voice from Jerusalem."[22] Yet not so very long afterwards a greater Judean prophet, standing in the Temple court perhaps on the occasion of an autumn festival, saw a theophany which he interpreted to imply judgment, in the first instance on the people of Judah with whom he identified himself. It seems to have been no priestly voice but the prophet's alone that reminded the worshipers in the Temple, upon some occasion that we cannot date, of the obligation to obey the ancient moral law of Israel. The priests were doubtless much too busy dealing with the sacrificial victims, which Yahweh did not want, to have time for the weightier matters of the Law.[23] This is perhaps the place to mention that it is among Isaiah's prophecies[24]—though the matter is complicated by the presence of a parallel passage in the Book of Micah—that we find expressed the eschatological hope for a Mount Zion that would yet be a true amphictyonic center not only for all Israel but also for the nations. There is no trace of this in Deuteronomy, which is only interested in the covenant with Israel, but the possibility must be allowed that the prophetic interest in the nations may have some connection with the royal theology, though significantly there is no mention of the king.

The reference to Micah serves as a transition to one of the most stimulating recent contributions to the debate about the continuity of the amphicytonic law. It has been made by a

[21] Am. 5:4, 6, 14.   [23] Isa. 1:10 ff.
[22] Am. 1:2.   [24] Isa. 2:1-5; Mic. 4:1-4.

young German scholar, Walter Beyerlin, who, in line with the well-known views of Artur Weiser about a long-surviving amphictyonic covenant festival in Jerusalem, makes a thorough examination of the Book of Micah in a monograph entitled *Die Kulttraditionen Israels in der Verkündigung des Propheten Micha*. His thesis is that throughout the oracles which can be claimed for Micah—more are here regarded as authentic than some scholars would admit—there is to be discerned the presupposition of the amphicytonic law as known to the prophet and his hearers. Not only so, but reference is made in Micah to a theophany which reminds us of that at Sinai,[25] while there is also found the usual covenantal recapitulation of the saving acts of the Lord.[26] Beyerlin makes one very interesting point right at the beginning of his book. He examines all the instances of Micah's use of the name "Israel" and shows that he is familiar with the sacral meaning attached to it as a designation for all Israel, the people of God. This, he argues, could only have been so if, right through the period of the monarchy down to Micah's own time, such a usage was still alive alongside the more limited employment of the name (which also appears in Micah) as a designation of the northern kingdom. Such a sacral use of the name, he claims, must imply the existence of the amphictyonic institution to which it properly belonged. Of course, it is possible that even though there may have been no separate amphictyonic festival in Jerusalem, the autumn festival—in which we know that the Davidic king took a prominent part—may still in Micah's time have been made the occasion for recollection in some form of the old amphictyonic law. We know from a well-known reference in Jeremiah[27] that Micah prophesied during the reign of Hezekiah, and to his protests is traced the change of heart on the part of the king. Yet we may well ask whether such references as there were to the moral law in the cult would be enough, apart from some more living link with the tradition, to rouse Micah's solitary conscience and to account for the prophetic activity of this man from the Judean Shephelah who

[25] Mic. 1:3 ff.
[26] Mic. 6:3-5.
[27] Jer. 26:17 ff.

claims to be "filled with power, with the spirit of Yahweh, and with justice and might to declare to Jacob his transgression and to Israel his sin."

That Micah was familiar with the status of the Davidic monarch is shown, Beyerlin claims, by a passage which he rightly regards as authentic.[28] In this passage Micah, like his greater contemporary Isaiah, looks forward, away from present realities, to the coming of a ruler from Bethlehem (and therefore presumably of the same clan from which David had come) who would prove to be all that the Davidic monarch was required to be. He even gives him virtually the same title as Isaiah did, "lord of peace."[29] It is significant that both Micah and Isaiah should have reacted to the royal cult in the direction of eschatology. Did the prophets in some way incorporate the purer tradition?

To sum up, Beyerlin has made a very impressive case for his view that Micah's prophecies should be understood against the background of the autumn festival at Jerusalem, at which time some kind of reminder was given of the old Hebrew historical and moral traditions. It should be remembered, however, that Micah prophesied before the reformation of Hezekiah and that the various reformations of which we read in the history of Judah scarcely suggest that the continuity of tradition in the cult was well maintained throughout the period of the monarchy. Perhaps it is too much of a simplification to say that continuity must have been cultic. Certainly it was a priestly movement which brought the usurpation of Athaliah to an end, but there is evidence that it was the prophetic movement which kept a critical eye upon the monarchy in Jerusalem. Probably a prophetic tradition played the decisive part in preserving the memory of Israel's past through times when the cultic continuity was virtually broken. The prophets reveal a democratic liberty of prophesying and of criticizing king, priest, and commoner. This does not suggest that they were completely de-

[28] Mic. 4:14-5:5 (Heb.).

[29] Isa. 9:5 (Heb.), zé šālôm in Mic. 5:4 (Heb.) being the equivalent of śar śālôm. (For this use of zé compare Arabic dhu. So Beyerlin, *Die Kulttraditionen Israels in der Verkündigung des Propheten Micha*, FRLANT 54 (1959), pp. 35, 84.)

pendent on a state-sponsored institution for their knowledge of the sacred traditions.

For knowledge of the state of affairs in the kingdom of Judah, of course, we have at our disposal, as has been already said, the so-called royal psalms and many other psalms which likewise may be claimed for the pre-Exilic Jerusalem ritual. It is right that we should look a little more closely at this source of information. The scholar to whom we are indebted above all in the English-speaking world for our better understanding of these psalms in the modern context of discussion is A. R. Johnson, whose challenging book *Sacral Kingship in Ancient Israel* has much to say that is relevant to the subject of our present study. It is impossible in the brief scope of this essay to do justice to the massive argument of that book, but a few observations may be permitted. Johnson has undoubtedly made a very impressive case for the view that the composers of these very beautiful psalms, which were put into the mouth of the king, sought to link the new covenant between Yahweh and David[30] with the old amphictyonic law belonging to the Sinaitic covenant. He is able to show that it was enjoined upon the king, by the very words he had to utter at the autumn festival, in which he played a special role, that he must consider himself as the guarantor of justice throughout his dominions. When it is remembered that the Davidic king was the final court of justice in his kingdom, it will be seen that, if he took his judicial duties seriously, he would have plenty of opportunities to administer justice and to right social wrongs. We know that at least one Judean king did take his duties to heart, so as to earn the commendation of the prophet Jeremiah;[31] that he did justice and righteousness and judged the cause of the poor and needy— and this, added Jeremiah, was indeed to know God. The royal psalms remind us that there were those in Jerusalem who took a very exalted view of the function of the king. In the thoughts thus expressed the old tribal brotherhood was now caught up into the more complex relations of the monarchy and, as Johnson puts it, "was set in the wider context furnished by the

[30] Ps. 89:4, 29, 35, 40 (Heb.) ; 132:11-12. Cf. II Sam. 23:5.
[31] Jer. 22:15-16.

thought of Yahweh as the omnipotent divine King, who is also the Creator and Sustainer of the universe,"[32] the Yahweh of Israel and the Elyon of Jerusalem being identified. It is claimed that these psalms give a glimpse of Yahweh's ultimate purpose to bring in "a universal realm of righteousness and peace, in which not merely the twelve tribes of Israel but all the nations of the earth should be united in one common life."[33] It was a high task that was thus entrusted to the successive occupants of the throne of David. These psalms must have been written for use in the royal cult in the Jerusalem temple, though we have no means of knowing whether they were in regular annual use, or how far their exalted and often amazingly beautiful language was taken seriously. It is doubtless because they were capable of being interpreted eschatologically that they were preserved and that they survived the collapse of the Davidic monarchy. That Isaiah felt impelled to voice the hope of a ruler upon the throne of David, who would indeed deserve to be described in superlatives and on whom the spirit of Yahweh would rest in full measure, makes it clear that, whatever words the empirical king may have taken on his lips, his performance fell very far short of the ideal he was supposed to set before himself.

It may be granted, then, that there is evidence of a cultic tradition in Judah associated with the king which was capable of keeping alive, for those who had ears to hear, the memory of Israel's high moral code. In many of the pre-Exilic psalms (not only the royal psalms), which may be associated with the worship of the Temple, we can discern that the elements of the old amphictyonic tradition are modified by being linked with the monarchy. It may be suspected that in actual practice most of the Judean kings were more interested in the divine legitimization of their rule than in the moral responsibilities of kingship. Moreover, what Micah and Isaiah in their day and Zephaniah and Jeremiah a century later had to say about the popular religion and the immoral behavior of their contemporaries would suggest that the ancient moral law was more honored in the breach than in the observance. Indeed, cult had come to mean

[32] Aubrey R. Johnson, *Sacral Kingship in Ancient Israel* (1955), p. 128.
[33] *Ibid.*, pp. 128-129.

in Judah, as earlier in the northern kingdom, not the recollection in the sanctuary of the great, decisive acts of God on behalf of his people as the ground of moral obligation, but the offering of sacrifices as a surrogate for just dealing between man and man and for considering the unfortunate and needy.

Priestly and royal rituals had their value, since what is expressed in word may always come alive in deed. We may well believe that something like this happened at the time of the Josianic reformation, though it was not so very long afterwards that Jeremiah despaired of finding anyone in Jerusalem who did justice or sought truth.[34] Josiah at least, as we have already seen, took his duties seriously. He did not merely cleanse the cult of foreign elements but seems to have taken to heart the moral injunctions of the Deuteronomic Code. Ps. 95, which Johnson treats[35] as belonging to "the liturgy of the great autumnal festival as celebrated in Jerusalem during the period of the monarchy," seems to show evidence of Deuteronomic influence and seems to incorporate Deuteronomic phraseology. Though Deuteronomy had doubtless a long prehistory we should probably not look for traces of it within the pre-Josianic royal tradition.

It seems to the present writer that, important as cultic continuity was for preserving the covenant traditions in pre-monarchic Israel, there is under the united monarchy and in the divided kingdoms the even more important continuity incorporated in those people, many of them doubtless humble folk, who received the traditions and responded in obedience of heart and life. This living continuity was able to bridge the gaps when cultic continuity was broken and it represented at all times the true Israel of the spirit. Though the prophets sometimes speak as if there was no such obedience at all,[36] we must always remember that there were the prophets themselves, who represented Moses[37] and exhibited the essence of Hebrew morality in that, when God laid his strict commands upon them, they obeyed in defiance of consequences. This is the true Israel, which pre-

[34] Jer. 5:1.
[35] *Op. cit.*, pp. 59-61.
[36] E.g., Hos. 4:1; Jer. 5:1 ff.
[37] Dt. 18:15-16.

pared the way for Christianity. We may go even farther than this and see the prophets as the spokesmen not only of God but of the obedient in Israel, through the living witness of whose lives they learned the tradition which they presupposed. When Jeremiah[38] looked forward to the new covenant when God's law would be in men's hearts, he gave us the hint that meanwhile the knowledge of God's will was communicated from man to man, and we may well believe that from the earliest days the education of the home played its part. There were doubtless many pious priests who did their duty of communicating *torah*. Deuteronomy reveals both priestly and prophetic influence.

Yet there is in the Hebrew prophets an element which we may almost describe as secular. They believed that God claimed life as a whole and not just the religious part of it, and the priest is always in especial danger of forgetting this, as religious history shows only too clearly. There is a sense in which we should look for the true Israel not so much where sacred words were uttered, whether by priest or king—important as the utterance of such words could be and not seldom was—but in the quiet villages of the land and even in the busy towns, where some men at least put into practice the injunctions of the ancient Law and, having learned obedience, insured the continuity of Israel. Of such came the prophets, who did more than echo ritual words which they had heard, though such echoes should be duly noted and given the weight that belongs to them. These men could face king and priest and people in the strength of a morality which in some measure, by the aid of God's spirit, they had been enabled to live and so to keep alive in days when, but for their obedience, whatever sacral tradition there was might have died out altogether. And to the prophets must be added the humble and quiet in the land who had no memorial but who were the salt of the earth.

[38] Jer. 31:31 ff.

III

The Lawsuit of God: A Form-Critical Study of Deuteronomy 32*

G. ERNEST WRIGHT

The "Song of Moses" and the "Blessing of Moses" in Dt. 32 and 33 respectively belong to the series of appendices attached to the Book of Deuteronomy (Chs. 31-34). They are set within *narrative* traditions concerning the final deeds of Moses, as distinct from the *liturgical* materials in Chs. 5-29 wherein Moses expounds the meaning of the covenant to Israel. Both poems must have been of sufficient antiquity at the time of the final editing of Deuteronomy for them to be ascribed to Moses. The antiquity of the tribal blessings in Ch. 33 (late eleventh century B.C.) has recently been demonstrated.[1] The "Song of Moses" in Ch. 32, however, has appeared too heavily influenced by the prophetic movement to be placed as early as the Blessing. Recently a monograph by Eissfeldt[2] and articles by W. F. Albright and Patrick W. Skehan[3] have set forth the view that the Song may

* I would like to express my gratitude to my colleague, Frank M. Cross, Jr., for many insights which clarified my own thinking in our frequent discussions of the topic of this paper, and also to Edward F. Campbell, Jr., who was kind enough to read the manuscript and offer several suggestions for its improvement.

[1] See especially Frank M. Cross, Jr., and David Noel Freedman, JBL, LXVII (1948), pp. 191-210.

[2] Otto Eissfeldt, *Das Lied Moses Deut. 32:1-43 und das Lehrgedicht Asaphs Psalm 78 samt einer Analyse der Umgebung des Mose-Liedes* (Berichte über die Verhandlungen der Sächsischen Akademie der Wissenschaften zu Leipzig. Philologisch-historische Klasse, Band 104, Heft 5, 1958).

[3] W. F. Albright, "Some Remarks on the Song of Moses in Deuteronomy XXXII," VT, IX (1959), pp. 339-346; Patrick W. Skehan, "The Structure of the

be dated as early as the late eleventh century B.C.[4] Since this type of problem has always been close to the center of Professor James Muilenburg's scholarly interests, the following attempt to restudy the issue is gladly and affectionately dedicated to him.

I. TRANSLATION (DT. 32:1-43)

1. Give ear, O heavens, and I shall speak,   (Section 1)
   And hearken, O earth, to the words of my mouth.
2. Let my teaching fall like the rain;
   Let my word distil like the dew,
   Like . ? .[5] upon the grass,
   And like heavy rain upon vegetation.
3. Surely the name of Yahweh I will proclaim.
   Ascribe majesty to our God!

4. The Rock—perfect is his work.
   Indeed all his ways are just.
   A God of faithfulness without deceit
   Righteous and upright is he.

Song of Moses in Deuteronomy," CBQ, 13 (1951), pp. 153-163. The latter judiciously does not give a precise date, but simply implies that it can be early.

[4] Earlier articles, cited by Eissfeldt, which argued for an early date of the Song are those by U. Cassuto (*Atti del XIX Congresso Internationale degli Orientalisti Roma 23-29 Settembre 1935* [1938] pp. 480-484), for whom the "no-people" (vs. 21) are the Canaanites and the events behind the Song the same as those behind Jg. 5; and M. Frank (*Tarbiz*, 18 [1946-47], pp. 129-138), for whom the enemies in the Song are the Moabites and Ammonites of the period of the Judges. Paul Winter (ZAW, 67, [1956], pp. 40-48) has attempted to solve the problem by assuming that the Song is an editorial union of an old *Preislied* and a later *Scheltlied*, the first deriving from tribal history and poetry, and the second from a time of crisis shortly before the fall of the Judean state.

[5] The Hebrew word here obviously means "rain" or "showers" (cf. the parallelism), but the background and history of the term are obscure (hence the attempts at emendation). Frank M. Cross, Jr., suggests to me the possibility of the Ugaritic root š-r-', "surging" (water). Cf. Cyrus H. Gordon, *Ugaritic Grammar*, III (1947), Glossary No. 2002; and H. L. Ginsberg on II Sam. 1:21 in JBL, LXII (1943), pp. 111 f., n. 5.

5.   . . . . (?) . . . . (?) . . . . . .[6]
      A crooked and twisted generation.
6.   Is this the way you deal with Yahweh,
      O foolish and unwise people?
      Is he not thy father who created you?
      Did he not make you and form you?

7.   Remember the days of old;   (Section 2)
      Consider the years, generation by generation.
      Ask thy father and he will inform thee,
      Thy elders, and they will tell thee.
8.   When 'Elyôn[7] gave the nations their inheritances,
      When he separated the children of mankind,
      He set the boundaries of the peoples
      According to the number of the sons of God,[8]
9.   But Yahweh's apportionment was his people;
      Jacob was his measured inheritance.

10.   He found him in a desert land,
      In a wasteland, a howling wilderness.
      He encircled him; he cared for him;

[6] The Hebrew of the first colon of vs. 5 is obscure. Contrast RSV, Eissfeldt, E. Henschke (ZAW, 52 [1934], pp. 279 ff.) , the commentaries, and the ancient versions. The idea is surely clear from the parallel colon and from the words "not his sons" and "blemish"; but, lacking clearer indicators, caution suggests a question mark rather than the variety of conjectural emendations.

[7] An old appellation of deity borrowed from Canaan. Eissfeldt thinks it alludes to the deity who was once head of a pantheon in which Yahweh was a subisidiary deity. In archaic and archaizing contexts in the Old Testament, however, it is simply an appellative for Yahweh (e.g., Num. 24:16, where it is parallel to 'ēl and šadday; II Sam. 22:14, where it is parallel to Yahweh; 1 Sam. 1:10 as corrected, where there is the same parallelism; Gen. 14:22, etc.) . Consequently, it appears venturesome to say more than that in early Israel it was simply an honorific epithet for Yahweh. Cf. Aubrey R. Johnson's equally questionable 'Ēl 'Elyôn cult in pre-Davidic Jerusalem: Sacral Kingship in Ancient Israel (1955) , pp. 43 ff.

[8] So generally now following LXX and 4Q Dt.; cf. Patrick W. Skehan, BASOR, 136 (1954) , pp. 12-15; Frank M. Cross, Jr., Ancient Library of Qumrân (1958) , pp. 135-136; W. F. Albright, op. cit., p. 343. The term means "divine beings" and it appears to have been borrowed early by Israel to designate the members of Yahweh's heavenly court. The Qumrân MS actually preserves the original reading as bᵉnê 'ᵉᵉlōhîm (in a fragment found by Cross after publication of Skehan's article) : see Skehan, JBL, LXXVIII (1959) , p. 22.

He guarded him like the prize of his eye,

11. Like an eagle he stirs his nest,
    Over his young (?) he soars;
    He spreads his wings; he takes him;
    He carries him on his pinions.

12. It was Yahweh alone who led him
    And there was with him no illicit god.

13. He made him ride on the back of *Arṣ*,
    And gave him to eat[9] the produce of the field.
    He made him suck honey from rock
    And oil from flint-rock.

14. The butter of cows
    And the milk of goats
    With the fat of lambs,
    And rams of Bashan-breed, and he-goats
    With the term of the wheat!
    And the blood of grapes you drank (as) wine.

15b   You are fat, thick, gorged![10]
       (And) Jacob ate and was filled.[10]   (Section 3)

15a   And Jeshurun became fat and kicked (?).
       And he abandoned the God who made him;
       And he acted stupidly against the Rock
           of his salvation.

16. They made him jealous with strange (gods)[11]
    With (foreign?)[12] abominations they vexed him.

17. They sacrificed to demons, not divine;
    (Unto those) too deaf to approach they came;

[9] So with the LXX and Sam. instead of MT "he ate." The preceding colon does not make good sense except as it is highly metaphorical. F. M. Cross suggests a Canaanite mythological allusion, *Arṣ* being another name for *Môt*, Death.

[10] Vs. 15b is here transferred with Eissfeldt to form the second colon of the third poetic line of vs. 14, which otherwise would be too short. This enables one to bring back into the text from the LXX and Sam. the missing first colon of which vs. 15a is the second. This missing colon is also found in a 4Q phylactery; see Skehan, JBL, LXXVIII (1959), p. 22.

[11] Inserting *'ēlîm* or *'aelōhîm* with Albright in a colon otherwise too short.

[12] Albright suggests the insertion of *zārôt* (or perhaps *rā'ôt*) to fill out the colon. If, however, the line (vs. 16) were simply left as an odd 2 plus 2 in a prevailing 3 plus 3 context, the meaning as interperted by the inserted words would still be understood.

    Gods whom they did not know,
        And whom their fathers had not known![13]
18. The Rock who gave you birth you forgot;
        And you lost remembrance of the God who bore you.

19. And Yahweh saw (it) and was vexed[14]   (Section 4)
        At the insults[14] of his sons and daughters.
20. And he said:[15]
        I shall hide my face from them;
          I shall see what happens to them,
        Because a fickle generation are they,
          Children in whom is no stability.
21. They have made me jealous with a no-god;[16]
        They have vexed me with their "nothings."
        Therefore I shall make them jealous with a no-people;
        With a foolish nation I shall vex them.

22. Indeed a fire is kindled in my nostril (s)
        And it will burn even to Sheol below.
    And it will consume the earth and its produce;
        And it will devour the foundations of the mountains.
23. I will sweep over him calamities;
        My arrows I will spend on them:
24. Ravages of famine,
        Attacked by pestilence,
          And bitter stinging.

[13] The cola of vs. 17 are rearranged with Albright, partly on the basis of the LXX. In the second colon (MT vs. 17c) the difficulty is easily solved by Albright's shift of *daleth* to *resh* in the first word, so as to read "deaf" instead of "new." In the same colon, however, I retain the MT verb *bā'û* for Albright's suggested *'alêhem*. The rearrangement of the cola is not required, however, because the MT could be understood as climactic parallelism.

[14] Following LXX and a 4Q phylactery which have "become jealous" for "vexed" (*wyqn'* for *wayyin'aṣ*): Skehan, JBL, LXXVIII (1959), p. 22.

[15] That this (*wayyómer*) is an original element is doubtful. In any event, it must be interpreted as nothing more than a rubric, not as a part of the poetry.

[16] Albright renders the colon as follows: "They set up a no-god as my rival." This brings out the sense of the original most clearly, but I have chosen here to stay as near as possible to the verbal (as against the nominal) form of the Hebrew. Albright also renders *ka'as* (here translated "vex" in the sense of "offend") more strongly as "to be angry," surely the proper sense of the original, even though its primary and somewhat milder imagery is left behind.

And the teeth of beasts I will send on them,
With the poison of gliders in the dust.

25. Outside the sword will bring bereavement,
    And inside terror
For both youth and maiden,
    For suckling child as well as for the gray-haired man.

26. I would have said, I will scatter (?) them,
    I will extinguish their memory among men,

27. Except that I dreaded vexation from the enemy,
    Lest their adversaries misconstrue (it);
Lest they say, Our hand is high,
    And Yahweh did not do all this.

28. For a nation lacking sense are they,
    And there is among them no discernment.

29. If they were wise, they would have understood this;
    They would have seen through to their end.

30. How can one man chase a battalion,   (Section 5)
    Or two put a regiment to flight,
Unless their Rock had sold them,
    And Yahweh had given them up?

31. Truly not like our Rock is their rock (s)—
    Are not our enemies themselves the judges?[17]

32. Truly from the vine of Sodom is their vine,
    And from the terraces of Gomorrah.
Their grapes are grapes of poison;
    Bitter clusters belong to them.

33. Their wine is the poison of dragons,
    And the deadly venom of vipers.

34. Is this not stored up with me,
    Sealed in my treasuries,

35. For the day[18] of punishment[19] and requital,
    For the time when their foot slips?

[17] Interpreting this colon with Albright: *ha-lô'*, if not a part of the original text, is at least understood as needed to interpret the context.

[18] Following LXX and Sam., *le-yôm* for *lî*.

[19] The term *nāqām* should not be translated as "vengeance." As George E. Mendenhall has pointed out in an unpublished study, it is divine vindication, which may be punishment or salvation depending on the context.

Indeed the day of their calamity is near,
And events prepared for them make haste.

36.   Truly Yahweh will justify his people,
And on his servants he will have pity,
When he sees that their power is gone,
With neither bond nor free remaining,

37.   And when one says, Where are their gods,
The rock in whom they trusted,

38.   Who ate the fat of their sacrifices,
And drank the wine of their libations?
Let them rise and help you!
Let them be a shelter over you!

39.   See now that I (alone) am the one;   (Section 6)
And there is no other divine being with me.[20]
I am the one who kills and makes alive;
I wound, and it is I who heals;
And there is no deliverer from my hand.

40.   As surely as I lift my hand to the heavens,
And swear, As I live forever,

41.   I shall whet my flashing sword
And my hand shall seize in judgment.[21]
I shall render judgment on my adversaries
And punish those who hate me.

42.   I shall make my arrows drunk with blood,
And my sword shall eat flesh,
From the blood of the slain and captive,
From the unkempt[22] heads of the enemy.

[20] On this line see Albright, *op. cit.*, pp. 342 f., and Eissfeldt, *op. cit.*, p. 13. The
hû' ("he") is surely not a divine name, but the common copulative pronoun.
The translation here attempts to interpret the feeling of the original, without
being literal. The phrase "no god with me" ultimately means what Albright
renders "no other God than I," but I have here retained the literal rendering of
the preposition to preserve the Hebrew nonspeculative mode of expression: no
other power than that of Yahweh is engaged in the saving events. Effective power
in action, in contrast to the impotence of other "powers," might be one defini-
tion of Hebrew monotheism.

[21] Vss. 40 and 41a-b are in the form of a solemn oath not easily rendered in
English idiom. God is represented as raising his hand and solemnly swearing, "I
shall whet my flashing sword," etc.

[22] In the sense of long hair flying loose.

43. Shout for joy, O heavens, before him;   (Section 7)
      Worship him, all (ye) sons of God!
    Shout for joy, O nations, with his people;
      Ascribe might to him, all (ye) angels of God.
    Truly the blood of his children he will requite,
    And will purge the land of his people.[23]

II. STRUCTURE

It must be admitted that a translator's conception of the form
and over-all meaning of the poem influences his arrangement of
the poetic lines and even his rendering of the Hebrew, particularly at ambiguous points. Skehan (see n. 3) has cogently argued, for example, that the poem divides naturally into three
equal parts (A, vss. 1-14; B, vss. 15-29; C, vss. 30-43), each one
of which contains precisely twenty-three verses, representing
the number of letters in the Hebrew alphabet with an extra *pe*
line added at the close of each cycle. Indeed, in the first and last
main letters of the poet's identification of the poem as the
"words of my mouth" in vs. 1 (*'imrê-pî*) the pattern *aleph-pe*
is suggested. Furthermore, Skehan continues, sixty-nine verses
in number is the author's way of writing a seventy-line
poem. According to tradition the sons of Israel who went into
Egypt were seventy in number, and the Masoretic text's reading of *b^enê Yiśrā'ēl* in vss. 8-9 may have recalled that number.

---

[23] This verse simply cannot be reconstructed with certainty. The LXX has a
full text of eight cola. Of these the MT has substantially cola 3, 5, 6, and 8. The
Hebrew text of 4Q Dt. (see n. 8) has cola 1, 2 (with "sons" omitted), 5, 6, 7, and
8. In general Eissfeldt follows the 4Q text. Albright assumes that the LXX must
approximate the original and that the other texts are to be explained as having
lost certain cola. Skehan and Cross independently conclude that the LXX text is
a conflation: its cola 1 and 3 are doublets of one original; so are cola 2 and 4,
while cola 6 and 7 are simply revisions of vs. 41c and d. To me their argument
for cola 6 and 7 is convincing, but I have not been able to follow them in reducing
cola 1-4 from four to two elements. My own reconstruction preserves cola 1
(changing "with" to "before" though with great hesitation), 2, 3, 4, 5, and 8. I
am by no means certain about it, but would point to the contrasting parallelism
of cola 1 and 3 (which I think must surely be original), wherein the angels and
inhabitants of the earth are both called to rejoice, just as they were called as
witnesses in vs. 1 (see below).

Or if the original text read *bᵉnê 'ᵃelōhîm,* as is probable (see n. 8), we may recall that the Table of Nations in Gen. 10 originally had seventy names, and later tradition (e.g., Enoch 89:59 ff.) supports the notion that there were thought to be just seventy nations, and therefore seventy angels over them. One remembers also the seventy sons of the goddess Asherah at Ugarit, Moses and the seventy elders, the Jewish Sanhedrin composed of three sections with twenty-three in each, etc.

Hence it is clear to Skehan that the poem is tripartite in form, and he reconstructs each stanza as containing precisely two lines. The problem in vss. 14-15 is resolved differently from the way I have done it here in order to obtain precisely twenty-three lines in vss. 1-14, and the two-line reconstruction of vs. 43 is also necessitated. In both instances Skehan may indeed be correct. If his over-all view is also right, then we must conclude that external features of style and form were the chief influences upon the author's poetry. Skehan's analysis is based mainly on late Jewish sources, and a real problem arises as to how much of such formal numerical structuring can be read back into classical Hebrew material. Because of doubt on the point I have preferred to interpret the poem's form as inherent within its content. More will be said on this point below. My reconstruction of the poem in seven sections is based on an attempt to identify thought units. The paragraphing within these sections is not an attempt to reconstruct a series of stanzas original to the author, because we simply do not know enough about that aspect of Hebrew poetry. These paragraphs are only my interpretation of more or less coherent units of thought. It is on the main sections, however, that I would place particular stress.

Section 1. Introduction (vss. 1-6). In vss. 1-3 the poet begins by calling on all elements in heaven and earth to hear his words, and concludes with a summons to praise Yahweh. In vss. 4-6 he continues with a brief introductory statement of his theme: the goodness and stability of God, and by contrast the faithlessness of Israel to the God who made them a people (note the use of the rhyming terms *qānâ* and *kûn* with reference to the formation and election of Israel in vs. 6).

Section 2. Kerygma: Appeal to the mighty acts of God (vss. 7-14). This is the first main section of the poem, and it consists of a call to remember what God had done for Israel. First comes his election or choice of Israel to be his people (vss. 7-9), stated in terms of a suzerain administering a vast realm. Over each grouping of people (nation) he placed as administrator or governor a member of his heavenly court, but he retained Israel as his own to rule directly, rather than mediately (cf. Dt. 4:19-20). Next is a poetic statement of the wilderness and conquest themes. The poet portrays this as a time of extraordinary demonstration of God's loving care and asserts that he is solely responsible for this marvelous direction and provision of need, until Israel is now become very well fed, indeed fat and gorged (vss. 10-14, 15b).

Section 3. Indictment (vss. 15-18). This is the poet's formal statement of the second part of the theme announced in vss. 5-6: in their satisfied condition, Israel abandoned their true Rock and turned to idolatry. If the poet's primary form is a legal one, as will be affirmed below, then these verses constitute the indictment.

Section 4. The Sentence or Penalty (vss. 19-29). As response to the indictment, Yahweh himself is now heard to deliver the sentence: Because of Israel's idolatry he will trouble them with a "no-people," a "foolish nation" (vss. 20-21); fire, warfare, pestilence, and beasts (that is, the unruly in both nature and history) will bring terror and destruction (vss. 22-25). The reason God did not decree complete destruction to Israel was not that they were undeserving of it; the only reason was that the enemy people whom he expected to use as his agent were so lacking in sense that they would think they had wrought the destruction by their own power (vss. 26-29). This sentence by Yahweh is introduced by vs. 19, in which the poet explains that when God saw what Israel had done, he acted. In other words, the sentence by its context may be understood as having been carried out. Israel has indeed suffered from the hands of an enemy, though not scattered or extinguished as a nation (vs. 26).

Section 5. The poet's assurance of salvation (vss. 30-38). It is quite obvious to the poet that Israel's trouble at the enemy's hand could only be a result of Yahweh's giving them up. It cannot be inferred that the gods of the enemy have done it; for everything belonging to them is vile and poisonous, and the time is near when God's just and punishing action against them will take place (vss. 30-35). Indeed, Yahweh will have pity upon his people and save them as soon as he sees that their power is gone and it is publicly acknowledged that the false gods to which they have turned are powerless to help them (vss. 36-39).

Section 6. The Word of Yahweh confirming the poet's words of hope (vss. 39-42). This second speech of Yahweh (see Section 4) stands parallel to, and is a confirmation of, the poet's statement to Israel of the grounds for hope in the present situation. Yet here the case is stated generally, as though quoted from past oracles. It need not be taken as a fresh word of promise applying directly to the present situation but is instead a hope derivable from God's former revelation of his will. Thus he begins by affirming that it is indeed he who has sent the punishment (cf. vss. 30-31), for he alone brings life and death and no one can save or be saved from his power (vs. 39). Furthermore, as surely as though God had sworn a mighty oath about it, one can take full confidence in his determination to punish all his enemies (vss. 40-42).

Section 7. The poet's final exhortation for praise (vs. 43). In this confidence the poet now turns back to those addressed at the beginning (vs. 1) and calls on the whole of God's heavenly assembly to shout for joy and to worship or praise him, for he will surely save his people and cleanse their land.

III. ATTEMPTS TO DATE THE SONG

Eissfeldt's survey of the main treatments of the poem in the past need not be repeated in detail here. Beginning over a century ago, the main attempts to interpret the historical background and date of the Song have centered around the identification of the enemy people who had afflicted Israel, according to vss. 19-29. Scholars have argued for the Arameans of the mid-ninth century, for the Assyrians in the second half of the eighth century, and for the Babylonians during the early sixth century.[24] In 1953 I decided that there was no way to choose between the three views with any confidence, though I felt that the poem was surely pre-Exilic.[25] Most scholars, however, have preferred a late date because, as Eissfeldt has summarized the argument (pp. 17-20); (1) the poem has many connections in style and vocabulary with Jeremiah, Ezekiel, Second and "Third" Isaiah; (2) its high religio-ethical concerns indicate a special relationship with prophecy (e.g., Cornill's description of the poem as a "compendium of prophetic theology"[26]); and (3) so also does its high conception of God.

To these arguments Eissfeldt's reply is cogent: (1) In cases of literary dependence it is difficult to establish the direction of influence. It is certainly as easy to argue that Dt. 32 is older than Jeremiah as it is to argue the dependence of the former on the latter. Furthermore, one must always reckon with the possibility that both have been influenced by a third but unknown source, or derived from common tradition. (2) We can no longer assume that the prophets are the originators of Israel's concern for ethics. They have rootage in an old tradition of ethical concerns which was believed to go back ultimately to Moses. In any event, the supposition that God had given his people over to an enemy because they had displeased him was not confined to Israel (cf. the ninth-century Mesha inscription in which Chemosh is said to have given Moab to Omri of Israel because he was angry with his land). (3) As for the idea of God in the Old Testament, it has been argued that in early Israel there was no denial of the existence of other gods; the sole lordship of God which is expressed in this poem is another influence

[24] We can probably exclude from consideration Sellin's attempt to date the poem in the fifth century by seeing the Samaritans as the enemy (ZAW, 43 [1925], pp. 161-173).

[25] IB, II (1953), p. 517.

[26] Quoted by A. Bertholet, Deuteronomium, KHC V (1899), p. 95.

of the great prophets, especially Second Isaiah. Yet today we must affirm, says Eissfeldt, that long before Second Isaiah, back in the time of Israel's struggle for a living space among the other peoples, there were surely great expressions of the incomparable individuality and power of Yahweh. Indeed, it would be precisely the time of the Conquest and of the United Monarchy when such a religious polemic would have its proper, or at least most vigorous, setting. Ps. 82, for example, in all probability belongs to such an early time, and, Eissfeldt continues, the so-called "enthronement psalms," even if not as early as the tenth century, surely rest on predecessors that were.

Eissfeldt's own argument for the Song's date is based on the attempt to identify anew the "no-people" of vs. 21. He believes that the best case can be made out for the Philistines of the period of the Judges, especially at the time between the catastrophe in which the Ark was lost and the first victories of Saul, a period which he would date between *ca.* 1070 and 1020 B.C. Hence he believes the poem to derive from a source among the central tribes in the eleventh century and to have been taken up by the Elohist and made a part of his work in the mid-ninth century. This view eliminates the problem of the poem's editorial setting in Dt. 31-32 because the document is indeed older, not later, than its context.

It must be admitted, however, that Eissfeldt's argument from direct historical allusions in the Song itself is no stronger than the arguments for the later enemies in the ninth, eighth, or sixth centuries. The strength of his case actually rests upon his comparison of the Song with Ps. 78 and upon his contention that both derive ultimately from the same Philistine events in the eleventh century. The two poems are very much alike in the way they rehearse the mighty acts of God as the background for the story of Israel's rebellion and faithlessness. In each case God has used an enemy to punish his people, and the explanation of the punishment appears to have been the occasion for the composition. In Ps. 78:9, 60-61 the historical reference is explicit: the Ephraimites were defeated because they did not keep God's covenant. Therefore God abandoned the tabernacle at Shiloh and delivered "his power" into captivity. This can only mean the Philistine defeat and capture of the Ark as narrated in I Sam. 4. Because of the similarity of the two poems it is clear to Eissfeldt that the vague references to the "no-people" in Dt. 32:21 must echo the same incident. On the other hand, it is also clear that Ps. 78 comes from Judah, indeed from the court of David in Jerusalem, at a time when the Philistine problem had been resolved in David's victories and in the theology of the covenant made with David. Dt. 32, however, is Ephraimite or Benjaminite and comes from a slightly earlier time when the victories over the Philistines were only beginning or were simply promised.

Eissfeldt's argument is very persuasive, although two unresolved problems remain: (1) What would a form-critical study conclude regarding the *Gattung* and *Sitz im Leben* of each of the two poems? In its present form Ps. 78 is a meditation on the marvelous works of Yahweh, introduced in the style of a teacher who asks that his teaching be heard ("Give ear, O my people, to my teaching"). The meditation recounts the history of God's dealings with Israel from the Exodus[27] to the reign of David, emphasizing the faithlessness of Israel, for which reason God abandoned Shiloh, gave his people to the sword, and "rejected the tent of Joseph" (vs. 67). Then Yahweh awoke, as though he were one asleep, smote his enemies, chose Judah, Mt. Zion "which he loves," "built his sanctuary," and "chose David his servant . . . to be shepherd over Jacob, his people" (vss. 65-66, 68-72). There can be no doubt that the psalm belongs to the literature of the royal enthronement in the Jerusalem court and Temple. While the saving acts of God are recited as backdrop for a confession of national sin, the tension is completely resolved in the new national security achieved by David. The setting is the Jerusalem court of the tenth century, but the form is difficult to specify in detail. It is not liturgical but didactic, the present purpose being to justify the hegemony of Judah over

---

[27] Vss. 44-51 rehearse the signs or "plagues" wrought in Egypt, following apparently the seven-plague tradition of J in Exodus. Contrast Ps. 105:27-36 which appears to follow the ten-plague tradition of P: see, for example, the forthcoming article by J. L. Mihelic and the writer on "The Plagues in Exodus," in *Interpreter's Dictionary of the Bible*.

Ephraim, of Jerusalem over Shiloh. Whether that purpose was the original one may be questioned (see below) but not finally answered with certainty.[28]

By contrast the form of Dt. 32 is much clearer; it is that of a *rib* or lawsuit, as will be argued in the next section, and the tension it creates is unrelieved except by means of generalized expressions of hope. One must agree with Eissfeldt that its source is northern, rather than Judean; but the assumption that its content reflects the same Philistine victory as that interpreted in Ps. 78, while attractive and possible, is by no means as certain as Eissfeldt claims, especially when the radical difference in form is taken seriously (but see below).

A second question is whether the archaic features in both poems may not be explained by assuming that their authors have employed old material, adapting it to a function different from its original one. One cannot avoid the suspicion that this is the case in both instances, though we lack a sufficient amount of old poetry to be able to prove this, especially with Ps. 78. It is the contention of this essay, however, that Dt. 32 is a "broken" *rib*, that is, a specific cultic form adapted and expanded by other

[28] A detailed treatment of Ps. 78 cannot be given here. H.-J Kraus' analysis is the most recent to be published (*Biblischer Kommentar: Altes Testament*, XV, Fasc. 7 [1959], pp. 535-548), but its positive results are disappointing. A detailed form-critical analysis is not undertaken and the dating of the psalm in the post-Exilic period, because of an assumed need to posit a time when its wisdom and supposed Deuteronomic elements could be combined, is completely unconvincing. The assumed dependence on the Deuteronomic circle is accepted from the argument of H. Junker, "Die Entstehungszeit des Ps. 78 und das Deuteronomium," *Biblica*, XXXIV (1953), pp. 493 ff. Of interest, however, is Kraus' suggestion that the singer in the psalm was originally a Levitical priest whose teaching is related to that in the work of the Chronicler (see G. von Rad, "Die levitische Predigt in den Büchern der Chronik," *Festschrift O. Procksch* [1934], pp. 113-124; reprinted in his *Gesammelte Studien zum Alten Testament* [1958], pp. 248-261; for von Rad's own remarks on the psalm see *ibid.*, pp. 19, 61 f.). A. Weiser in his *Die Psalmen*, ATD (1959), 15, pp. 366-369, also considers the psalm to be priestly *torah*, but because it contains no allusion to the destruction of the Temple he believes it clearly to be pre-Exilic. As to its relationship to Deuteronomy, he asks whether it is a purely literary dependence, or whether both derive from a cultic tradition which is clearly older than its literary witnesses. Weiser obviously inclines to the latter view, though he does not desire to commit himself further (see also n. 60).

themes to serve a more generalized purpose in confession and praise.[29]

IV. PRIMARY FORM: THE COVENANT LAWSUIT

Because the Song appears to contain a mixture of elements, it has not permitted clear form-critical analysis. In one place Aage Bentzen discusses it in relation to Pss. 78, 106, 50, 81, and 95 as a versified penitential address from a circle of cultic prophets, a type which is the presupposition of the prose sermons (e.g., in Dt.) and prophetic exhortations, just as many other psalms are the prototypes of prose prayers, etc.[30] A few pages farther along, however, he sees in the Song a mixture of styles (wisdom, prophetic sermon, parenetic meditation on history); this strongly suggests that it is comparatively late, though it had a separate history before being placed in its present context.[31] Indeed, about the only point on which scholarship agrees is that the poem represents a mixture of forms, the *Sitz im Leben* of which is unclear.

[29] Albright, *op. cit.*, does not present a detailed argument for the antiquity of Dt. 32. He says only that cases of archaic morphology and vocabulary are common, and that it is difficult not to see instances of archaic consonantal spelling without *matres lectionis* at the end of words, a factor which generally suggests an original not later than the tenth century B.C. The poem is later than the compositions like those in Jg. 5 and Ex. 15, which are characterized by archaic repetitive parallelism. While examples of repetition following Canaanite patterns appear, they are relatively few. Instead the style points toward the tenth century, when paranomasia tends to replace the older repetitive style. One of the difficulties with the poem, however, is precisely that it possesses its own style and so lacks a sufficient number of specific characteristics to place it precisely within the typological history of early poetry which Albright has slowly been constructing. One thing is clear, it seems to me: the poem almost totally lacks the personifications of nature and the elaborate quotation of borrowed images and phrases from Canaanite poetry which were so frequent in the more ornate compositions of pre-ninth-century Israel. Vs. 13a is probably an exception (see n. 9 above), while vss. 13, 18, 36, and 39 clearly show archaic orthography, and the repeated use of *mô* as the third plural pronominal suffix is an old element.

[30] Aage Bentzen, *Introduction to the Old Testament* (1948), Vol. I, p. 160.

[31] *Ibid.*, pp. 208-209; Vol. II (1949), p. 40. Gunkel and Begrich likewise list it as a "Mischgedicht" (*Einleitung in die Psalmen* [1933], p. 330).

It seems to me that we are now in position to probe the mixture and assert that basic to the Song is one distinguishable form
which the psalmist has elaborated. This is the divine lawsuit, or
rîb. Gunkel dealt with the form in his psalm-studies under the
title *Gerichtsrede,* along with the associated terms *Schelt-,
Droh-,* and *Mahnrede,* all of which are derived from the form
criticism of prophecy.[32] Indeed, Gunkel treats them under the
heading "Das Prophetische in den Psalmen." New emphases,
beginning with an important article by H. Wheeler Robinson,
have contributed much to clarify the form.[33] It presupposes a belief which Israel shared with Canaan, in a heavenly assembly of
divine beings, an *ʿᵃdat ʾēl* (Ps. 82:1), *a môʿēd, sôd,* or *qāhāl,* the
members of which are designated by a variety of terms, among
them *bᵉnê ʾᵃlōhîm* (see above, n. 8), or simply *ʾᵃlōhîm,
malʾākîm* ("angels" or "messengers"), *qᵉdôšîm* ("holy ones"),
etc. Together they also may be designated as the "army (*ṣᵉbâ*)
of heaven" (e.g., I Kgs. 22:19; cf. Dt. 4:19) as well as "assembly"
or "council."[34]

In prophecy, as H. Wheeler Robinson pointed out so clearly,
the dominant picture is that of the heavenly assembly serving as
a court of law. The prophet understood himself to be one who
not only could hear what went on during the heavenly *rîb,*[35]
but also to have been appointed as an officer of the court
(a *malʾāk,* "messenger" or "herald") to announce its verdict, and
perhaps even to expound the verdict and to reveal some of the
proceedings in the heavenly trial. The Micaiah story in I Kg. 22

[32] Gunkel and Begrich, *op. cit.,* pp. 33 ff., and especially pp. 361-367.
[33] H. Wheeler Robinson, "The Council of Yahweh," JTS, XLV (1944), pp. 151
ff.; and subsequently his *Inspiration and Revelation in the old Testament* (1946),
pp. 167 ff. See also my discussion of it in relation to Ps. 82 in *The Old Testament
Against Its Environment* (1950), pp. 30 ff.; Frank M. Cross, Jr., "The Council of
Yahweh in Second Isaiah," JNES, XII (1953), pp. 274-277; James Muilenburg's
commentary on Isa. 40-45 in IB, V (1956).
[34] See further the writer, *op. cit.,* pp. 32-36; and especially Cross, "The Council
of Yahweh . . . ," nn. 1 and 3, for a concise summary of the evidence and the
Canaanite parallels. It is now time for the evidence to be assembled and sifted in
detail.
[35] For a study of the usages of this term in the Old Testament, see especially
B. Gemser, "The *Rib*—or Controversy—Pattern in Hebrew Mentality," *Wisdom
in Israel and in the Ancient Near East,* M. Noth and D. W. Thomas, eds., Suppl.
VT, III (1955), pp. 120-137.

and the calls of both First and Second Isaiah (Isa. 6 and 40) are excellent examples of the conception.[36]

That the lawsuit pattern is the central form in Dt. 32 may be seen from the official summons to the witnesses in vs. 1, the indictment in Section 3 (vss. 15-18), and the verdict of the Judge in Section 4 (vss. 19-29). In the delivery of the sentence God as the Judge is quoted directly by the psalmist. Otherwise in vs. 1 and during the indictment the psalmist speaks as the officer of the court, convening the witnesses and reciting the formal charges as they have been made in the heavenly court. The Gunkel-Begrich analysis of this particular form has been put into outline form by Herbert B. Huffmon as follows:[37]

I. A description of the scene of judgment
II. The speech of the plaintiff
    A. Heaven and earth appointed judges
    B. Summons to the defendant (or judges)
    C. Address in the second person to the defendant
        1. Accusation of the defendant in question form
        2. Refutation of the defendant's possible arguments
        3. Specific indictment

In Dt. 32 we may perhaps see II.A and all of II.C; the psalmist here (like the prophet) speaks for the plaintiff. II.A is vs. 1 although, as we shall see, "heaven" and "earth" in these contexts are scarcely to be considered "judges." II.C.1 may be seen in vss. 4-6; II.C.2 is in Section 2 (vss. 7-14) although, as we shall see, there is probably a better interpretation of it; and II.C.3 is our Section 3 (vss. 15-18). To be added to the Gunkel analysis of the form, however, is another section: the verdict or sentence of the heavenly Judge, addressed either by him directly to the defendant (Israel) or by the prophet as the royal spokesman (or by the latter quoting the Judge's words). Indeed, in pre-Exilic

[36] For this interpretation of Isa. 40, see especially the works of Cross and Muilenburg cited in n. 33.

[37] See his article, "The Covenant Lawsuit in the Prophets," JBL, LXXVIII (1959), pp. 285-95. An alternate form need not concern us here since it is based almost solely on Ps. 82. In one paragraph on pp. 288-289 Huffmon has stated the same conclusion regarding the primary form of Dt. 32 as that being independently argued here.

prophecy this divine sentence is the basic subject matter, while in Dt. 32, as previously stated, it constitutes the fourth section (vss. 19-29).[38]

The appeal to "heaven" and "earth" in vs. 1, however, needs a more adequate explanation. Four other excellent poetic examples of the divine lawsuit, which include this formula, appear in the Old Testament. Isa. 1:2 is the closest example. Mic. 6:2 calls to the "mountains" and to the "foundations of the earth" to hear the case of Yahweh against his people. In Jer. 2:4-13, vs. 12 mentions the heavens in a similar context as a witness to the indictment; and the parallel colon may well have had "mountains" (*hārîm bô* for *hārᵉbû*).[39] Ps. 50 also derives from, or uses, the lawsuit form and in vs. 4 heavens and earth are summoned (cf. the allusion in Job 20:27). And finally three especially interesting examples appear in the hortatory prose of Deuteronomy: 4:26; 30:19; and 31:28. In each passage Moses is warning Israel of the consequences of disobedience to the covenant; and in each case, in legal style, the call is given to heaven and earth to serve as witnesses of the broken covenant (the Hiphil conjugation of *'ûd;* see n. 48). These passages appear in sections which are supplementary to the main core of the Book of Deuteronomy (chs. 5-28) and which refer to that core as "this Book of the Law."[40] The background of Deuteronomy in the Mosaic covenant theology (as distinct from the Abrahamic or Davidic covenant pattern), and in the liturgical renewal of that covenant once celebrated at Shechem, has been much stressed in recent exposition.[41] Thus it is clear from these passages that in the Deuteronomic tradition the celebration of covenant renewal in the course of time embodied elements of the lawsuit. Were it

[38] It is, of course, obvious that no Biblical example contains all of the elements that might have been supposed to belong to the heavenly trial. The Biblical authors use the theme in different ways, differing elements being emphasized. They are primarily interested in the exposition of the *meaning* of the trial, rather than in a detailed report.

[39] See Cross, "The Council of Yahweh . . . ," p. 275, n. 3; and Huffmon, *op. cit.,* p. 288.

[40] See the writer in IB, II (1953) , pp. 311 ff.

[41] See especially G. von Rad, *Gesammelte Studien,* pp. 33ff., *Studies in Deuteronomy* and the writer, IB, II, pp. 311 ff.

otherwise the lawsuit would not have been understood as the form of Moses' warning.

Inasmuch as all of the passages cited above have to do with the Mosaic covenant tradition (as distinct from the Davidic) and with the threatened or actual breach of that covenant, Huffmon is surely correct in saying that they possess the form of a "covenant lawsuit."[42] In the past it has been quite difficult to understand the meaning of the appeal to heaven and earth, except as a purely poetic device to secure attention for something deemed most serious. Huffmon is again correct in seeing that this discussion has reached a turning point with the study by George E. Mendenhall, *Law and Covenant in Israel and the Ancient Near East* (1955).[43] His discovery of the form lying behind the Mosaic covenant, the suzerainty treaty between an emperor and his vassal, turns attention particularly to the Hittite treaties of the Late Bronze Age.[44] The sanctions of the treaties are purely religious, appeal being made to the gods of the contracting parties to serve as witnesses. Following the detailed listing of divine names, there appears the summarizing formula, "the mountains, the rivers, the springs, the great sea, heaven and earth, the winds (and) clouds—let these be witness to this treaty and to this oath"—or the like.[45] In this context heaven and earth are meant to refer to all the gods who have charge over the universe. When the treaty form was adopted to depict the meaning of God's election of Israel, this element of the treaty for obvious reasons had to be set aside or reinterpreted. In Ex. 19-20 and 24 there is no mention of witnesses. In Jos. 24 it is the people who are witnesses of their own oath (vs. 22, *'ēdîm 'attem bākem*). Only in the "later" poetic and hortatory contexts, as indicated above, does the reference to the natural elements as treaty testators reappear.

Huffmon has difficulty, however, in interpreting the precise role which "heaven and earth" were supposed to play in the

---

[42] Huffmon, *op. cit.*, pp. 291-295.

[43] Reprinted from BA, XVII (1954), Nos. 2 and 3.

[44] See ANET, pp. 199-206, and particularly Viktor Korošec, *Hethitische Staatsverträge* (1931).

[45] Cf. also the later treaties cited by Huffmon, *op. cit.*, pp. 291-292, n. 23.

lawsuit. Although the judicial function of the divine assembly is known,[46] he cannot accept the thesis of Cross and myself that the prophetic lawsuit-oracle originated in the conception of God's heavenly assembly acting as a court. The reason, he says, is that there is no direct evidence that "heaven and earth" as such served as members of the council. The only passages that might have some relevance are those in which heaven and earth are called upon to sing or rejoice (e.g., Isa. 44:23; 49:13; Jer. 51:48; I Chr. 16:31; Ps. 96:11; etc.). The natural elements are addressed in the lawsuit-oracles, Huffmon continues, "because they are witnesses to the (prior) covenant," as the Hittite treaties indicate, but "the precise function of these witnesses is still not clear. The formal analogy with court procedure would strongly suggest that heaven and earth serve as judges, for Yahweh is the plaintiff and Israel the accused. Heaven and earth as judges may be a literary fiction, but it would be more appropriate if the judge could serve as the executor of the sentence in actual court practice. . . . since the natural world served to carry out the curses and blessings."

It seems possible to say more than this, even though our knowledge of ancient judicial procedures is limited. First of all, it is doubtful whether one should expect to find the mountains, rivers, heaven and earth, etc., listed per se as members of the heavenly assembly. If my interpretation of the witness section in the Hittite treaties is correct, the natural elements listed after the divine personal names are not *additional* gods, but rather summarizing categories into which all gods, known and unknown, would have fallen in polytheistic thought. That they never appear as members of the divine assembly is, therefore, not surprising, and means nothing as far as our problem is concerned.

Secondly, at the root of the problem is Gunkel's mistaken assertion that "heaven and earth"[47] are summoned in the Biblical

---

[46] See Thorkild Jacobsen, for example, "Primitive Democracy in Ancient Mesopotamia," JNES, II (1943) pp. 159-72; Ps. 82; Zech. 3.

[47] Or in Mic. 6:2 the "mountains" and "foundations of the earth" (i.e., evidently the cosmic mountains supporting the dome of heaven, and those supporting the earth) in the deep below.

form to act as judges. It is impossible, in my judgment, to make coherent sense of the passages on such an interpretation. *The heavenly lawsuit implies a Suzerain, one who claims authority over all powers on earth, and who is presiding over the highest tribunal in the universe. Furthermore, it implies a covenant which the Suzerain has granted a vassal, a covenant which the vassal has broken.* It is inconceivable in such a situation that the Suzerain would call in a third party as judge and jury in a case where his own prerogatives and stipulations have been violated, especially when that third party can only be a subsidiary being or beings in the Suzerain's domain. Instead, the Suzerain has only to call in the witnesses to the original treaty and let them hear the charges, not to act as judges but simply to testify that they had been witnesses of the original oath which the vassal has now broken.[48] In a sense, then, the witnesses were perhaps a special type of "jury." As powers of nature in the original polytheistic setting, they were also agents of the Suzerain for the execution of the natural curses stipulated in the treaty for its violation.

In no case should these witnesses be conceived as holding or wielding power. Here the Suzerain is himself the real Judge, Plaintiff, and Jury; he is the one who has been violated, and since there is no power above him he wields power himself, both accusing and sentencing. The heavenly assembly is in this case only witness and counsel (cf. I Kg. 22:20-22), nothing more. Consequently neither the example of the "primitive democracy" in the Mesopotamian divine council (see note 46) nor that of any polytheistic pantheon is entirely relevant to the interpretation of the Israelite divine lawsuit. More to the point would be some knowledge of what formal proceedings were undertaken by the Hittite suzerain when one of his vassals broke the oath that bound him. Since we do not have this information, we can only make inferences like those above, for which a considerable amount of evidence from our sources can be amassed.

[48] "To witness" or "testify against" (Hiphil of *'ûd* plus the preposition *b*) in this context thus means to confront the accused with his broken oath, or to witness in court against one who has violated an oath.

A final question with regard to the witnesses, "heaven and earth," may now be asked. What did Israel mean precisely by them? Two possibilities may be suggested. One is that Israel simply took the polytheistic mode of expression poetically as a designation for the "angels," that is, for all those divine powers whom God associated with himself as his "ministers" or assistants in the administration of his universal realm, with duties over both heavenly and earthly spheres. The other is a suggestion of R. B. Y. Scott that heaven and earth in the contexts being discussed "are not elements of the natural world, but are called upon as population areas—the heavenly hosts and the people on earth respectively. . . ."[49] That the terms were taken to mean angels and men in later eras of interpretation is probable, especially since Judaism demythologized the heavenly assembly conception.[50] The occasional poetic call to various peoples to witness God's indictment of Israel could be taken as evidence for such a reinterpretation of the mythological conception at least as early as the eighth century B.C. Am. 3:9 ff. calls on Assyria and Egypt to assemble in the mountains of Samaria as witnesses of the great disorders in Israel, and perhaps even to "hear and testify against the house of Jacob" (vs. 13). In a different context this call to the people is, of course, common in the trial theme of Isa. 41 ff. In Ps. 96:10-11 the exultant cry is proclaimed among the nations that Yahweh reigns, that "he will judge the peoples with equity." Thereupon the heavens and earth are called upon to rejoice and be glad. In Ps. 97:6 in parallel cola are "the heavens" and "all the peoples." That one should beware of too complete a rationalization of the term "earth" in the passage cited, however, is suggested by Ps. 148, in which there are two main sections: "Praise Yahweh from the heavens" (vss. 1-6), and "Praise Yahweh from the earth" (vss. 7-13). In this case "earth" includes not only kings and all peo-

---

[49] See his brief reference in his commentary on Isa. 1:2, (IB V [1956]). A lengthier treatment of "The Literary Structure of Isaiah's Oracles" by the same author is in *Studies in Old Testament Prophecy*, by H. H. Rowley, ed. (1950), pp. 175-186. I owe these references to Huffmon, *op. cit.*, p. 290.

[50] The indictment in Ps. 82 was understood to refer to human, Israelite judges (cf. Jn. 10:34), and the original reading, *bené 'aelōhim*, in Dt. 32:8 was changed to *bᵉné Yiśrā'ēl*.

ple, but also sea monsters, deeps, fire, hail, snow, wind, mountains, trees, animals, and birds! Nevertheless, in the light of such evidence it appears only reasonable to conclude that vs. 43 of our poem may be used as evidence for Israel's reinterpretation of the polytheistic expressions.

If these contexts are followed, one could affirm that Israel demythologized the meaning of the term "earth" in the covenant lawsuit to the extent that it no longer conveyed the notion of divine beings in charge of earth, as in the Hittite treaties, but simply the entities visible on earth. This would, of course, mean that there was no sense of nature's being inanimate in either heaven or earth; instead the various elements all possessed some kind of psychic life.[51]

Now that we have identified the covenant lawsuit form in Dt. 32, but before we attempt isolation of its elements, let us discuss the Mosaic covenant form, reconstructed by Mendenhall from the Hittite suzerainty treaties,[52] on which form the lawsuit rests for its legal basis.

Form of the Mosaic Covenant Renewal

1. Yahweh as Suzerain, or his representative who leads the covenant-renewal ceremony, recites his benevolent acts to Israel (the Credo, or Old Testament kerygma).

Yahweh speaks, or is quoted, in the first person, addressing Israel as his vassal. The precise content is not stereotyped but varies with the situation, though it is always set within the chief elements of the kerygma: the leading of and promises to the Patriarchs; the deliverance from Egypt, including the marvelous acts of power demonstrated in the defeat of Pharaoh; the kindly and benevolent leading through the terrible wilder-

[51] Cf. H. Wheeler Robinson, *Inspiration and Revelation in the Old Testament* (1946), Chap. I.

[52] Mendenhall, *op. cit.;* and also James Muilenburg, "The Form and Structure of the Covenantal Formulations," VT, IX (1959), pp. 347-365. Cf. also now Klaus Baltzer, *Das Bundesformular* (1960).

ness; and the gift of the Promised Land. This recitation will usually be preceded by a preamble in which the Suzerain is identified or identifies himself. (Ex. 20:2; Jos. 24:2-13; cf. I Sam. 10:18; 12:6-8; Dt. 6:21-23; 29:2-9 [Heb. 1-8]).

2. Next are read the stipulations of the covenant, the will of the Suzerain, to which the vassal (Israel) vowed solemn obedience (Ex. 19:7-8; 24:3-7; Jos. 24:23-26; cf. I Sam. 10:25; II Kg. 23:2-3; Neh. 8:2 ff.; Dt. 6:24-25).

The primary form of these stipulations, or, as Mendenhall has put it, the legal *policies* given the community by the Suzerain, were his "Words," the Decalogue (Ex. 20:1; 24:3-4, 8; 34: 27-28;[53] Dt. 5:22), which were kept in a special portable coffer, called the "Ark of the Covenant" (or in the tradition of the Jerusalem priesthood, the "Ark of the Testimony"—ʿēdût; Ex. 25:21-22; 26:33).[54] Various collections of legal procedures

---

[53] Frank M. Cross, Jr., and I believe we have demonstrated in an unpublished article that these verses in Ex. 34 do not refer to a supposed "ritual decalogue" (which only with the gravest difficulty can be "found" in the preceding vss. 18-26). Instead, Ex. 34 once contained the Yahwist document's rendition of the covenant; but only two of the commandments are preserved in the parenetic setting (see vss. 10, 14, and 17). The remainder for some unexplained reason has been displaced or omitted, and a ritual calendar inserted (vss. 18-26), another form of which is preserved also in Ex. 23:12-19 (plus Ex. 12:12-13; cf. 34:19-20).

[54] Discussions about the Ark have always been troubled by the problem of harmonizing two emphases found in the traditions. In one it is the most sacred object of the Tribal League, containing within it the covenant document, the Decalogue. The other (P), while knowing the contents of the chest, emphasizes the lid with the cherubim, which symbolized the throne of God and which was called the *kappōret* (AV and RSV "mercy seat"). In this case the Ark symbolizes not so much the covenant unity of the tribes in treaty with Yahweh as the holy place where Yahweh may be met for purposes of revelation and atonement (cf. Ex. 25:22). In the past when the literary-critical school assumed the idea of the covenant to be late theocratic doctrine, the title "Ark of the Covenant" was also considered a late phenomenon. With our present knowledge, I think a more reasonable case can be made for the assumption that the title is original and that the object was indeed the chest which held the holy "Words." The emphasis on the *kappōret* may well have been elaborated later, especially in the time of David, when the Mosaic covenant theology had lost its vigor and was virtually displaced in Jerusalem by the theology of the Davidic covenant. For the great influence of the reign of David on the climax and end of the Tabernacle or desert-tent institution, see especially the preliminary treatment of Frank M. Cross, Jr., BA, X, 3 (1947), pp. 63-65. In addition, we may note Albright's discovery that P's ʿēdût reflects an older ʿâdôt, meaning "covenant" (*From the Stone Age to Christianity* [Anchor Books ed., 1957]), p. 16.

(*mišpāṭîm, ḥuqqîm*) were made at different times and places, however. Whatever the original purpose of the collections, those preserved in the Old Testament have been used liturgically in covenant renewal ceremonies, as is clear from the parenetic setting, especially the conclusions affixed to each (see further below). This is evident in the "Book of the Covenant" (Ex. 21-23), the "Holiness Code" (Lev. 17-26), and the Deuteronomic Code (Dt. 12-26). In fact, the latter, in its framework and in the Deuteronomic history of Israel (Jos.-II Kg.), is repeatedly referred to as "this book of the *tôrâ*," on the basis of which covenant renewal was vowed. Deuteronomic tradition records that Moses ordered it to be placed by the side of the Ark of the Covenant in the sanctuary (Dt. 31:26).

3. At the conclusion of the reading of the *tôrâ* vows were taken; evidently there was a statement concerning the witnesses and a declaration of the vassal's solemn obligation to be loyal and obedient to the Suzerain's stipulations.

As pointed out above, there are two traditions in the Old Testament concerning witnesses, one reinterpreting the polytheist expression "heaven and earth," and the other abandoning it in favor of the view that the vassals were themselves the witnesses of their own vow (cf. Jos. 24:22). The latter verse, along with Ex. 24:8 ("Behold, the blood of the covenant which Yahweh has made with you on the basis of all these words") and Dt. 26:16-19 (cf. also I Sam. 12:20-25), suggests that the ceremony of the vows and witnesses concluded with a solemn declaration of the binding nature of the covenant and the obligation now to keep it.

4. Finally, there was the parenetic recitation of the benefits and the terrors consequent on obedience and disobedience.

Only in the Deuteronomic tradition (Dt. 27-28) are these specifically called "blessings and curses," as also in the Hittite treaties, though the identical idea is present elsewhere even when not given this specific formulation (cf. Ex. 23:20-33; Lev. 26:3-45).

Put succinctly, then, the covenant-renewal form was as follows: (1) recital of the Suzerain's benevolent acts (the Credo), preceded by a preamble which identifies the Suzerain; (2) the stipulations of the covenant; (3) vows, witnesses, and solemn declaration; (4) blessings and curses.[55]

An attempt to recover the form of the covenant lawsuit from Dt. 32 and related passages discloses a logical outline of major elements which obviously are based on the covenant-renewal form.

Form of the Covenant Lawsuit

1. *Call to the witnesses to give ear to the proceedings.* Where these are not "heaven and earth" but Israel herself, the prophet may begin by calling Israel to hear Yahweh's word (e.g., Am. 3:1; 4:1; 5:1; etc.). In other words, the lawsuit begins at the third point in the covenant-renewal form.

2. *Introductory statement of the case at issue by the Divine Judge and Prosecutor or by his earthly official* (cf. Dt. 32:4-6; Isa. 1:2b-3; Mic. 6:2; Jer. 7:3-4).

3. *Recital of the benevolent acts of the Suzerain.* The form, content, and unstereotyped nature of this recital are precisely parallel to the first main part of the covenant renewal (cf. Dt. 32:7-14; Mic. 6:3-5; Jer. 2:5-7a; etc.).

4. *The indictment* (Dt. 32:15-18). This is the element most commonly found in prophecy, since it is the basis of the prophet's mission. It may be the quotation of the Word of God, which is then expanded, interpreted, and defended, or it may appear in a variety of guises.

5. *The sentence* (Dt. 32:19-29). There is, of course, a large

---

[55] This outline is very similar to the projection of von Rad from the Book of Deuteronomy (see his "Das formgeschichtliche Problem des Hexateuch," *Gesammelte Studien*, p. 34). The main difference, and an extremely important one which cannot be further argued here, is with regard to the content of the first point, the Credo. The covenant form, as here understood, is incomplete without the Credo; it is precisely what holds the Exodus and Sinai traditions together. To separate these traditions is to have a Credo without a *Sitz im Leben*. The fact that such Credos appear separately must be explained otherwise, probably by a variety of factors, including the Davidic covenant's disruption of the old cultic practices. But there is no covenant without Credo, and no Law without Gospel.

group of passages, particularly from prophecy, which illustrate this section. Most commonly, God says that he will give Israel into the hands of an enemy which serves as his agent. This is the case in Dt. 32. That is, a foreign power becomes the Suzerain's arm to enforce the treaty and to punish its infraction. Since, however, the involvement of the ultimate powers in and over heaven and earth was integral to the original treaty form, natural evils also are normally a part of the "blessings and curses" and, therefore, of the sentence. The very structure of the natural order had been called upon, through the series of gods of heaven, earth and the waters, to guarantee the treaty. Once it was broken, the curses become operative and the whole of nature could be considered in convulsive disruption. In other words, the intimate relation between historical and natural "evil" in Old Testament prophecy and apocalyptic may well have had its origin in the conceptions lying at the root of the suzerainty treaty. In Dt. 32:19-29, enemy action, fire that consumes the foundations of the mountains, famine, pestilence, and wild beasts—all are mixed together in a cosmic reaction against Israel for breach of covenant with Yahweh.

Both the covenant renewal and the covenant lawsuit, then, ultimately rest upon the suzerainty treaty form. (See. Part VI of this essay for discussion of the possible source and setting of the lawsuit.) The question is whether the evidence implies that behind the passages cited above two *liturgical* forms actually exist. That the covenant renewal was celebrated seems probable; but was the lawsuit anything other than a conceptual image, a teaching form, an interpretative device? Would a people celebrate a report of a heavenly proceeding in which God dissolved the covenant?

However this may be, it is quite clear that none of the extant materials dealing with the subject was composed for liturgical purposes. The most that can be said is that liturgical practice is *reflected* in the Old Testament literature, or that the original forms of celebration have given form to present compositions. Yet in every case these literary forms are incomplete, or "broken," or elaborated in a manner and for a purpose very different from those contemplated in the "pure" liturgical forms, if the latter ever existed at all.[56] We must now turn to a brief statement of the adaptations evident in Dt. 32.

V. EXPANSION OF THE PRIMARY FORM

The first clear evidence in Dt. 32 of the expansion and adaptation of the primary lawsuit form for a wider and more generalized purpose appears in vs. 2. Here the psalmist, who in vs. 1 and in succeeding sections is the spokesman on earth for the Suzerain-Plaintiff of the heavenly courtroom, hints that the whole setting, and presumably the very form of the lawsuit which he uses, is only an instructional device. The interpretation of vs. 3 is not entirely clear; but the call to unspecified persons to give glory to God in vs. 3b is most easily interpreted as referring to the witnesses of vs. 1, in which case vs. 3a may represent the announcement of Yahweh's entrance into his court. If so, then vs. 3 is a part of the original form which is interrupted by vs. 2. On the other hand, it is possible that vs. 3, along with vs. 2a, represents a further adaptation of the form in which the psalmist announces his purpose of praise and calls on his hearers to do likewise.

Vs. 2 has led former commentators to see a wisdom motif mixed in the composition, for the psalmist here speaks like a wisdom teacher. The word employed for his composition, translated "teaching" (liqḥî), is comparatively rare, appearing elsewhere only in the wisdom literature except for Isa. 29:24, which is in a "wisdom" context. Also the combination of teacher-giving-instruction and the comparison to the refreshing, revivifying dew and rain on the vegetation reminds one of Job 29:21-23. There Job pictures himself as a great wise man for whose counsel men waited as (the earth waits) for rain.

[56] In other words, current liturgical studies in Old Testament literature, while very rewarding, must be careful not to claim too much, because they always face this barrier. There were a variety of interests in ancient Israel, many of which are preserved in the canon. But the liturgical and the cultic, important as they are, constitute only *one* of these interests, and in the final form of the literature even they are not dominant (if "cultic" is used in its properly narrow sense).

The original *Sitz im Leben* of none of these motifs, however, is really clear on close inspection; and as a matter of methodology one must surely avoid the temptation to pronounce a late date when the typological history of a given motif is not clear. If Proverbs represents a dominant form of wise teaching in which an elder teaches the young, then we may certainly say that Dt. 32 lacks the motif, for in it a teacher addresses all Israel. Pss. 49 and 78 are surely pre-Exilic psalms which also contain the teaching form, each making use of old motifs or material in its own way.[57] The latter is a composition from within the circles of Jerusalem's royal theology (see above). The early composition, "The Last Words of David," in II Sam. 23:1-7 already has both the teaching form and the comparison to rain, but because of apparent textual corruption the subject of the comparison is by no means certain.[58] Another royal psalm contains the same rain motif, including two of the words used in Dt. 32:2 (*māṭār* and *rᵉbîbîm;* Ps. 72:6). In other words, neither the teaching nor the rain motif can be confined to the later wisdom literature. The latter motif surely appears in pre-Exilic royal-theology literature; and the widely spread teaching motif, as indicated, for example, by von Rad's studies in Levitical teaching and preaching, had a more complex history than the simple ascription to the "wisdom movement" might suggest.[59]

[57] Both, for example, employ the *rîb* device as a way of beginning: "Give ear," those addressed being all mankind in the one case, and Israel in the other. In neither instance does the psalmist continue directly with an indictment, but instead with a statement concerning his teaching.

[58] For a review (with bibliography) of arguments for and against a tenth-century date of this short composition, see A. R. Johnson, *Sacral Kingship in Ancient Israel* (1955), pp. 14-17 and nn. 2 and 3.

[59] See von Rad's *Studies in Deuteronomy* (cited in n. 41) and his discussion of Levitical preaching in the Chronicler's work (cited in n. 28). In addition, one may point to "wisdom" elements in the tenth-century "Court History of David," and particularly to the figures of Ahithophel and Hushai. Cf. also II Sam. 14:17, 20, where wisdom like that of a member of the heavenly assembly is ascribed to David. Furthermore, not only the traditional setting of wisdom in the court of Solomon, but the very antiquity of the figures of the counselor and wiseman in the ancient Near East should warn against oversimplifying the wisdom problem in the evolving culture of ancient Israel. See, for example, Albright, *From the Stone Age to Christianity*, pp. 367 ff., and especially his "Canaanite-Phoenician Sources of Hebrew Wisdom," *Wisdom in Israel and in the Ancient Near East*, Suppl. VT (1955), pp. 1-15, and other articles in this same volume, e.g., those especially of A. Alt, P. A. H. deBoer, J. Lindblom, N. W. Porteous, and R. B. Y.

The second and major instance of expansion in the Song is to be found in the last thirteen verses (vss. 30-43). The tension created by the *rib*, and particularly by the indictment and sentence, is now relieved by an expression of hope and trust in God's salvation. Inasmuch as the lawsuit form was employed as a means of public confession in a time of calamity, the psalmist here has followed the "confession" with the "absolution": that is, with the affirmation of faith and trust in the mercy of God to provide salvation for his people, though admittedly they do not deserve it. In this vein, then, the author ends his composition in vs. 43 with the call to the heavenly assembly and to the people of earth to raise a doxology unto Yahweh, the savior of the oppressed.

The subject of the "original" composition, if such existed, was a particular catastrophe; and Eissfeldt may indeed be right in pointing to the eleventh century B.C. for its appropriate setting.[60] In the composition as finally received, however, the treatment is generalized, as is necessarily the case in all great hymns, in order to make possible its repeated use on various historical occasions in Israel's subsequent history. One might also venture the remark that the hymnic expansion of the poem is most *uncharacteristic* of the wisdom movement, a further warning against reading too much into vs. 2.

The original setting of the type of material used in vss. 30-43 is fortunately somewhat clearer. As pointed out in Part II of this essay, vss. 30-38 (Section 5 of the poem) represent the psalmist's reflection on the meaning of the present situation: (1) It is God himself who has given Israel up to the enemy; (2) the gods ("rock") of the enemy and the enemy themselves are evil and the day of Yahweh's requital is at hand; and (3) this

---

Scott. Cf. also W. Baumgartner, "The Wisdom Literature," *The Old Testament and Modern Study*, H. H. Rowley, ed. (1951), pp. 210-237, with excellent bibliography.

[60] Following this lead, Arthur Weiser ("Samuels 'Philister-Sieg,'" ZTK, 56 [1959], pp. 253-72) revises Eissfeldt's thesis and considers Dt. 32 to derive from the same circle of tradition as I Sam. 7. The Song further proves, he believes, that Israel's defeat by the Philistines and the loss of the Ark were cultically celebrated as a *Gerichtsrede*—a view which in turn revises and perhaps strengthens that of Würthwein (see n. 64). The question is, however, *how* the event was used cultically (see below), and *what type* of *Gerichtsrede* is in question.

means that God's judgment upon his people will be followed by his mercy on them when he sees that their power and idolatry are at an end. In Section 6 (vss. 39-42) Yahweh, confirming the psalmist's meditation, speaks for the second and final time: (1) It is indeed I who have done it, for all issues of life and death are in my hands alone; and (2) I solemnly swear that I shall indeed whet my sword and give judgment against my adversaries. On this basis, the psalmist rests his call to the angels and peoples to shout for joy, for God will "avenge" his people and "make atonement for" (or ritually "cleanse") his people's land (vs. 43 or Section 7).

Extensive comment on this type of material cannot be given here. It must suffice to suggest that the themes in the final speech of Yahweh are closely paralleled in various places, for example, in the Song of Hannah (I Sam. 2:1-10), which, as Bentzen remarks, is a royal psalm (cf. vs. 10) used in its present context as a Song of Praise.[61] Furthermore, one should note the dominance of the imagery of Yahweh as Warrior against his foes, and also the dominance of legal language. Central to these sections are the words *nāqām* (both noun and verb) and *šillēm* (vss. 35, 41, 43), commonly rendered "avenge, requite." Actually, both are legal terms, often misunderstood in English, which refer to the action of the royal Judge or Suzerain against those who rebel against him, who will not acknowledge sovereignty. God, who stands as the guarantor of justice, thus assumes the form of Warrior to assure justice.

The original setting of this ideology and type of expression is surely to be sought in the tradition of Holy War in pre-monarchical Israel. This was the time of the "Wars of Yahweh." In Judah the Holy War ideology, with its legal and martial means of expression, survived and was taken up into the royal theology and its cultic expression in the Jerusalem court. Von Rad has pointed out how in North Israelite religious tradition the ma-

[61] Bentzen, *op. cit.*, Vol. I, p. 163. I change his "Song of Thanksgiving" into "Praise" because Hebrew has no term comparable to our "thanksgiving." See especially Claus Westermann, *Das Loben Gottes in den Psalmen* (1953), pp. 16 ff., a small work that has not received the attention it deserves; it is an excellent corrective to Gunkel's description of the various *Gattungen* in the Psalms. Cf. also Jean-Paul Audet, O.P., RB, LXV (1958), pp. 371-399.

terials now surviving in Deuteronomy preserve the ideology.[62] Yet the Deuteronomic circle employs the theme differently from the way cultic circles in Jerusalem used it; it preserves the traditions in order to emphasize the utter loyalty, obedience, and trust demanded by the covenant faith.[63] Thus, for example, the Song of Hannah affirms the same things as Dt. 32:39 ff., but the former is from Jerusalem while the latter is North Israelite.

It is clear, therefore, that our psalmist has used the covenant lawsuit as his primary form and has expanded it by using a type of hymnic material originally associated with Holy War, so that confession and praise are carefully associated. By the insertion of vs. 2 he indicates his purpose: he is a teacher, and he prays that his words may be like dew, like rain, upon the vegetation.

VI. THE RÎB AS A MEANS OF DATING THE SONG

If there is merit in the above analysis, then the problem of dating the Song would appear very difficult, not only because of the obscurities involved in identifying the "no-people" in vs. 21, but also because of the distance that may well separate the psalmist from the original catastrophe, as well as his re-use of older forms and themes. Consequently, even if Eissfeldt's identification of the enemy with the Philistines before the reign of Saul were correct it does not follow that the Song dates from the eleventh century. Nor does the united monarchy of the tenth century appear to be a proper time to memorialize a severe defeat as a public confession and as a call to faith and praise. On the other hand, a sixth-fifth century date in the Exilic or post-Exilic time seems hardly commensurate with the implication of vss. 26 ff. that the people are not exiled but only oppressed; and such a date on the ground of a supposed influence from a (datable?) "age of the wisemen" must be abandoned as without merit.

[62] See von Rad, *Studies in Deuteronomy*, pp. 49 ff., and *Der Heilige Krieg im alten Israel* (1951), pp. 68 ff.

[63] As, for example, in both the ninth- and eighth-century prophets also (cf. Isaiah before Ahaz, Isa. 7:7-9). While these remarks need more extensive discussion, the point is not crucial for the main thesis of this essay.

It seems to me that more precision might be achieved if we were able to trace the history of the lawsuit form. It is a question, however, as to whether this is now possible. Here I can only touch upon certain pieces of evidence that seem to be relevant and important.

1. First of all, as previously noted, the breach of the covenant and the consequent heavenly *rib* is the conceptual setting of Israel's classical prophecy. It is not certain, however, whether that fact necessitates the supposition that the *rib* was an actual liturgical celebration with which the prophets were well acquainted.[64] It is only necessary to suppose a given theological tradition and the symbolic world view, in which alone the prophetic self-understanding is meaningful.

2. On the other hand, to me it appears possible that at one time in North Israel the covenant-renewal celebration was revised and turned into a penitential service by the use of the *rib* motif. This involves an acceptance of von Rad's arguments concerning the liturgical elements in Deuteronomy, their origin in North Israel (see also A. C. Welch and others), and the existence there of a covenant-renewal ceremony, originally celebrated at Shechem. Yet, there is more in the Deuteronomic tradition than this. Indeed, the theme of the Deuteronomic History of Israel in the Promised Land (Jos.–II Kg.) is God's gift of the land, followed by his struggle with a faithless people in the period of the Judges; and his provision for monarchical government as a gracious concession to Israel's sinfulness, followed by his controversy with the kings and through them with both Israel and

---

[64] Ernst Würthwein, "Der Ursprung der prophetischen Gerichtsrede," ZTK, 49 (1952), pp. 1-16, gives an excellent analysis of the *Gerichtsrede*-form in prophecy as well as the history of its exegesis in German Old Testament scholarship. He makes a valiant attempt to prove the liturgical background of the *Gattung*, but in my judgment he does not succeed. It cannot be denied that Mendenhall's comparison of the Mosaic covenant form with the suzerainty treaty has thrown the whole subject into an entirely fresh perspective. Lacking that perspective Würthwein is unable to clarify differences in the circles of tradition, and he resorts to the enthronement psalms, where God appears as Judge of the peoples of the world, to establish his case. To me this is unfortunate because the enthronement theme is a different matter with a different *Sitz im Leben* from that under consideration here. Finally, he has given no consideration to the question of the heavenly assembly, with the result, for example, that the real significance of Ps. 82 is not grasped. A similar critique could be offered of Arthur Weiser's important reconstruction (see his *Die Psalmen*, ATD 14 [1959], pp. 21, 30-35).

Judah for faithlessness. In other words, the very theme of the Deuteronomic history is the *rib:* the goodness of God in providing for the people, God's indictment because of the people's rebellious response, a series of historical punishments by God, culminating in the destruction of the northern kingdom (II Kg. 17) and reform under Hezekiah and Josiah, with the final outcome, if not initially recounted by the historian, at least indicated by way of warning.[65]

The data for this theme, that is, for the presumed use of the *rib*-idea in penitential liturgy, are also found in the Book of Deuteronomy itself. The only covenant known in Deuteronomy is a broken covenant; the literature has a somber, serious tone. From beginning to end Deuteronomy is an exposition of the covenant theology with warnings to hearken, to obey, to love, to cleave unto Yahweh, for the issues at stake are none other than life and death. The curses receive more elaboration than the blessings in order that Israel may be warned and "prolong your days in the land." As already noted, Dt. 4:26, 30:19, and 31:28 summon "heaven and earth" as witnesses of the blessing and especially the curse. Israel's whole history is seen to be one of ingratitude and rebellion (e.g., Dt. 9:6 ff.). The curse has been invoked, or certainly will be, with the result that Israel is, or will be, scattered among the nations—although after repentance God will have compassion, gather them again and "circumcise" their heart so that they may truly love him (30:1-10). Indeed, the *rib* theme could not have been unfamiliar in the Deuteronomic circles, at least in their later period, as may be seen from the setting provided the Song in Dt. 31:16-22. There Yahweh tells Moses that after his death Israel will play the harlot, break the covenant, and bring upon themselves the curses. Moses, therefore, is commanded to write the Song in Dt. 32:1-43 and teach it to Israel, that it "may be a witness for me against the people of Israel." When Israel suffers hardship, "this song shall confront them as a witness (for it will live unforgotten in the mouths of their descendants)" (vss. 19, 21; EVV).

---

[65] The problem of whether the original work ended with the reign of Josiah, and was supplemented later (as I believe), or whether the whole was initially composed in the mid-sixth century must here be left undiscussed.

These remarks offer no proof for an actual covenant-lawsuit ceremony. They do suggest, however, that the theme was well known in Deuteronomic circles, and indeed that the celebration of the Deuteronomic covenant involved a definite *rîb* element, the latter qualifying the covenant-renewal ceremony in the light of actual experiences which were interpreted in terms of the curses of the Mosaic covenant. It cannot be said that Deuteronomy brings us immediately within the liturgy of such a celebration of worship. But the book as a whole, especially the framework of the older sections and the history of Israel which is based on it, show close familiarity with the *idea;* and it is a simple postulate that an actual didactic (if not liturgical) form lies ultimately behind the material.

3. Can we say when the alteration of the covenant-renewal ceremony by means of the *rîb* conception took place? Hypothetically there is no reason why the *rîb* could not have been conceived in the days of the Tribal League, particularly as an attempt to comprehend the meaning of the defeat by the Philistines. It may be noted, however, that the literature which expresses the royal theology of the Jerusalem royal court contains little suggestion of the *rîb* motif. The covenant lawsuit derives from another circle than that of the Davidic dynasty. Ps. 78 is an excellent case in point because, of all the expressions of royal theology, it comes nearest to the *rîb*. Its aim is simply to show how God resolved the Philistine problem by choosing Judah, Zion, and David. Israel had sinned, had broken God's covenant (vs. 9), had forgotten all he had done for his people. As a result, they provoked him to anger and he delivered them over to their foes. In this Jerusalemite treatment of the eleventh-century disaster there is no hint whatever of the *rîb*. There is no call to the witnesses of the covenant, no heavenly assembly, no indictment or sentence within that assembly's legal proceedings. The issue is handled very simply: Israel rebelled and God punished. Consequently, there is some justice in Eissfeldt's comparison to Mesha's statement on the Moabite Stone that Chemosh was angry with his land and gave it into the power of Omri of Israel in order to humble it.

As the covenant lawsuit had no primary setting in the royal theology in Jerusalem, so also there is no evidence for it among the traditions of the Jerusalem priesthood (P). We are thus left with the Deuteronomic traditions and with prophecy, northern and southern. In both, the *rib* is dominant. Ultimately, the Deuteronomic traditions are to be traced back to the covenant-renewal ceremonies of the Tribal League; but within that tradition itself there is no evidence whether the *rib* motif was original to it or a subsequent reformulation of it. The latter constitutes the more probable hypothesis. Also it is simpler to believe that Ps. 78 represents the most common way that defeat was interpreted during the earlier days of the nation (as well as later, for that matter).[66] Yet this is supposition, not proof.

4. The problem might be capable of solution if we could answer this question: How is it possible for the *rib* theme to be shared by both Deuteronomic and prophetic circles?

Whether the *rib* was an actual liturgical form or simply a dynamic form for a theological conception, it seems unexplainable apart from the office of prophecy. That is, only a charismatic official of the divine government could reveal in Israel actual proceedings presumed to have taken place in heaven. Without the prophetic office no *rib* would have been announced in Israel. Hence the *rib* form must have originated in Israelite circles where the theology of the prophetic office was seriously regarded as a vital part of God's rule over Israel. This must have been in North Israel, judging not only from the history of the

---

[66] It seems to me that the Court History of David (II Sam. 9-20; I Kg. 1-2) may also suggest a tenth-century non-*rib* treatment of the problem of divine judgment in a manner typical of tenth-century Jerusalem. While this work has generally been considered as "objective" historiography with little theology in it (e.g., R. H. Pfeiffer, *Introduction to the Old Testament* [1941], pp. 356-359), von Rad has attempted to stress the theological character of the work ("Der Anfang der Geschichtsschreibung in alten Israel," *Gesammelte Studien*, pp. 148-188). In support of von Rad's judgment, I would simply point to the centrality of the Bath-sheba incident, and especially of the judgment of God as pronounced by Nathan upon David (II Sam. 12:7-12). While the judgment has certain elements of the *rib* form (statement of God's benevolent acts followed by sentence), the prophet stands in relation to king, instead of to the whole people; the Mosaic covenant is not in view. Where the Court History once began is a debated problem. In any case, in II Sam. 9-12 David is an older man at the height of his glory. After the Word of God by Nathan comes the detailed statement of the troubles of David in his later years. In other words, God's judgment on the king, as announced by the prophet, is central to the work, and it is followed by the narration of the steps by which the judgment was carried out (cf. for one detail the question of the concubines: II Sam. 12:11-12; 15:16; 16:20-22; 19:5; 20:3).

prophetic office but from the special interest in prophecy shown in both the Elohist and Deuteronomic strata of the Pentateuch (e.g., Gen. 20:7, where Abraham is understood to be a prophet; Num. 11:29; 12:6; Dt. 18:9-22, the office as God's primary means of revelation; cf. 13:1-5, etc.). The royal and priestly theologies of Jerusalem never make a statement comparable to that found, for example, in Dt. 18:9-22.

At this point, we must pause for a few brief remarks about the history of the office of prophecy. Without going into details regarding the ecstatic and formal influences on the Israelite office,[67] it is clear to me that the establishment of the monarchy under Samuel's leadership was the time when the office became a formal part of Israelite government. During the period of the Tribal League, God had ruled directly, making use of charismatic leaders as the need arose. With Saul political and military leadership resided permanently in one man, but the ideology of the Tribal League was preserved under the assumption that he would exercise his authority only at God's direction, given by a charismatic spokesman—that is, by Samuel in the role of God's prophet (herald or messenger of the divine throne). The function of the prophet as the charismatic official at the right hand of the governing power in Jerusalem seems to have continued throughout the tenth century, although positive evidence is limited largely to the figures of Nathan, Gad, and Ahijah (II Sam. 7; 12; 24:11 ff.; I Kg. 11:29 ff.). During subsequent centuries also, dominant prophetic figures were not infrequently associated closely with the kings, even within the court of Ahab (note the prophet roles in the stories in I Kg. 20 and 22).[68]

[67] See for example, W. F. Albright, *From the Stone Age to Christianity*, pp. 17-19, 301 ff. For the significance of the office of *apilum* in the Mari documents, see the writer, *Biblical Archaeology* (1957), pp. 96-97; Martin Noth, "History and the Word of God in the Old Testament," BJRL, XXXII (1950), pp. 194-206; A. Malamat, "Prophecy in the Mari Documents" (in Hebrew), *Eretz Israel*, 4 (1956), pp. 74-84.

[68] Recent discussions of the "cultic prophet," while in many respects very rewarding, have always seemed to me to come off rather badly because they have generally failed to get at the *central* point about Israelite prophecy. That is not its "cultic" role in the special, technical sense of that term, but its "political" role. The prophet was an official of the divine *government* of Israel; hence, the "politics" of the office, not its "accidental" features, whether cultic or psychological, is what is centrally important; cf. the writer's interpretation in *The Rule of God* (1960), Lecture 6.

It is precisely in the ninth century, however, that prophecy begins to assume a new role in relation to the whole nation. Ahijah announced that the division of the kingdom was decreed by God because of the sins of Solomon (I Kg. 11:31 ff.). There is a great distance between that statement and the prophecy of Amos in the mid-eighth century: "Hear this word that the Lord has spoken against you, O people of Israel, against the whole family which I brought up out of the land of Egypt . . ." (Am. 3:1). The belief, expressed in legal terms, that God was in controversy not simply with the kings but with the whole Chosen People must have originated between Ahijah and Amos, that is, during the time of civil wars that resulted from the division of the kingdom, of the dynasty of Omri, which, having no prophetic legitimation whatever, shook the very foundations of Yahwism and led to subsequent weakness and disastrous troubles at the hands of the Arameans. It was during this pivotal period in North Israel that a fresh and revolutionary form of interpretation took shape: The Chosen and Covenanted People were now the *object* of the divine "avenging" action. They had been indicted and found guilty in the heavenly assembly. The story of the prophet Micaiah in I Kg. 22 (vss. 17-22) furnishes the first documented and datable portrayal of the heavenly *rîb,* even though the sentence of the divine court is, in this instance, simply the death of King Ahab. Elijah on Mt. Carmel (I Kg. 18) calls to all Israel, not simply to the king, for fateful decision. On Mt. Horeb (I Kg. 19:14 ff.) he complains that the whole people has abandoned the covenant, torn down the altars of Yahweh, and killed the prophets, so that he alone is left. And in his fresh commissioning of the prophet God affirms that the sword of Hazael and that of Jehu will bring about a terrible carnage in Israel, although there remain seven thousand in Israel who have not bowed to *Ba'al.* The same thematic interpretation of the Aramean defeats of Israel appears in the Elisha cycle of tradition (e.g., II Kg. 8:12-13), and, of course, this in turn is used by the Deuteronomic historian (e.g., II Kg. 13:3-6).[69]

[69] The Chronicler knew of a letter written by Elijah to King Joram (Jehoram) of Judah to the effect that since he had led all Judah and Jerusalem into faith-

It is unfortunate that we do not have more literature which is definitely datable to the middle and second half of the ninth century. During this obscure time fateful issues were being decided; and the Elijah movement surely began a new era for at least a number of teachers and prophets. In that time the theological reformulation of the Mosaic covenant tradition was surely undertaken. Its fruits are only partially preserved for us in the canonical prophets, in the Levitical teaching and liturgical elements preserved in the Book of Deuteronomy, and—one may now be permitted to add—in Dt. 32.

CONCLUSION

The above proposal concerning the *Sitz im Leben* of the *rib* form has by no means been proved beyond question. Yet it appears to be a hypothesis which is at least bolstered by a considerable degree of probability. The covenant-lawsuit theme, in this view, was a reformulation of the covenant-renewal theme. The reformulation took place in North Israel among those who had preserved the amphictyonic traditions and particularly the traditions of the era of Samuel, whose understanding of the role of the prophet in the divine government of Israel was considered normative. The prophet was no longer the charismatic spokesman to the royal court alone (cf. n. 67 for the Mari "prophet"

---

lessness, the royal household, the people, and the king himself would be punished (II Chr. 21:12-15). The Chronicler, it will be noted, makes much of the traditions concerning the prophets and writes a highly personalized history of events firmly within the royal theology of Jerusalem. For him the Chosen Davidic King and the Chosen City remain the center of history and the ground of hope for the post-Exilic community. Hence, his narrative attempts to interpret success and defeat, wherever possible, by the prophet-traditions: this-and-that took place at the Word of Yahweh by such-and-such a prophet making announcement to the king. This is the tenth-century pattern, as already noted, which presumably remained fixed in Jerusalem court traditions. The Deuteronomic tradition, while to a large extent following the same line, nevertheless has a larger perspective, one which envisages the fall of the whole people to the enemy and their end as an independent entity.

who formally was of this simple, royal type); he also became the spokesman to the nation of God's judgment upon the whole people. This took the form of the heavenly lawsuit, the proceedings of which were publicly announced. In both north and south the canonical prophets of the eighth to the sixth centuries found in this reformulation the central meaning of their calling and office, while Levitical teachers and poets in the north took it up and made considerable use of it, although unfortunately little of their literature has survived. The royal and priestly circles in Jerusalem did not accept it, at least before the reforms of Hezekiah or Josiah.

With regard to the Song of Moses, this view suggests the following conclusions:

1. The historical catastrophe lying behind it cannot now be dated. Following Eissfeldt, I consider the eleventh-century Philistine defeat of Israel, the destruction of the amphictyonic center at Shiloh, and the capture of the Ark as the most probable situation, and I believe that Ps. 78 is a different treatment of the same defeat within a different circle (the Jerusalem court). If the "no-people" of vs. 21 are not the Philistines, then the Arameans of the latter part of the ninth century would be the most likely candidate.

2. The primary structure of the Song is the covenant lawsuit, which suggests that, however the defeat had once been treated, the present form of the Song does not antedate the ninth century.

3. The primary lawsuit form was then expanded by hymnic themes drawn from Holy War traditions. Thus the *rib* became a mode of confession, the hymnic portions resolving the tension into an expression of hope and faith in God for deliverance. Finally, vs. 2 indicates that the psalmist intends the whole poem to be a tool for teaching. Whether both the *rib* and its expansions are by one and the same original author simply cannot be decided now, and from the standpoint of form criticism is not an essential question.

4. Since the poem is a "broken" or expanded *rib*, I would still be inclined to say the same thing as I did in 1953: a date *within* the three-hundred-year period (900-600 B.C.) seems clear,

but a closer determination is difficult.[70] My preference is the period around 815 to 805 B.C. in the reign of Joahaz (Jehoahaz) of Israel (ca. 815-801 B.C.—Albright), before the Assyrian destruction of the power of Damascus ca. 802 B.C.[71] Not only from the Biblical tradition, but from archaeological sources as well, we know that at that time both Israel and Judah were brought almost completely to their knees by Hazael, and that Samaria, Hazor, and Megiddo among other Palestinian cities were attacked and destroyed with violence.[72] We are told that Hazael reduced the army of Israel to a mere bodyguard for the king and a police force for the nation (II Kg. 13:7). Yet the first part of the Assyrian crisis before 721 B.C. might also serve as the *rib's* immediate focus and point of relevance. Certainly the seventh century appears too late. These suppositions and preferences, however, do not constitute either proof or even a high probability for one century instead of another. Only the linguistic archaisms (see n. 29) might tip the balance in favor of the ninth century, except that they may also be survivals from an earlier stage of the material.

[70] See above, n. 25.

[71] Cf. John Bright, *A History of Israel* (1959) , pp. 235 ff., especially p. 237. For the inscriptions of Adad-nirari III which tell of this event, see ANET, pp. 281-282.

[72] Cf. the writer's "Israelite Samaria and Iron Age Chronology," BASOR, 155 (1959) , Chart, and p. 14, n. 4.

IV

The Background of Judges 17-18

MARTIN NOTH

What is to be made of the narrative found in Judges 17-18 is not evident at first glance. It is generally recognized that this narrative of Micah's graven image, its theft by the land-seeking Danites, and its erection in the city of Dan contains many highly interesting details regarding the history of the Israelite tribes and of their cultic practices—details which apparently rest upon direct knowledge of the subject matter. There is no doubt, however, that the story has not been constructed in order to communicate these details. The concrete details, rather, are in the service of the expansive narrative style which characterizes the section. For this reason, the older commentaries on Jg. 17-18 hardly deal with the issues adequately when they confine themselves to pointing out the ancient and reliable character of the tradition and then proceed to interpret the details.

It is still a debatable question, to be sure, whether we actually have one narrative or two parallel "sources," which have only secondarily been combined by literary means.[1] Since, however, even the majority of the representatives of the "two-source" hypothesis, which has become standard in the period since Wellhausen, stress the fact that the two "sources" are very similar, I shall not deal with the literary-critical problem. Let me

---

[1] A. Murtonen, VT, I (1951), pp. 223 f., even assumes three literary strata, an "original narrative" and two "later narratives."

only remark that I am in agreement with the more recent and latest works on the Book of Judges,[2] which hold to the essential literary unity of Jg. 17-18. This is not to deny that the original story was later distorted somewhat by a few alterations and additions.[3] Such particulars may be left aside here, since they are not essential to the following remarks. Later on we have to take up only the question of the literary originality of the last two verses (18:30-31).

Somewhat more complicated is the traditio-historical question. The chief theme is that of the cult object which is finally erected in the city of Dan. The narrative begins with this chief theme by relating how the image came to be made; and it also ends with the same theme by reporting how the image attained what was then thought of as its permanent resting place in Dan.[4] A Danite tradition dealing with the origin and early history of the image worshiped in ancient times at Dan is probably the basis of this chief theme. If so, we must assume that the Danites took delight in telling the story of how their immigrating forefathers brought along the image from the mountains of Ephraim. A second theme is joined to the chief theme: the story of the "Levite" from Bethlehem. This theme is introduced in 17:7 with a formula similar to the one which introduces the first in 17:1. To me it appears doubtful that the antecedent history of the "Levite," which is briefly reported in 17:7-9, has its own special basis in tradition. It is reasonable to suppose that here we have only a typical picture of a "Levite" such as was common in ancient Israel. In support of this judgment is the fact that Jg. 19:1 ff. gives a picture of a "Levite" that is similar in some respects, although it is not to be assumed that one story depends on the other in a traditio-historical or even in a literary way.

---

[2] See, among others, F. Nötscher, *Das Buch der Richter*, Echter-Bibel (1950), p. 66=Echter-Bibel, *Altes Testament*, I (1955), pp. 686 f.; H. W. Hertzberg, *Die Bücher Josua, Richter, Ruth*, ATD, IX, (²1959), p. 239; E. Täubler, *Biblische Studien, Die Epoche der Richter* (1958), pp. 45 f.

[3] The adherents of the "two-source" hypothesis also cannot dispense with the assumption of secondary alterations and additions.

[4] To me it seems certain that portions of the two concluding verses (18:30, 31) belong to the original narrative, at least either vs. 30a or vs. 31a.

Whether the connection with Bethlehem[5] belongs to this type
of "Levite" is a matter that pertains to the early history of the
"Levitical" office, which cannot be discussed here. In any case,
the reference to Bethlehem in 17:7-8 can hardly support the
thesis that chs. 17-18 represent a Judean tradition. Rather, this
theme surely originates from the place at which the journey of
the "Levite" in Jg. 17-18 comes to an end, namely, Dan. It is
true that the Levite theme is essentially finished in 18:20; only
in 18:24 is "the priest" mentioned once more in passing, while
the concluding statements of the narrative in its original form
do not refer again to the "Levite" explicitly.[6] Yet according to
18:20 it was the unambiguous sense of the narrative that the
"Levite" became a "tribal priest" of Dan and probably also—
although this is not explicitly stated—the prototype of a "Levitical" tribal priesthood in Dan. Thus this theme may also be of
Danite origin. The Danites took pleasure in pointing out that
their forefathers brought with them on their migration a "Levitical" priest as well as the cult image.

A further theme found in Jg. 17-18 is that of the Danite conquest. This theme begins in 18:1b and comes to an end in 18:29.
Traditio-historically considered, it belongs to the circle of the
conquest traditions of the individual tribes and may be compared at various points with the conquest traditions of other
Israelite tribes. Here it is not necessary to deal with this matter.
It should only be pointed out that this tradition is certainly
Danite in origin and transmission. This fact is not refuted by
the etiological note in 18:12b, which traces the locality *maḥ⁼nê
dān* in the environs of the city of Kiriath-jearim back to an in-
terim encampment of the land-seeking Danites. No matter how

---

[5] In 19:1 ff. the relationship of the "Levite" to Bethlehem consists in the fact
that he had a concubine from Bethlehem. This does not necessarily mean that he
himself had come from Bethlehem and only subsequently sojourned in "the
farthest parts of the mountains of Ephraim."

[6] From this it is clear that I regard the note in 18:30b as a later addition. Of
course, the addition tacitly identifies Jonathan, the ancestor of the Danite priesthood, with the "Levite" mentioned in the previous narrative. On this matter, cf.
Ch. Hauret, "Aux origines du sacerdoce Danite," *Mélanges bibliques rédigés en
l'honneur de André Robert* (1958), pp. 108 f. The fact that the "Levite," who
has remained nameless throughout the entire narrative up to that point, suddenly
receives a name is certainly not original.

the name of the locality came into being and what its original meaning may have been,[7] it is easy to see that this place-name was known to the Danites, that it must have reminded them of the name of their own tribe, and that they connected it with the antecedents of their conquest. From this etiological note the conclusion cannot be drawn that the Danite conquest tradition as it appears in Jg. 17-18, or the entire narrative in these chapters, received its present form in Judah.[8] The specific statement in 18:12a that Kiriath-jearim lies "in Judah" is, rather, an indication that the note has been formulated outside of Judah.[9]

The above-mentioned tradition themes, introduced one after another in 17:1 and 17:7 and 18:1b, have been woven together into the larger narrative of chs. 17-18 in a very ingenious literary manner. This masterful composition, however, has a strange ring. Dissonance accompanies the development of the themes. According to content, the entire narrative could be designated as a legend of the founding of the sanctuary at Dan. Yet this would be but a caricature of such a legend; for an unmistakably "pejorative" element is found in the whole narrative. It does not have the serious effect which should be expected from a foundation legend. Again and again we encounter motifs which shift the reported events into an atmosphere of ridicule or even contempt. This characteristic feature of the narrative can hardly be accounted for in terms of the naïveté and coarseness of ancient Israelite narrators, who liked to adorn even a serious subject matter with jocular traits which make for narrative effect.[10] The composition of Jg. 17-18 is too artful, too devoid of naïveté, and the "pejorative" motifs are inserted and elaborated too consciously, to permit such an explanation.

[7] It is by no means improbable that this place-name actually contains the name of the tribe of Dan. The region of Kiriath-jearim is not far at all from the Danite area of settlement in the neighborhood of Zorah and Eshtaol (see Jg. 18:2).

[8] So Hertzberg, op. cit., pp. 238 f.

[9] Moreover, in 18:12a "Judah" is to be understood as the state, not the tribe of Judah. For Kiriath-jearim, a pre-Israelite city which along with its pre-Israelite neighbors affiliated at first with the tribe of Benjamin (according to Jos. 9), never became a "Judean" city in a tribal sense; it only became a part of the territory of the Judean state after the death of Solomon.

[10] So, for example, W. Nowack, Richter-Ruth, HKAT, I, 4, 1 (1900), pp. 140 ff.; recently also Täubler, op. cit., pp. 49 ff.

This negative manner of description affects, above all, the chief theme: the cult image. A positive nucleus, based perhaps upon a genuine Danite tradition, could possibly be discerned in the statement that the cult object is a costly piece made from silver. Unfortunately nothing at all is said about the shape[11] and workmanship of the image. According to 17:4 it was made by a silversmith. Accordingly, one is inclined to think of a solid silver statue or statuette. But this is hardly certain. It is just as plausible to suppose a wooden core overlaid with silver. This view, of course, cannot be supported by the double designation *pésel úmaśśēkâ*, since these terms can also be understood as a hendiadys in the sense of a "plastic image cast from metal."[12] The narrator presupposes an acquaintance with the Danite cult image and therefore he says nothing at all about its appearance. However, he may intend to say that, although made of precious silver, it was only a very small object. For according to 17:4, 200

[11] The conjecture of H. Gressmann, *Die Anfänge Israels* (*Die Schriften des Alten Testaments in Auswahl*, I, 2 [³1922], p. 254), that the image represented a bull like the image later set up at Dan by Jeroboam I has no substantiation whatever, as Gressmann himself acknowledges.

[12] The double designation appears in 17:3, 4; 18:14 (17, 18), while in 18: (20), 30, 31 only the shorter expression *pésel* occurs. This fact itself indicates that only *one* object is meant (note also the singular of the verb in 17:4b). Accordingly, the separation of the two parts of the double designation into "the wooden core" and "the external metal plating" (so G. von Rad, *Theologie des Alten Testaments*, I [1957], p. 214, n. 57) is questionable. In the enumeration of the cult objects in Jg. 17-18 some confusion has arisen later on. The differences in the enumerations, however, hardly provide occasion for undertaking a division into "sources." To me the facts of the case seem to be simple and originally coherent. After the cult image has been introduced under the double designation *pésel úmaśśēkâ* in 17:3, 4, it is reported that Micah has outfitted his "house of God" for cultic activities. For this purpose he first made the "ephod and teraphim." Inasmuch as this statement immediately precedes the reference to the installation of a priest, it is reasonable to assume that the "ephod and teraphim" here are paraphernalia for the priest in his cultic role. Then after "ephod and teraphim" and *pésel úmaśśēkâ* are quite appropriately mentioned together in 18:14 as valuable objects found in the house of Micah, the four words are repeated in irregular sequence in the following verses. Originally 18:17, 18 referred only to *pésel úmaśśēkâ* (the five Danite spies stole the cult image from the house of Micah) and 18:20 spoke only of "ephod and teraphim" (the priest, having decided to accompany the Danites, took along the "ephod and teraphim" which belonged to his cultic apparatus). Later redactors no longer understood these distinctions and have rather carelessly filled out the text in a manner considered to have been necessary.

shekels of silver sufficed for making it, that is, about two and one-half to three kilograms, depending upon what weight of the shekel is presupposed here. This was actually not very much, not any more than the quantity of silver which Achan stole, along with other precious objects, from Jericho and buried in the ground beneath his tent (Jos. 7:21), and it was only a fraction of the amount of silver which the Philistines promised to Delilah for the betrayal of Samson (Jg. 16:5).[13] Unfortunately, we have no appropriate comparative evidence for estimating how much precious metal was commonly used in ancient Israel to make a "normal" cult image, whether of solid or only of metal-plated construction. Therefore we cannot say for sure whether the figure for the quantity of silver used in making the image is intended to say something negative about the image. However that may be, the report about the previous history of the silver manifestly intends to represent the cult image from the very first in an unfavorable light.[14] The particulars about the silver in 17:2-4, with which the narrative opens, are too detailed to be understood as anything more than amusing narrative accessories. The two hundred shekels of silver were only one part, and a relatively small part, of a stolen silver treasure; and they were devoted to a "holy" purpose in order to render ineffective the curse uttered when the theft was committed, by a then unknown party. Had not Micah of the mountains of Ephraim stolen the silver treasure from his mother, the image would never have been made at all. The further history of the image corresponds with this beginning. The private sanctuary of Micah, for which the image was first intended, was not a very distinguished establishment, according to 18:19; and the image finally was stolen from there by the migrating Danites. A *chronique scandaleuse!*

Even the figure of the "Levite" is not treated with sympathy

[13] Perhaps it is a mere coincidence that the number given in 16:5 is identical with that in 17:2, 3, unless in ancient times—for reasons unknown to us—"1100 silver shekels" used to be a current designation for a rather large treasure of silver.

[14] A different but unconvincing explanation is given by Täubler, *op. cit.*, pp. 50 ff. On p. 46 Täubler gives a good explanation of 17:2-4, a text which is perhaps not entirely intact, and he offers an illuminating textual reconstruction which does not alter essentially the substance of this section.

in the narrative. True, the picture in Jg. 17-18 of a "Levite" moving from place to place and seeking any kind of work and livelihood simply reproduces in all probability the customary picture of the "Levite" in ancient Israel, without saying anything particularly unfavorable about him. But a "Levite" was not a very respectable figure, even in this ancient time,[15] at least in the view of some circles within Israel. Such a "Levite" admittedly had one advantage: he was especially well fitted to administer a priestly office. This is not to say that in those days every priest had to be a "Levite" (cf. 17:5b); but one could count himself fortunate if he were able to engage a "Levite" for the priestly office. That view was prevalent in Israel, and Micah in Jg. 17-18 shared it. He spared no effort in securing the "Levite" who was passing by as a priest for his "house of God" (17:10-12), thereby securing for his cult a particular blessing from Yahweh, as he believed (17:13). Of course, the narrator of Jg. 17-18 hardly shared this view. Deliberately he depicts how Micah soon became bitterly disappointed in his high estimate of the "Levite." Within the context of the narrative, the full description of the installation of the "Levite" in 17:10-12, which provides us with so many interesting details concerning the possible terms under which a priest might be installed, clearly aims to make the subsequent conduct of the "Levite" appear particularly ungrateful and unpleasant. The man whom Micah treated so well at his installation later acted with great disloyalty toward his benefactor. When the Danites on their journey to the north passed by the homestead of Micah, and the five Danite spies who were already acquainted with the locality took away Micah's cult image from its place, the priest who after all was responsible for the image merely stood quietly at the "entrance of the gate" (18:17ba)[16] and finally brought himself to ask the

---

[15] Jg. 17-18 is a very important source for the early history of the "Levitical" office, a subject which cannot be dealt with here.

[16] For an understanding of the section 18:13-20, the text of which is not nearly so marred as is commonly assumed, it would be important to know the local conditions which are here presupposed but not made explicit. Since the expression pétah haššá'ar (vss. 16, 17) normally refers to a city gate but not to the door of a house, it is evidently thought that Micah's house was located within a walled settlement—a fact that is not expressly stated but also one that need not have

lame question, "What are you doing?" (18:18b). He did not consider warning his benefactor Micah, perhaps for fear of the 600 armed Danites. In any case, he made no serious effort to protect his master's property. Hence Micah was first informed of what had happened by his servants and neighbors when the Danites, with their booty and the faithless "Levite," had already gone some distance (18:22). Again it must be observed that the remarkable prolixity in the description of the scene must have its special purpose and that this purpose is to be sought in the portrayal of the "Levite's" questionable conduct. This questionable conduct consists above all in the fact that he offered no resistance to being taken along by the Danites, having in mind the advantages to be gained. In pointing out to him that a tribal priesthood was preferable to a household priesthood (18:19b), the Danites did not have in mind just the fact that a tribal priest had a superior position; they were thinking more of the higher income. The Levite must have understood their words in this way, even as it was intended that he should; and so this element of the narrative was probably understood generally in ancient Israel. Leaving out of account the special terms of the installation (which in contrast to 17:10 are not mentioned here), a priestly position at a tribal sanctuary is a definite improvement over a priestly role in a private sanctuary in view of the fact that many more worshipers visit a tribal sanctuary and accordingly the priest's share of the sacrificial offerings is greater. With this in mind, the "Levite" immediately and gladly accepted the proposal of the Danites. The narrator has brought this out very subtly and clearly. While formerly the "Levite" was finally "contented" to remain with Micah because of the latter's extremely generous offer to him (17:11a), "his heart" became "glad" over the offer of the Danites and he at once fetched the priestly paraphernalia, the "ephod and teraphim" which belonged to Micah (17:5ba), in order to take them along.[17] Then he "set out in the

___

been said. Ample room remains for speculation concerning the relationship of the "house of Micah" to the "house of the young Levite" (vs. 15) and to the "houses which were near to Micah's house" (vs. 22), and its relationship to the spatial scene of the whole event.

[17] On this point see p. 72 above, n. 12.

midst of the [armed] people" so as to place himself under their protection in the event of a possible appearance of Micah (18:20). In all of this, it seems to me, the narrator has given unambiguous expression to his negative judgment upon the "Levite."

It is not certain that the Danite conquest in Jg. 17-18 is also evaluated unfavorably. True, the Danites, acting upon the report of their spies (18:9, 10; cf. vs. 7), fell upon, conquered, and annexed a prosperous, self-confident, remote region, whose people—so isolated that there was no possibility of neighborly assistance in case of attack—were living quietly. Yet from the point of view of the Israelites of the period of the Conquest, such action was not necessarily blameworthy. Nevertheless it is striking that the supposed security and the actual helplessness of the pre-Israelite inhabitants of this region are stressed so often and so deliberately (18:7, 10, 28). In making this emphasis it is suggested that the Danites did not accomplish a particularly praiseworthy feat when they conquered and destroyed (18:27b) the indigenous population of the territory destined to belong to the tribe of Dan—a population which was utterly unable to offer serious resistance. Unambiguously, however, the theft of Micah's cult image and the taking of his "Levitical" priest by the Danites is stigmatized as malicious and brutal. When the Danites arrived at Micah's house, their spies secretly approached the untrustworthy "Levite" and greeted him (18:15), while their armed forces remained threateningly in the background. Then after the spies had taken the cult image, apparently at first without the immediate knowledge of the priest, and after the Danites had enticed the priest to accompany them, they answered the despoiled Micah—who had finally learned what had happened and had called them to account—with scoffing and contemptuous words (18:25). The narrator has formulated this answer in such a way as to show quite clearly that mere power prevails over justice. Thus he unequivocally characterizes the conduct of the Danites as disgraceful. Even in the perspective of the crude life of an ancient time, such behavior could hardly be considered praiseworthy or admirable.

If a negative, "critical" tone dominates the whole narrative of Jg. 17-18, then a definite intention must lie behind it. This is not to assume that the narrative acquired this form only in order to hand down something that was historically unusual from early Israelite times[18] or to report, without a value judgment,[19] something curious from ancient times for the enjoyment of later hearers or readers. Rather, the narrative has a "bias" (*Tendenz*), although the narrator does not labor this *Tendenz* but envelops it in a masterful composition, letting it come out only in a very few places.[20] The art of the author consists precisely in the fact that he suggests, without being clumsily obtrusive, that judgment upon the narrated event which he deems correct.

Now one particular *Tendenz* has frequently been found in Jg. 17-18: an indirect polemic against the one cultic practice which elsewhere in the Old Testament is associated with the city of Dan, namely, a polemic against the state cult established in Dan by King Jeroboam I of Israel, with its cult image of a "golden calf" (I Kg. 12:28, 29). So W. Vischer[21] regards Micah's graven image in Jg. 17-18 as a "precursor of the golden calf that Jeroboam . . . created," and he bases his view on the quite apposite observation that the concluding remark in Jg. 18:31 "is not meant so innocently as it sounds." F. Nötscher[22] properly notes the "quiet mockery" which "sounds" throughout Jg. 17-18 and adds that "for people in the time of the Israelite monarchy who were acquainted with the zealous attacks of the prophets upon the 'sin of Jeroboam,' upon the offensive cult in Bethel and Dan, no more explicit language was necessary." H. W. Hertzberg[23] points out that the sanctuary of Dan, the establishment of which is the climax of the narrative of Jg. 17-18, was "according to I Kg. 12:29 f. the sanctuary, along with Bethel, established by Jeroboam and particularly eminent for its bull-worship," and that "consequently it is understandable why its origin is painted in dark colors." But is this interpretation of the "bias" of Jg. 17-18 really probable and illuminating?

Even if one supposes that the "golden calf" of Jeroboam was

[18] So E. Jacob, *La tradition historique en Israël* (1946) , p. 69.
[19] So Hauret, *op. cit.*, pp. 110 f.
[20] On 17:6; 18:1a, see below, pp. 79 ff.
[21] W. Vischer, *Das Christuszeugnis des Alten Testaments*, II (1942) , pp. 135 f.
[22] Nötscher, *op. cit.*, p. 66 (= p. 687) .
[23] Hertzberg, *op. cit.*, p. 239.

erected at Dan on the very spot where formerly the silver image of Jg. 17-18 stood (which is nowhere stated and is by no means self-evident) and that therefore the "calf" has superseded and replaced this cult image, nevertheless the cult objects are entirely different and accordingly different cultic practices are involved. One can hardly polemicize against the one when he has the other in mind. In almost all other respects as well, the two cultic establishments differ from one another. Whereas the earlier sanctuary was a recognized tribal sanctuary according to the explicit notation in Jg. 18:19b, the one established by Jeroboam I at Dan was a royal sanctuary.[24] Also, he fashioned it in a correspondingly new form by having a $b\bar{a}m\hat{a}$-house"[25] erected, and therefore he gave a new character to the whole thing,[26] even though the spot was perhaps the same one where the tribal sanctuary had been located. The same applies to the priesthood. According to Jg. 17-18, the tribal sanctuary attached great importance to having a "Levitical" priesthood; but Jeroboam I, according to I Kg. 12:31b, installed non-Levites as priests in his state sanctuaries. Thus very little remains of concrete agreements between the two reports: only a general polemic against cultic establishments in the city of Dan and perhaps agreement that these establishments were located in the same place. For the rest we are dealing with phenomena of a quite different character and from different times.

In my opinion, therefore, Jg. 17-18 cannot be understood as a polemic against the royal sanctuary established by Jeroboam I at Dan. The "bias" of Jg. 17-18 must be sought in another—and, as it will become clear, entirely opposite—direction. The observations found in Jg. 17:6 and 18:1a provide the key to an adequate interpretation of the intention of Jg. 17-18. Admit-

[24] Bethel, which is mentioned in connection with Dan in I Kg. 12:29, is expressly designated in Am. 7:13 as a "royal sanctuary" with a "state temple."

[25] On the meaning of $b\bar{a}m\hat{a}$, see W. F. Albright in Suppl. VT, IV (1957), pp. 242-258. Precisely what is meant by a $b\bar{a}m\hat{a}$-house cannot be determined with certainty. It must have been in each instance a structure built for cultic purposes.

[26] In I Kg. 12:31a the establishment of "$b\bar{a}m\hat{a}$-houses" is not explicitly connected with the sanctuaries of Bethel and Dan mentioned in the preceding verses (the genetival relationship is conceived as a unit; thus only the second word is inflected); this connection, however, is probably intended.

tedly, the originality of these observations must first be defended and their purpose examined.

In Jg. 17:6 is found the following observation: "In those days there was no king in Israel; every man did what was right in his own eyes." A briefer observation appears in Jg. 18:1a: "In those days there was no king in Israel." These short notes have often been considered secondary and redactional.[27] Of course, they may be removed from their contexts without difficulty and without leaving lacunae. But this fact alone is not sufficient justification for denying that they belong to the original narrative. Suspicion could better be aroused by the fact that the same formulas also appear in Jg. 19-21, the shorter form in 19:1a and the full form in 21:21; and indeed in Jg. 19-21 these formulas do appear to be redactional. The half-verse 19:1a precedes the normal narrative introduction found in 19:1b (cf. 17:1, 7), and the concluding verse of the entire narrative complex (21:25) seems superfluous. It should be noted, however, that the formulas in Jg. 17-18, unlike those in Jg. 19-21, are located in places which are not so much exposed to redactional additions as are the beginning and the end of narrative units. In Jg. 17-18 they are found, rather, in the midst of the narrative and at conspicuous places: at the junctures between the beginning of the chief theme and the first subsidiary theme, and between the introductions of the two subsidiary themes. This means that they have been placed in their present location by someone who comprehended the interior structure of the narrative, and most probably this was the author himself. Accordingly, we come to the conclusion that probably the formulas in Jg. 19:1a and 21:25 have been taken over editorially from Jg. 17-18, where they once intrinsically belonged. It can still be asked whether in Jg. 17-18 the two sentences should be understood as closing remarks to what precedes or as introductory words to what follows. If they have not been placed at the two junctures primarily

[27] So, among others, G. F. Moore, *A Critical and Exegetical Commentary on Judges*, ICC (1895), p. 369; Nowack, *op. cit.*, p. 144; Gressmann, *op. cit.*, p. 252; Hauret, *op. cit.*, p. 110; also with certain reservations K. Budde, *Das Buch der Richter*, KHC, VIII (1897), p. 112; A. Schulz, *Das Buch der Richter und das Buch Ruth*, HSAT, II, 4, 5 (1926), pp. 90 f.

to cast light upon the entire narrative, then they are better understood as concluding judgments upon what precedes, since a new stage in the narrative follows them.[28]

The contents of the two sentences are most remarkable and astonishing; their significance has hardly been correctly evaluated up to now. They do not merely make a chronological statement, demonstrating that they and the narratives of which they are a part come from the "time of the monarchy."[29] They contain a quite unusual judgment upon the kingship.[30] Elsewhere in the entire Old Testament there is hardly a passage which assumes such an absolutely positive attitude toward the institution of the historical kingship. The Old Testament contains various traditions glorifying a definite royal figure who is called by name: this is true of some of the Saul narratives and above all of a portion of the David tradition, up to and including the Chronicler's representation of David. The same is true of the well-known favorable judgments of the Deuteronomist upon a few of the Judean kings referred to by name. But it is quite unusual that the "king" as such should be evaluated as positively as he is in the sentences under discussion. Obviously these sentences do not envisage an idealized, unreal kingdom and still less do they envisage a future "Messianic" kingship; rather, as the text makes clear, they refer to a real, historical kingship which the author knows. In addition, in Jg. 17:6, 18:1a the regulative authority of the king strangely is claimed to extend right into the cultic sphere. If the two sentences are taken in relation to the whole narrative of Jg. 17-18, they show that in general a "royal" regulation in the cultic sphere is a blessing. But if they are connected especially with what precedes in each case—and in both instances the preceding subject is the installation of a priest—then above all it is eminently clear that

---

[28] So, for example, V. Zapletal, *Das Buch der Richter*, EHAT, VII, 1 (1923), pp. 255, 259; Nötscher, *op. cit.*, p. 67 (= p. 688).

[29] Cf. Budde, *op. cit.*, p. 112. Only by doing violence to the sentences can we assign them to the post-Exilic period "which views the kingship in a glorious light" (so Moore, *op. cit.*, p. 369; cf. Nowack, *op. cit.*, p. 144).

[30] This applies equally to the shorter formulation in 18:1a, which is only a reference to the full formulation just preceding it and is to be understood in the same sense as the latter.

the activity of the "king" in installing priests is assumed to be desirable. Reflection upon this matter will disclose the extraordinary position which these two sentences have in the Old Testament. And when seen from this viewpoint, it is quite improbable that they can rightly be regarded as redactional glosses.

The question then arises as to what picture of kingship is reflected in Jg. 17:6; 18:1a. These texts refer in general terms to a "king in Israel." There were, however, various historical expressions of kingship in "Israel." Which special form is meant here? In so far as these two sentences have received serious attention before now, and have not just been thought to refer vaguely to some ideal image of kingship, they have been taken to mean—and at first glance this would seem obvious—"the kingship of David as the deliverance from the crisis of the period of the Judges,"[31] and thus the author of Jg. 17:6; 18:1a has been viewed as "an admirer of the [Davidic] monarchy."[32] Yet a closer examination shows that this view is hardly correct. The very fact that in Jg. 17-18 we have not Judean but North Israelite tradition before us speaks against it. Granted, David and Solomon were also kings of " (North) Israel." But it should be kept in mind that the story in Jg. 17-18 comes not from "North Israel" in general but from Dan in particular; and it neither is reported in tradition nor is in itself probable that David and Solomon had anything at all to do with cultic matters in Dan. Jeroboam I was the first king about whom anything of this sort is reported; he undertook that well-known intervention in cultic matters at Dan (I Kg. 12:28 ff.). If in a Danite tradition we hear of the regulative hand of the "king" in cultic matters, we must think—on the basis of what we know—of Jeroboam I, even though the special tradition in question gives quite a different evaluation of the cultic measures taken by this king than is found in I Kg. 12:28 ff. and, further, in the stereotyped treatment in the Deuteronomic historical work. Thus I am led to the conclusion that the polemical narrative of Jg. 17-18 stems from the circle of the royal Israelite sanctuary of Dan which was

[31] So Vischer, op. cit., p. 136.
[32] So Hauret, op. cit., p. 113; also Hertzberg (op. cit., pp. 239, 241) probably has a similar understanding, although he does not say so explicitly.

established by Jeroboam I.[33] This would account concretely for the fact that the ancient sanctuary at Dan, whose origin is reported in Jg. 17-18, is in almost every respect the opposite of the later royal sanctuary at Dan: a silver statuette of questionable origin, not a "golden calf" established by the king; a tribal sanctuary of a small tribe, not a sanctuary erected by the king of all " (North) Israel"; a priesthood consisting of "vagabond" Levites, not a royally commissioned priesthood.

The narrative of Jg. 17-18 thus sheds light upon the cultic conflicts of the early monarchy. And if there were such conflicts, one must assume that it was necessary to justify the royal measures taken at Dan. The justification took the form of a polemic against opposition which, relying upon ancient cultic traditions, resisted the king's innovations.[34] The fact that the narrative of Jg. 17-18, so understood, stands quite isolated in the Old Testament need not prevent us from deriving this very understanding from its text. It is thoroughly understandable why the Deuteronomist did not take the narrative up into his historical work, so that only secondarily was it inserted into his portrayal of the "time of the Judges." For even though he shared completely the scorn for the silver cult image, he could hardly have approved the positive statements concerning the "king" and even less the manner in which the conduct of the "Levite" is depicted.[35] The polemic against the "Levite" shows at the same time that it was not just an act of serious neglect and irresponsible disregard of the divine will when Jeroboam I gave preference to non-Levites as priests; rather, there were reasons to mistrust the "Levites" and to engage non-Levites as priests.

There still remains the historical question of the relation between the earlier tribal sanctuary and the later royal sanctuary

[33] Intentionally I state the matter in this indefinite manner, since obviously nothing more can be demonstrated about the author than the spiritual standpoint from which he evaluated the cultic conditions in Dan.

[34] The basic elements in Ex. 32 acquaint us with the other side of the polemic against the Danite cult. Here also—at least in a later addition—the "Levites" play a role (vss. 25-29). Of course, the role is a positive one here, in accordance with the contrasting viewpoint of the narrative. From Dt. 33:11b it is also clear that there were conflicts over the Levitical priestly claims.

[35] The entire story does not fit well at all into the Deuteronomistic conception of the "period of the Judges." According to that conception, such a questionable act of founding the sanctuary in Dan would have issued in a divine punishment.

in Dan. Connected with this question is the problem of the originality and significance of the two concluding verses, 18:30, 31, and their individual parts. On this point we can hardly go beyond conjecture. The historical question is whether the Danite tribal sanctuary was replaced by the royal sanctuary in Dan, or whether the former continued to exist alongside, and in the shadow of, the latter. In other words, is the polemic in Jg. 17-18 directed against the adherents of a cult of the past or against those of a cult still in existence? An answer to the question may be sought in the two divergent dates given in 18:30bb and in 18:31b. It is self-evident that the two dates are irreconcilable.[36] Offhand there is much to be said for the view that the time indication in vs. 30bb, which is so much later than that found in vs. 31b, is secondary. Furthermore, in vs. 30bb the end of the state of Israel is evidently presupposed, while in 17:6; 18:1a the presence of a "king in Israel" is still taken for granted. Moreover, since vs. 30ba is clearly a gloss[37] and since vs. 30a anticipates what is said again in vs. 31a, it seems reasonable to consider the entire verse as a later gloss. Even this addition, however, makes an important assertion which has hardly been invented and which therefore must be taken seriously. According to the addition, there were priests of the tribe of the Danites up to the end of the state of Israel and up to the time of the deportation of the upper stratum of its population, among whom the victors probably would have included the priesthood.[38] This Danite tribal priesthood had originated with a certain Jonathan ben Gershom.[39] It has already been indicated that this Jonathan was, in the view of the glossator, identical

[36] Frequently the reading "at Laish" instead of "at Shiloh" in vs. 31b has been considered to be the original text. This is, however, pure conjecture which has no textual support and is only supposed to overcome the contradiction between the two time indications. This conjecture is all the less acceptable in that after vs. 29 one does not expect the name "Laish" to appear again.

[37] See above, p. 70, n. 6.

[38] From II Kg. 17:25-28 we learn explicitly that the Assyrians deported the priestly classes of the state of Israel. It is true that the reference is specifically to the province of Samaria and to the former royal sanctuary at Bethel. But the Assyrians certainly acted similarly in the other sections of the state of Israel.

[39] The connection which this priesthood is thought to have had with "Moses" (or "Manasseh"), according to Jg. 18:30, is not to be discussed here. This is a matter of the early history, or ideology, of the "Levitical" office.

with the unnamed "Levite" of the preceding narrative.[40] The gloss thus witnesses to the presence of a tribal priesthood of Gershomites in Dan during the period of the existence of the state of Israel, a priesthood which claimed for itself—with whatever right—a "Levitical" origin.[41] The question is only whether this priesthood still had at its disposal the old sanctuary of Jg. 17-18 or whether the royal sanctuary of I Kg. 12:28 ff. had in the meantime taken its place, so that the Gershomites could function among the Danites perhaps only in the role of oracle givers, cultic advisers, or the like.[42]

An answer to this question seems to be given by vs. 31. According to this verse, the cult image of Micah stood in Dan only "as long as the house of God was at Shiloh." If the whole of vs. 30 is viewed as a gloss, then at least vs. 31a must have belonged to the original narrative as the appropriate conclusion to it. There is no reason at the outset not to include the time indication in vs. 31b with the original narrative as well. On the other hand, it is true that this time indication is added in such a way that it could also be regarded as a secondary addition without difficulty; nothing essential would be missing from the conclusion of the narrative. Yet even if it should be a gloss, it would still be so unusual in content that one would have to take its factual character seriously. In so far as vs. 31b contains a time designation, it indicates that the cult image of Micah, and accordingly the old Danite tribal sanctuary as well, existed only during the time of the Judges, and that later the Danite tribal priests from the house of the Gershomites were no longer able to exercise their office in the ancient tribal sanctuary. This must be considered historical information; no sound objection based on the tradition at our disposal can be raised against its factual

[40] Here the question may be left open as to whether the glossator has adopted something which is historically correct; whether, that is, the Danite tribal priests were actually from the beginning "Levites," or whether they only later declared themselves to be "Levites," as for example in the case of the Zadokites of Jerusalem.

[41] In the later Levite genealogies Gershon (Gershom and Gershon may be identical) assumes a prominent position (cf. Num. 3:17, etc.) .

[42] The glossator, who added vs. 30, evaluated the narrative of Jg. 17-18 positively; he did not take account of the polemical bias of the story.

accuracy. It is another question as to why the duration of the "house of God" at Shiloh serves as a measure of time. It is not very probable that the Philistines, at about the same time they destroyed the central sanctuary at Shiloh,[48] should also have brought to an end the remote tribal sanctuary at Dan. It is much more likely that this end came with the establishment of the royal sanctuary in Dan by Jeroboam I. However, the period of time between the destruction of the "house of God in Shiloh" and the reign of Jeroboam I is not inconsiderable. We may reasonably assume, therefore, that vs. 31b is concerned not only with a temporal but also with a factual (sachlich) declaration; and for that reason the imprecision of the time indication was simply accepted as a matter of course, especially since a certain objective (sachlich) connection existed between the two events despite their separation in time. Since presumably the "house of God in Shiloh" is referred to in a positive sense, perhaps one may trace vs. 31b to a (North Israelite) adherent of the "good old times" who wanted to say something like this: As long as the central shrine at Shiloh was still in existence, as long as David had not yet appropriated the sacred Ark for his city of Jerusalem, as long as an Israelite king, Jeroboam I, had not yet had occasion to establish sanctuaries in Bethel and Dan as rivals to the Davidic sanctuary in Jerusalem and thereby bring to an end the old Danite cult; in short, as long as kings had not yet interfered with the cultic traditions of Israel, everything was better than it is today. On the basis of such an anti-royal *Tendenz,* then, the notice in vs. 31b must be excluded from the original part of the narrative in Jg. 17-18 and must be regarded as a later addition.

[48] Cf. Jer. 7:12, 14; 26:6, 9. On this matter see M. Noth, *The History of Israel* (²1960), pp. 166 f.

V

The Prophetic Call of Samuel

MURRAY NEWMAN

I Sam. 3:1-4:1a is the story of the prophetic call of Samuel. It is the final part of the larger collection of traditions concerning the birth and boyhood of Samuel that begins with chapter one. Martin Noth terms the material found in I Sam. 1:1-4:1a *"eine in sich geschlossene Prophetentradition, deren Ziel in 3. 19-20 ausdrücklich angegeben wird."*[1]

The structure of the story of Samuel's call is similar to the accounts of the call of certain of the classical prophets such as Isa. 6, Jer. 1, and Ezek. 1-3.[2] The narrative recounts a story of the young Samuel sleeping before the Ark in the sanctuary at Shiloh. When he hears a voice calling to him, he assumes that it is Eli who is asleep in a neighboring room. After Samuel has come to the old priest for the third time, Eli perceives that it is Yahweh who is calling and sends the lad back to the Ark with the proper liturgical reply. Thereupon the word of Yahweh comes with the announcement of the divine determination to destroy Eli's house. The old priest accepts the will of God as good and Samuel is accepted as a prophet by all Israel. "And Samuel grew, and Yahweh was with him and let none of his words fall to the ground. And all Israel from Dan to Beer-sheba knew that Samuel was established as a prophet of Yahweh. And

---

[1] *Überlieferungsgeschichte des Pentateuch* (1948), pp. 60-61.

[2] It is actually closer to Jeremiah's call than to those of Isaiah and Ezekiel. Unlike Isaiah and Ezekiel, there is no visual evidence of Yahweh's presence in either I Sam. 3 or Jer. 1; the emphasis is exclusively upon audition.

Yahweh appeared again at Shiloh, for Yahweh revealed himself to Samuel at Shiloh by the word of Yahweh. And the word of Samuel came to all Israel" (3:19-4:1a).

What the story seems to be saying is that the prophet in Israel, as personified by Samuel, succeeded and took over the functions formerly exercised by the house of Eli. Thus I Sam. 3 might be termed an *etiological legend* which seeks to explain the emergence of the prophet in Israel. That the theological circles responsible for this tradition viewed the prophet as the successor to an earlier priesthood is somewhat strange and calls for further examination. The key to an understanding of the story of Samuel's call would seem to be the *Ark*.

In another study[3] the present writer has sought to show that the E covenant legend[4] in various of its early oral forms was used in connection with the Ark as the cult legend of the covenant-renewal ceremony of the twelve-tribe amphictyony of Israel. At the yearly autumnal festival some form of the E covenant legend was read and re-enacted. Thus it would have been used first at Shechem, when that city was the central cult site of the amphictyony, and later at Shiloh.[5]

Ex. 20:18-21 is probably the etiology for the office of covenant mediator in this northern covenant ceremony.[6] The covenant mediator was the cult official who presided at this regularly observed covenant rite. Appointed by the people (Ex. 20:19 E; contrast 19:9a J), he would have performed the role of Moses in the re-enactment of the Sinaitic covenant. Thus in the ceremony the covenant mediator (1) spoke for Yahweh and in his name (Ex. 20:1-2a); (2) spoke to the whole people of Israel,

[3] *The Sinai Covenant Traditions in the Cult of Israel*, Diss., Union Theological Seminary, New York (1960).

[4] In its final written form to be found in Ex. 19:2b-6, 10-11a, 14-17, 19; 20:18-21, 1-17; 24:3-8.

[5] The J covenant legend (Ex. 19:19a, 11b-13, 18, 20; 34:1-4; 33:18-23; 34:5-8, 10-28; 19:7-8; 24:1-2, 9-11), on the other hand, can be associated with the Tent of Meeting at Hebron in the premonarchical period. In an early form it was a cult legend of the southern six-tribe amphictyony. On the southern six-tribe amphictyony see Martin Noth, *Das System der zwölf Stämme Israels* (1930), pp. 107-108, and *The History of Israel*, (1958), p. 81.

[6] On the covenant mediator see especially Hans-Joachim Kraus, *Gottesdienst in Israel* (1954), pp. 58 ff., 110 ff.

i.e., the twelve-tribe amphictyony (Ex. 19:3, 6; 24:4); (3) recalled Yahweh's mighty deeds (Ex. 20:2b; cf. 19:3-6); (4) proclaimed the apodictic law which expressed the righteous will of Yahweh (Ex. 20:3-17).

That Joshua performed this function at Shechem when that site was the cult center of the twelve-tribe amphictyony is indicated by Jos. 24 (cf. 8:30-35). Subsequently a Levitical priest may have served as covenant mediator in the ceremony, as might be concluded from Dt. 27:9 ff., 14 ff., and 31:9-13 (cf. Dt. 33:8-10). It is also possible, as Hans-Joachim Kraus has suggested,[7] that the judges mentioned in Judges 10:1-5; 12:7-15 served in this capacity. This suggestion is not necessarily antithetical to the view that a Levite could fulfill the function, since the Levitical priesthood was evidently a flexible phenomenon in the period[8] and these judges could have been Levites. In fact, it may have been characteristic of the office of covenant mediator that there were no set genealogical or ecclasiastical requirements for the one who so functioned. Ex. 20:18-21 indicates that the appointment of the covenant mediator came directly from the people and was not dynastic in character. In this respect it would have been more of a charismatic than dynastic office.[9]

When the Ark was moved from Shechem to Shiloh, the latter site became the cult center of the Israelite amphictyony. This is the situation that obtains in the early chapters of I Samuel. Presumably the annual festival which was celebrated at Shiloh (I Sam. 1:3, 21) had as its central theme the renewal of the covenant.[10] With the Ark would presumably have been an early form of the E covenant legend, which was used as a liturgical

---

[7] *Ibid.*, p. 64.

[8] W. F. Albright, *Archaeology and the Religion of Israel* (4th ed., 1956), pp. 109-110.

[9] That there was a dynastic office of covenant mediator in southern Palestine during this period seems probable, as is suggested by the J covenant legend which had its *Sitz im Leben* in the covenant ceremony at Hebron. Ex. 34:27; 19:9a; 24:1-2, 9-11 indicate that an Aaronic dynastic priesthood was viewed in southern theological circles as standing in legitimate succession to Moses, the original covenant mediator. This priesthood was regarded as the real center of the life of the covenant people and its office was to continue "for ever" (19:9a).

[10] See John Bright, *A History of Israel* (1959), p. 149, and Noth, *History*, pp. 97-98.

legend in the covenant ceremony. It would seem to follow, then, that an important function of Eli, the priest at Shiloh, was to serve as covenant mediator in the covenant festival.

But the central point of I Sam. 3 is that the house of Eli is to be destroyed and Samuel, the prophet, is the legitimate successor of this priestly house. The prophet succeeds the priest! The meaning of the story evidently is that the prophet in Israel performed certain functions of the covenant mediator of the old amphictyony.

Significantly Dt. 18:15-22 also relates the office of covenant mediator to the prophet. In the future, this tradition says, Yahweh will raise up from among the Hebrews a prophet like Moses. Divine words will be placed in the mouth of the prophet and he will speak what Yahweh commands him. One should observe that vs. 16 refers specifically to the etiology of the covenant mediator found in Ex. 20:18-21. Yahweh raises up the prophet to succeed the Mosaic covenant mediator. The similarity of the functions of the two is clear. Like the covenant mediator, the prophet too (1) spoke for Yahweh and in his name; (2) spoke to the whole people of Israel; (3) recalled Yahweh's mighty deeds; (4) proclaimed the law and righteousness of Yahweh.

I Sam. 3, however, seems to be relating Samuel directly to this development. Samuel, who later anoints the first king of Israel and thus is a decisive figure in the transition from tribal amphictyony to monarchy, is depicted in this story as the one in whom the transition from covenant mediator to prophet also occurred. It is quite possible that the tradition has preserved an authetic historical memory in this respect.

Samuel appeared at a point in Israel's history when the amphictyony was breaking down under the blows of the Philistines. In the early part of his life the Hebrews suffered a crushing defeat at the hands of these enemies (I Sam. 4-6). The Ark, the sacred shrine of the amphictyony, was lost, and Shiloh, its central cult site, was destroyed. Moreover, with the death of Eli and his two sons the priesthood of the central sanctuary came to an end. The office of covenant mediator would also have ceased, at least temporarily. For the continuation of the life of Israel as the covenant people of Yahweh, however, it was necessary for the basic functions of the covenant mediator to be perpetuated. This was evidently a concern of Samuel. The traditions in I Sam. 1-3 connect him with the central amphictyonic cult at Shiloh and ch. 3 specifically associates him with the Ark. Whether I Sam. 3 gives a literal account of Samuel's call might be open to question; but that it preserves the memory of some charismatic experience in his life which was determinative for his subsequent career is not improbable. In any case, by associating him with the Ark the chapter would seem to indicate that in his youth he was imbued with a knowledge of the basic cultic and theological traditions of the Yahweh-worshiping amphictyony. He would have possessed a knowledge of an early form of the E covenant legend with its distinctive theological emphases and its tradition of the covenant mediator. He would have understood the profound importance of this office, which involved the regular proclamation of Yahweh's mighty deeds and his righteous law to his covenant people. These concerns would have remained with Samuel as he passed from youth to maturity.

The various traditions in I Sam. concerning Samuel's adult career are not at all easy to interpret. In one tradition he is a seer, a man of God who is consulted in connection with the loss of some asses (ch. 9). Elsewhere he appears as a judge whose circuit seems to be restricted to the limited area of Ramah, Bethel, Gilgal, and Mizpah (7:16-17). In another tradition he is depicted as a judge over all Israel, and indeed, like the charismatic judges before him, a conqueror of Israel's enemies (7:3-14). And of course he is the king-maker who anoints (chs. 9-11) and deposes (13:7b-15a; ch. 15) Saul and then anoints David as Saul's successor (16:1-13).

It is significant that after ch. 3 he is not again called a prophet in I Sam.[11] That he was a prophet in the classical sense, as might be concluded from I Sam. 3, is therefore unlikely. In two traditions, however, he is specifically associated with the ecstatic groups of prophets who appear for the first time in Israel's history during this period. In I Sam. 10:5-6 Samuel tells the newly

[11] I Sam. 9:9 is an explanatory gloss.

anointed Saul that as he goes on his way he will "meet a band of prophets coming down from the high place with harp, tambourine, and lyre before them, prophesying. Then the spirit of Yahweh will come mightily upon you, and you shall prophesy with them and be turned into another man." The tradition in I Sam. 19:18-25 likewise authentically associates him with these prophetic groups. Here he is pictured as "standing as head over them" (vs. 20).

These ecstatic groups seem to have been the first to bear the name *nābî'* in Israel.[12] Such religious ecstasy was not unique with Israel, of course, and it seems particularly to have been associated with Canaanite religion, as evidenced by the Story of Wen Amon as well as by the tradition of Eiljah's contest with the prophets of Baal at Mt. Carmel (I Kg. 18). It is therefore probable that this cultural form came to Israel from the Canaanites. When they first appear in the time of Samuel, however, the Hebrew prophetic groups are already firmly established in Yahwism. Their salient characteristic is a fanatical devotion to Yahweh with a particular concern for the amphictyonic institution of Holy War. Since they bear the same name, *nābî'*, these prophetic groups can be regarded in a definite sense as forerunners of the classical prophets.

Also it would seem reasonable to conjecture that Samuel was instrumental in the development from charismatic prophet to classical prophet. Samuel was probably concerned with transferring the basic functions of the covenant mediator to the prophetic groups and thus insuring that these functions be perpetuated for the people of Yahweh. This must have been an important result of his association with the groups.

To be sure, an Amos did not emerge immediately from these prophetic communities of Samuel's day. Several centuries were required for the completion of the transition from the charismatic to classical prophet. The charismatic prophets first appear in the eleventh century in the age of Samuel. They are not mentioned again until the middle of the ninth century in the

[12] Those who are called *nābî'* before this period probably bear the name anachronistically: Abraham, Gen. 20:7; Moses, Dt. 18:15; 34:10; cf. Hos. 12:13; Miriam, Ex. 15:20; Deborah, Jg. 4:4; Gideon, Jg. 6:8.

time of Elijah and Elisha. And it is not until the eighth century that Amos, Hosea, Isaiah, and Micah appear as the first of the classical prophets. Undoubtedly there were many factors which influenced this development during these centuries.

It has recently been pointed out that an important root of the classical prophetic movement was the *apilu* mentioned in the Mari texts.[13] The *apilu* was the unasked and unbidden messenger of a god. His message came to him by inspiration and he appeared suddenly to deliver it orally. In these respects the *apilu* parallels the classical prophet of the Old Testament. Since this kind of messenger seems to be confined to the Mari texts and the Old Testament, and in view of the several other affinities between these two bodies of literature, it is likely that there is an historical connection between the *apilu* and the classical prophet. However, there are also differences between the two. The content of their oracles differ. The message of the *apilu* was delivered to the king and was mainly concerned with gaining his favorable attention toward the cult of the god involved. There is no proclamation of divine control and involvement in the events of human history nor of any demands in regard to the righteous conduct of human life, both of which are hallmarks of the classical prophets. Another significant difference is that the message of the *apilu* was intended for the *king*. In this regard, he is like the court prophet of the Old Testament, such as Nathan and Gad, but not the classical prophets. The classical prophets, although on occasion delivering oracles to the king, were primarily concerned with speaking to the *whole people Israel*. One might suspect, however, that in so far as the phenomenon of the *apilu* did affect the development of the prophetic office in Israel, the influence came through the royal court at Jerusalem.

Among the various roots of the classical prophets, the most authentically Yahwistic was the covenant mediator of the old amphictyonic covenant ceremony. This root extended back through Samuel to Moses himself.[14] One should observe, how-

---

[13] Noth, "History and the Word of God in the Old Testament," BJRL, XXXII (1950), pp. 194-206, and G. E. Wright, *Biblical Archaeology* (1957), pp. 96-97.
[14] Could it perhaps be for this reason that Moses and Samuel are coupled in Jer. 15:1 and Ps. 99:6?

ever, that the prophet as covenant mediator differed in certain respects from the original cultic covenant mediator.

1. For one thing, while the latter functioned once a year on the occasion of the great autumnal festival, the former seems not to have been limited by any chronological restrictions. He spoke when the Spirit moved him and the *kairos* demanded it.

2. Nor did he function only at the central cult. He could deliver his oracles at Bethel, as did Amos; but he could proclaim his message elsewhere too. He was not bound to any one place.

3. Further, while the cultic covenant mediator seems to have proclaimed the traditional apodictic law which was already formulated, the prophet was a charismatic interpreter of Yahweh's law and righteous will. He applied the law to the particular historical situation by which he was confronted.

Of course, it is not necessary to think that the cultic office of covenant mediator came suddenly to an end in the time of Samuel, to be immediately replaced by the prophet. As has been suggested, it was undoubtedly a gradual process in which the functions of the cultic covenant mediator were assumed by the charismatic prophets. And it is quite possible that in the northern kingdom the cultic covenant mediator was functioning at an annual covenant ceremony in Bethel at the same time that prophets like Elijah and Elisha, Amos and Hosea were carrying on their activities as prophetic covenant mediators.

The foregoing discussion in regard to the historical significance of I Sam. 3 leads directly to the question concerning the circles responsible for it. What kind of group would have preserved, formed, used, and transmitted this tradition? Certain things would seem obvious in regard to the character of the group. It would have been a northern prophetic community with a vital concern for the covenant faith of the old twelve-tribe amphictyony. If chs. 1-3 of I Sam. belong to the "Samuel" source of that book, as many critics believe, the group would have been strongly antimonarchical. The legend would have reached its present form, of course, after the emergence of the individual prophet in Israel who spoke in Yahweh's name to the whole covenant people and normatively experienced a call. This would seem to indicate that these circles would have to be dated in the ninth century, the period of Elijah and Elisha, or later.[15]

This characterization might point to prophetic circles of the eighth century who shared the general theological outlook of Hosea. He was a northern prophet who spoke to the people of Israel and who emphasized the Exodus event and the covenant. He alludes to his call and is grimly opposed to the institution of the monarchy. If the Elohist epic is to be dated in the eighth century, this might be further reason for relating I Sam. 3 to Hoseanic circles. That Hosea was acquainted with the Elohist tradition is generally recognized. In view of this fact, it is significant that there are definite affinities between the call of Samuel and E's account of the call of Moses. There is the repetition of the name "Samuel, Samuel" (vs. 10; cf. vs. 4 in the LXX), which finds its parallel in "Moses, Moses" of E (Ex. 3:4; cf. Gen. 22:11; 46:2, both of which are E). Even more significant is the absence in both traditions of any *visual* evidence of Yahweh's presence in connection with the call. Unlike J, who speaks of a theophany seen by Moses (Ex. 3:2-4a), E knows only audible signs of Yahweh's presence at the call of Moses (vss. 4b, 6, 9 ff.). Also in I Sam. 3 there is exclusive emphasis upon hearing. Yahweh "comes" and "stands forth" (vs. 10), but he is not seen; not even his glory is visible; he is only heard.

If, however, E is dated earlier than the eighth century, as is quite possible, an earlier date for I Sam. 3 might be called for. Ninth-century prophetic circles associated with Elijah could well have been responsible for the formation, preservation, and transmission of the legend.

The Elijah narratives in I Kg. 17-19; 21; II Kg. 1-2 are legendary and episodic, so they cannot be expected to provide anything approaching a complete and accurate account of Elijah's prophetic activity. But they do reveal the theological concerns of the late ninth-century circles that preserved them and, if used cautiously, can even provide authentic insight into the central emphases of Elijah's ministry itself.

Elijah clearly was a proponent of Mosaic Yahwism as interpreted by northern amphictyonic circles. A man whose life is said

[15] Prophets such as Nathan and Gad seem to have been court officials rather than amphictyonic covenant mediators.

to have begun and ended in the wilderness, he seems on at least one occasion to have visted Horeb, the mountain of Moses' call and the site of the covenant (I Kg. 19).[16] His commitment to the covenant faith was deep and he had a particular concern to uphold the first commandment of the Decalogue. At Mt. Carmel he stood firmly for Yahweh's claim to the exclusive allegiance of his people over against the challenge of Baalism (I Kg. 18:17-40). He was committed to the other apodictic laws of the covenant faith with equal firmness and he vehemently condemned Ahab for violations of the Mosaic prohibitions of murder and theft (I Kg. 21). Although there is no evidence of a direct attack by Elijah upon the institution of the monarchy as such, he was certainly not its friend and is specifically said to have been involved in a plot to overthrow the house of Omri (I Kg. 19:15-17).

Elijah was not only a proponent of Mosaic Yahwism but also a *prophet* who championed this faith. As a prophet, he stood on the threshold of the classical prophetic movement. Like Samuel he was associated with the prophetic bands (II Kg. 2). Like the covenant mediator and classical prophet he spoke in Yahweh's name and proclaimed Yahweh's righteous will to the whole covenant people. Indeed, although he left behind no written oracles, there is a real sense in which he can be considered the first of the classical prophets.

It is probably with definite intention that the tradition in I Kg. 18:17-40 depicts the contest between Eiijah and the prophets of Baal at Mt. Carmel in terms reminiscent of the covenant assembly at Shechem under Joshua (Jos. 24; cf. Jos. 8:30-35; Dt. 11:26-32; 27:1-26) and of the E account of the original covenant at Sinai.[17] Like Moses, Joshua, and Samuel in I Sam. 12,[18] Elijah appears here as a covenant mediator. "All the people of

[16] Although aware of the problems involved, the present writer believes that for all practical purposes Horeb and Sinai are identical. Horeb is the expression that E and D use, while J and P prefer Sinai.

[17] For the possible historical situation reflected in I Kg. 18 see Albrecht Alt, "Das Gottesurteil auf dem Karmel," *Kleine Schriften zur Geschichte des Volkes Israel*, II (1953), pp. 135-149.

[18] Dr. Muilenburg has demonstrated that I Sam. 12 depicts Samuel as a covenant mediator and belongs in the same tradition stream as Ex. 19:3-6 and Jos. 24 in his provocative article "The Form and Structure of the Covenantal Formulations," VT, IX (1959), pp. 347-365.

Israel," i.e., the covenant assembly, are gathered together at Carmel (I Kg. 18:19, 20), as had happened at Shechem (Jos. 24:1; cf. Ex. 19:2b, 3). Elijah calls the covenant people to a decision in behalf of Yahweh, the covenant God who claims the exclusive allegiance of his worshipers (I Kg. 18:21). In similar language Joshua had challenged the people at Shechem to commit themselves to Yahweh alone (Jos. 24:14-15; cf. Ex. 19:3-6; 20:3). At Carmel the people respond by acclaiming Yahweh as their God (I Kg. 18:39), as had the Israelite tribes in the time of Joshua (Jos. 24:16-18, 21; cf. Ex. 24:3, 7). Finally, Elijah takes twelve stones to build the altar upon which the sacrifices are offered (I Kg. 18:30 ff.). At Shechem, too, Joshua had made an altar of stone for covenant sacrifices (Jos. 24:26; 8:30-31).[19] It would thus seem that there is a clear attempt by the author of the Carmel tradition to present Elijah as a covenant mediator in terms of Joshua and Moses.

If I Kg. 18 presents Elijah as a covenant mediator, I Kg. 19 would seem to depict him as a prophet who is called. Although the story of his experience at Mt. Horeb in its present position in I Kings does not come at the beginning of his career, it does exhibit certain features which suggest affinities with the prophetic call of Samuel. Samuel was called before the Ark of the Covenant at Shiloh. In the time of Elijah the Ark had long been in the Holy of Holies of the Jerusalem Temple and thus was not accessible to him. Horeb, however, was the sacred mountain where the Ark had originated. In fact, the Ark had long been regarded as a kind of miniature Horeb. Just as Yahweh, according to E,[20] had been enthroned upon the mountain in the Mosaic age, so he was subsequently enthroned upon the Ark. The logical site for this experience of Elijah, therefore, was Horeb, the mountain of the call of Moses, of the covenant, and of the Ark. And it is certainly not fortuitous that the expression "Yahweh, the God of hosts," which first appears in connection

---

[19] Note that in the E covenant legend twelve pillars, corresponding to the twelve tribes, are erected along with the altar at Sinai (Ex. 24:4), just as twelve stones are used by Elijah to build the altar at Carmel (I Kg. 18:31).

[20] J, on the other hand, thinks of Yahweh as being enthroned in heaven (Ex. 24:9-11) and on occasion he "comes down" (*yārad* 19:11, 18, 20; 34:5) to the mountain.

with the Ark, is mentioned twice in this chapter (vss. 10, 14). When Yahweh manifests himself to Elijah on this occasion, as with the call of Samuel and E's version of Moses' call, he is only heard, not seen.[21] Yahweh is present in neither the wind, the earthquake, nor the fire. The only indication of his presence is a *qôl*, the "sound (*qôl*) of stillness" (vs. 12), a "voice" (*qôl*) which is that of Yahweh (vs. 13). The "voice" of Yahweh "calls" Elijah, just as it called Samuel and Moses before him and the classical prophet after him. He is called and commissioned to act for Yahweh in the accomplishing of his righteous will in human history.

I Kg. 18 and 19, therefore, seem to depict Elijah, the ninth-century Israelite who embodied Mosaic Yahwism, first as a covenant mediator and then as the prophet called by Yahweh. In so doing they place him in the succession which began with Moses, to which Joshua and Samuel belonged, and which continued with the classical prophets of the eighth century and after. It would seem clear that the circles which preserved and shaped the Elijah legends were informed by the same theological concerns that motivated those who preserved, shaped, and used the story of Samuel's call. Though we cannot be certain about such matters, it is possible that they were one and the same group.

---

[21] In this respect Elijah's encounter with Yahweh is unlike the similar experience of Moses recounted by J in Ex. 33-34. Although Moses cannot see Yahweh's face, according to J, he is permitted to *see* the back of Yahweh's glory as he passes by. Elijah sees nothing.

VI

The Prophet as Yahweh's Messenger

JAMES F. ROSS

If one may be permitted to anticipate the verdict of those who will write the history of Biblical studies in the twentieth century, the contribution of James Muilenburg seems to be clear. Both in the classroom and on the printed page he has done much to advance our understanding of and appreciation for the depth and breadth of Hebrew literary form. His articles on the subject[1] give evidence of his sensitivity not only to the sequence of the words but also to the theological significance of a given *Gattung*. To date his most extensive effort is the masterly introduction to and commentary upon Isaiah 40–66.[2]

This article stems from a reference in one of Muilenburg's most recent studies of literary forms.[3] Commenting on Ex. 19: 3b, he notes that we have "the characteristic speech of the messenger, the rôle which Moses is to assume here."[4] The questions arise: What are the characteristics of the messenger speech? What is the relationship of the messenger to the sender, and the locus of his authority? Finally, what is the task and responsibility of the messenger; what does he actually say and do? Let us examine these questions in terms of their bearing upon the form and content of Old Testament prophecy.

---

[1] "The Literary Character of Isaiah 34," JBL, LIX (1940), pp. 339-365; "Psalm 47," *ibid.*, LXIII (1944), pp. 235-256; "A Study in Hebrew Rhetoric: Repetition and Style," Suppl. VT (*Congress Volume, 1953*), pp. 97-111.

[2] IB, V (1956), pp. 381-773.

[3] "The Form and Structure of the Covenantal Formulations," VT, IX (1959), pp. 347-365.

[4] *Ibid.*, p. 354 and n. 2.

I

Ludwig Köhler was among the first to demonstrate the existence of the prophetic *Botenspruch*.[5] In his classic analysis of the stylistic elements in Deutero-Isaiah he isolated numerous passages where the prophet assumes the role of a messenger and couches his oracles in the standard messenger style; we have not only the usual opening, *Kô 'āmar yhwh*, followed by qualifying titles, but also the standard conclusion, *ne'um yhwh*.[6] Köhler finds no less than sixty-one examples, more or less completely preserved, and concludes that Deutero-Isaiah uses the *Botenspruch* much more freely than his predecessors.[7]

It is surprising that so few scholars have made use of Köhler's suggestions.[8] For the comparative material is not confined to these opening and closing phrases alone. It is obvious that the verb ordinarily used to describe the sending of a messenger, *šālaḥ*, is common both in the accounts of the prophets' inaugural visions and in the introductions to subsequent oracles.[9] Other features of the messenger narratives may also be discerned. For example, when Jacob sends messengers to Esau, he commands them, "Thus shall you say to my lord, to Esau: 'Thus says your servant, Jacob . . .'" (Gen. 32:4-5—EVV 32:3-4).[10]

[5] *Deuterojesaja (Jesaja 40–55) stilkritisch untersucht*, BZAW, 37 (1923), pp. 102-109.

[6] This is the full form, best preserved in 45:11-13, "*ein formstrenger Botenspruch*," (*ibid.*, p. 195).

[7] *Ibid.*, p. 109.

[8] See, however, Victor Maag, *Text, Wortschatz und Begriffswelt des Buches Amos* (1951), where passages such as Am. 1:3–3:2; 3:12a; 5:3; 5:4-6; 5:16-17; and 8:3 are called *Botensprüche;* cf. also Edmond Jacob, *Theology of the Old Testament* (1958), pp. 130-131, and Rolf Rendtorff, "*prophḗtēs ktl,*" TWNT, VI (1959), p. 810. See now Claus Westermann, *Grundformen prophetischer Rede* (1960).

[9] Yahweh sends (*šālaḥ*) a divine messenger ("angel") : Gen. 24:7, 40; Ex. 23:20; 33:2; Num. 20:16; Jg. 13:8; etc.; a man sends (*šālaḥ*) a man: Gen. 32:4, 6—EVV 32:3, 5; 37:13-14; 42:16; 46:28; Num. 20:14; 21:21; 22:5; Jos. 2:1; 7:22; Jg. 6:35; 7:24; 9:31; 11:12, 14, 17, 19; etc.; Yahweh sends (*šālaḥ*) a prophet: Ex. 3:10, 13-15; 4:28; 5:22; 7:16; Num. 16:28; Dt. 34:11; Jos. 24:5; I Sam. 12:8; Mic. 6:4; Ps. 105:26 (all Moses) ; I Sam. 15:1; 16:1 (Samuel) ; II Sam. 12:1, 25 (Nathan) ; 24:13 (Gad) ; Isa. 6:8; 61:1; Jer. 1:7; 7:25; 19:14; *et passim* Jer.; Ezek. 2:3-4; Hag. 1: 12; Zech. 2:12, 13, 15—EVV 2:8, 9, 12; 4:9; *et passim* Zech.; Mal. 3:23.

[10] Cf. also Gen. 45:9 (Joseph to Jacob) ; I Kg. 14:7 (Ahijah to Jeroboam) ; 22:27 (Ahab to his officials concerning the imprisonment of Micaiah) ; II Kg. 1:6 (Elijah to Amaziah) ; 18:19 (Rabshakeh to Hezekiah) ; 19:6 (Isaiah to Hezekiah) . All of these accounts have the form, "Say to . . . 'Thus says. . . .'"

Almost exactly the same language is used in the introductions to many of the prophetic oracles. The word of Yahweh comes to Nathan, "Go and say to my servant David, 'Thus says Yahweh' " (II Sam. 7:4-5, 8); Yahweh says to Ezekiel, "The people also are impudent and stubborn: I send you to them; and you shall say to them, 'Thus says Adonai Yahweh' " (Ezek. 2:4; cf. 3:11).[11] Or a messenger may begin, "Hear the word of [the sender] . . . ," and continue, "Thus says [the sender] . . ." (II Kg. 18:28-29); this form is particularly characteristic of Jeremiah (7:2-3; 17:20-21; 22:2-3). There are exceptions to this pattern, however; the expression ne'um yhwh, which so frequently concludes the prophetic Botenspruch, is found only once in this meaning outside the prophetic books or narratives: as a parenthesis in a message of the mal'ak yhwh (Gen. 22:18).

A comparison of prophetic Botensprüche with those found in extra-Biblical sources may also be of interest here. The most striking example is to be found in the Mari texts.[12] In one of these a man has a dream in which Dagan tells him, "Now go! I send you to Zimri-lim [the king of Mari]: [to him] you yourself shall say: Send me thy messenger. . . ."[13] Two other letters have been discovered in which a "man of the god Dagan" (awîlum mu-uḫ-ḫu-um ša ᵈDa-gan) says that the god has sent (šaparu) him to say, "Send speedily to the king" (or, "thy Lord").[14] Noth comments that we have here not only the phenomenon of a messenger of God, but also a remarkable similarity in wording to the prophetic oracle; he cites in this connection the well-known narrative of Wen-Amon, where we find a reference to a messenger of Amon.[15]

The Ras Shamra texts also contain material parallel to the Old Testament message form. Ugaritic letters commonly begin,

---

[11] Other examples may be found in Isa. 7:3-4; Jer. 8:4; 11:3; 13:12; 15:2; et passim Jer.; Ezek. 6:3; 11:5; 12:10; 14:6; et passim Ezek.; Hag. 2:2-6; Zech. 1:3; 6:12.

[12] Martin Noth, "History and the Word of God in the Old Testament," BJRL, XXXII (1949-50), pp. 194-206; cf. also H. H. Rowley, "Ritual and the Hebrew Prophets," JSS, I (1956), p. 340, n. 5, where further references are given.

[13] Noth, op. cit., p. 197.

[14] Ibid., pp. 197-198. The second of these passages is imperfectly preserved.

[15] Ibid., pp. 198-199.

"To NN [sometimes qualified by adjectives or titles], say: 'Message of NN [similarly qualified] . . . .' "[16] The Hebrew equivalent is *'ᵃᵉmōr lᵉ* NN *kô 'āmar*. Similarly messenger narratives in the mythological texts usually begin, "Say [rgm] to NN; message [*thm*] of NN [variously qualified]";[17] occasionally *thm* is paralleled by *hwt*, "word."[18]

We may conclude that the form of the prophetic oracle was often derived from that of the typical ancient Near Eastern *Botenspruch* as found both in Biblical narratives and in the literature of Israel's neighbors.

II

It would seem that the question of the messenger's authority could be answered simply: it is that of the one who sends him. Thus a messenger is to be treated as if he were his master. Rahab is rewarded for her reception of Joshua's messengers (Jos. 6:17, 25); Abigail washes the feet of the messengers sent by David to take her to him as his wife (II Sam. 25:40-41); conversely, the disgraceful treatment of the messengers sent by David to the king of Ammon results in warfare between the two countries (II Sam. 10).[19] The existence of this close relationship between

[16] E.g., Gordon 89:1-5: 1. *mlkt adty rgm thm. tlmyn bdk;* cf. also texts 18, 21, 95, 117, and PRU, II, p. 30, no. 14. In 54, 138, and PRU, II, p. 31, no. 15, we have *thm* (sender), *rgm* (addressee). Note also the Akkadian form *a-na* NN (often qualified) *qi-bi-ma-um-ma* NN . . ., "To NN, my lord my son, etc., say: Thus NN. . ."; Amarna letters *passim;* PRU, III, texts 16.112, 15.178, 10.046, 16.116, and, with the transposition of *um-ma* and *a-na*, 13.7, 15.77, 8.333, etc. Cf. Köhler, *op. cit.*, p. 102.

[17] E.g., 137 (III AB B) :16-17, 33: Krt (KRT A) : 248-249; cf. also Krt 125, 268, and 305.

[18] 49 (I AB) : IV:34; 51 (II AB) : VIII:32-34; 67 (I* AB) : I:12-13; III:10-11, 17-18.

[19] Cf. also I Sam. 8:7, where Yahweh (the sender) tells Samuel (the messenger) that the people "have not rejected you, but they have rejected me from being king over them." A broken passage in Ras Shamra 137 (III AB B) :38-42 may be relevant here. El has granted the request of Yamm, brought by his messengers, that Baal be surrendered to him; Baal is angry and seizes weapons, but is restrained by Ashtoreth (and Anath or Asherah?). They apparently ask how he can presume to strike a messenger, for "a messenger has upon his shoulders the word of his lord" (*mlak . bm . ktpm . rgm . b'lh;* cf. Isa. 9:5—EVV 9:6). This reconstruction of the text by Gordon, *Ugaritic Manual, Analecta Orientalia*, 35 (1955) , p. 168, is followed by H. L. Ginsberg, ANET, p. 130; cf., however, G. R. Driver, *Canaanite Myths and Legends, Old Testament Studies*, III (1956) , pp. 80-81, where a radically different restoration and translation is proposed. Note

master and servant may also account for the occasional confusion between Yahweh and his *mal'āk*. The *mal'ak yhwh* appears and speaks to Hagar, but she thinks she has seen God himself (Gen. 16:7-13); the narrative in Gen. 18 oscillates between Yahweh and the three men; Jacob, in blessing Joseph, apparently makes no distinction between *'aelōhîm* and his *mal'āk* (Gen. 48:15-16); it is the *mal'ak yhwh* who appears in the burning bush, but it is Yahweh himself who sees that Moses has taken notice (Ex. 3:2-4).[20]

Passages such as these, however, merely illustrate the way in which the messenger was received. For the real source of his authority we must step behind the scenes, so to speak, into the divine council itself. For just as a human group can and does commission messengers,[21] so also Yahweh is conceived as acting in concert with his council of "holy ones" (*qedōšîm*) when sending his emissaries.

This council is sometimes called a *qāhāl* or an *'ēdâ* (Ps. 89:6— EVV 89:5 and 82:1 respectively), but the more precise term is *sôd*.[22] A *sôd* was a small, intimate group of close friends; the psalmist laments the treachery of his companion with whom he walked *sôd* (used adverbially), and Job complains that all the men of his *sôd* turn away from him in disgust.[23] Jeremiah says, somewhat wistfully, that he did not join the *sôd* of the merrymakers; rather, he "sat alone" (Jer. 15:17). But a council was not merely a chance collection of individuals. It had a purpose; in it decisions were made and plans laid after mutual discussion.[24] And although we have no reference to the sending of

---

also Ereshkigal's wrath when her messenger, Namtar, is not shown due respect (ANET, pp. 103-104).

[20] See also the theophanies in Jg. 6 and 20, and for a general discussion, Johannes Pedersen, *Israel: Its Life and Culture*, III-IV (1940), p. 497; Jacob, *op. cit.*, p. 76.

[21] Gen. 42:16; Num. 21:21; Dt. 1:22; 19:12; Jos. 6:17; 10:6; Jg. 11:17, 19; 20:12; 21:13; etc.

[22] Jer. 23:18, 22; Ps. 25:14; 89:8—EVV 89:7; Job 15:8. Cf. also Job 29:4, where, however, the text should probably read *besôk* (see *BH³* mg.). On Am. 3:7 see below, p. 103.

[23] Ps. 55:15—EVV 55:14; Job 19:19; cf. Pedersen, *op. cit.*, I-II (1926), p. 307.

[24] Pedersen, *op. cit.*, I-II, p. 130; Ludwig Köhler, *Hebrew Man* (1956), pp. 87-88; cf. also H. Wheeler Robinson, *Inspiration and Revelation in the Old Testament* (1946), p. 170, n. 4.

messengers from a human *sôd,* we may assume that this was a common practice. For the word *sôd* came to mean not only the council itself but also a decision ("secret") emanating from it;[25] this decision was probably transmitted by a messenger.

The divine council was of the same order.[26] Its members were the "holy ones," the "sons of God," or simply "the gods."[27] It has been thought that its meetings were held only once a year, on New Year's Day;[28] the language in Job 1:6 and 2:1 (literally, "And it was the day, and the sons of God came . . .") would at least seem to point to some regularity. Like the human *sôd,* the divine council also made decisions. The first person plural pronouns in Gen. 1:26 ("Let us make man in our image, after our likeness. . ."); 3:22 ("the man has become like one of us. . ."); and 11:7 ("Come, let us go down, and there confuse their language. . .") probably have the divine council as their antecedent.[29] As in human affairs, the word *sôd* can thus be used for the "counsel" proceeding from the "council"; this is the meaning of the term in Am. 3:7. And we may assume that messengers were again used to carry out the "counsels"; this may be the significance of the *mal'ākîm,* who ascend and descend the ladder between heaven and earth (Gen. 28:12). Certainly a "spirit" can be sent from the council ("to entice Ahab"—I Kg. 22:20-22); similarly Satan proceeds from a meeting of the "sons of God" to test Job (Job 1:12; 2:7). So also the Mesopotamian "assembly of the gods" imposes the death sentence on a rebellious god, decrees the flood, decides to destroy a city, and

---

[25] Pr. 11:13; 20:19; 25:9. We read that "without counsel [*sôd*] plans go wrong" (Pr. 15:22) . On the dual meaning see S. R. Driver and G. B. Gray, *A Critical and Exegetical Commentary on the Book of Job,* ICC, II (1921) , p. 95.

[26] For a general description see Robinson, *op. cit.,* pp. 167-169; *idem,* "The Council of Yahweh," JTS, XLV (1944) , 151-157; G. Ernest Wright, "The Faith of Israel," IB, I (1952) , pp. 360-361; *idem., The Old Testament Against Its Environment,* SBT, No. 2 (1950) , pp. 30-41.

[27] In addition to the passages listed on p. 102, see also Dt. 33:2, where Yahweh comes from "the ten thousands of holy ones." For a discussion of the possibility that the heavens, the earth, and the mountains were members of the council, see Herbert B. Huffmon, "The Covenant Lawsuit in the Prophets," JBL, LXXVIII (1959) , pp. 290-291.

[28] Julian Morgenstern, "The Book of the Covenant," HUCA, V (1928) , pp. 48-50.

[29] See, among others, Robinson, "The Council of Yahweh," pp. 154-155.

in general "fashions" or "proclaims" destinies.[30] Furthermore the assembly sends forth agents to carry out its decisions; various gods participate in the creation of the primeval flood.[31]

Thus it is probable that the ultimate source of the messenger's authority was in a council, and that he is to be regarded as the means by which the deliberations of that body are made effective. When we turn to the Old Testament prophets, we find a similar phenomenon. The inaugural visions of Isaiah of Jerusalem and Deutero-Isaiah are to be interpreted against the background of the *sôd yhwh:* Yahweh says, "Whom shall I send, and who will go for *us?*" (6:3), and uses the plural imperative in ch. 40.[32] The most instructive example, however, is to be found in Jer. 23:18, 22. In the course of his diatribe against the false prophets Jeremiah asks,

For who among them has stood in the council of Yahweh [*b*e*sôd yhwh*]
    to perceive and to hear his word,
    or who has given heed to his word and listened?[33]
and concludes,

But if they had stood in my council [*b*e*sôdî*]
    then they would have proclaimed my words to my people,
and they would have turned them from their evil way,
    and from the evil of their doings.[34]

It is interesting to note that the latter verse is preceded by the

[30] ANET, pp. 68, 94, 458, and 70 respectively. Cf. Thorkild Jacobsen, "Primitive Democracy in Mesopotamia," JNES, II (1943), pp. 159-172.

[31] ANET, p. 94.

[32] See Muilenburg, IB, V (1956), pp. 422-423; Robinson, "The Council of Yahweh," p. 155; P. A. H. DeBoer, *Second Isaiah's Message, Oudtestamentische Studien,* XI (1956), p. 40; and especially Frank M. Cross, Jr., "The Council of Yahweh in Second Isaiah," JNES, XII (1953), pp. 274-277, where other passages are listed.

[33] Strictly speaking, the Hebrew seems to imply that *no one* has ever stood in the council; since this contradicts vs. 22, many add *mehem* after *mi* (e.g., Rudolph; thus the RSV), while others (e.g., Volz) regard the verse as an addition based upon Job 15:7-8, where Eliphaz asks Job, "Are you the Urmensch? . . . Have you listened in the council of God (*b*e*sôd 'aelôah*) ?"

[34] Cf. Ezek. 13:9, where it is said that the false prophets will not be in the council (*sôd*) of Yahweh's people.

statement that Yahweh has neither sent (*šālaḥ*) nor spoken (*dibbēr*) to these prophets.[35] Clearly Jeremiah claims that his ultimate authority as God's messenger is to be found at the highest level, in the divine council itself. He has heard words and has seen visions; he is under constraint to make the people hearken, to carry out the decision of the *sôd*. And while the term *sôd* is used only here in connection with the prophet's authority,[36] it is probable that the *idea* of the divine council is to be seen as the background of the prophetic *Botensprüche* as a whole.

III

A comparison of the actual content of the nonprophetic *Botenspruch* with that of the prophets themselves shows that the former is usually a promise or a blessing. The divine *mal'āk* or *'iš 'ᵃelōhîm* announces the forthcoming birth of a child (Gen. 18; Jg. 13); he rescues those in distress (Gen. 16:7-12); he goes before or accompanies someone on a dangerous journey (Gen. 24:7, 40; Ex. 23:20; 33:2); he fights against the people's enemies (Ps. 35:5-6; cf. Jos. 5:13-14; II Kg. 19:37). The function of the human messenger is similar. He, too, announces births (Jer. 20:15); he carries back the news of victory on the battlefield (I Sam. 31:9; II Sam. 18:19-33; cf. Ps. 68:12-13—EVV 68:11-12); he consoles the bereaved (II Sam. 10:2). The "herald of good tidings" (*mᵉbaśśēr, -éret*) of Isa. 40:9; 41:27; and 52:7 announces the advent of Yahweh, the rise of Israel's deliverer, and the reign of God. Only rarely does a messenger convey bad news or proclaim judgment. A messenger of God calls for the curse of Meroz and threatens to destroy Jerusalem (Jg. 5:23; II Sam. 24:16); on one occasion a *mᵉbaśśēr* reports military defeat and the capture of the Ark (I Sam. 4:17); the news of various disasters is brought to Job by messengers (1:14, 16, 17, 18).

The prophetic "message" is, of course, similar in many respects. The prophet also announces a birth (Isa. 7:14), predicts victory (the 400 prophets of Yahweh in I Kg. 22:6, 11), consoles (Isa. 40:1) (where Deutero-Isaiah is to be conceived as

[35] Cf., the parallelism between "send" and "go for us" in Isa. 6:8, quoted above, p. 104.

[36] Cf., however, Am. 3:7, *supra*, p. 103.

standing in the *sôd yhwh*), and tells of Yahweh's coming (Hab. 3). Many other parallels will occur to the reader. Nevertheless, there is a difference of emphasis. Whereas the ordinary messenger and the divine *mal'āk* usually bring good tidings, and only rarely news of defeat or a threat of judgment, just the reverse is the case with Israel's prophets. While we should not make the common error of assuming that the earlier prophets preached "woe" while their successors promised "weal," we must admit that the relative emphasis upon doom and mercy changes with the times.

Perhaps this emphasis upon Yahweh's coming judgment in the pre-Exilic prophets accounts for the fact that they never use the actual *word* "messenger" in describing themselves or their task. As noted above, the ordinary message is one of peace. It often begins with *šālôm* (I Sam. 25:5-6; II Sam. 18:28; cf. Jg. 21:13; Dt. 2:26).[37] But the pre-Exilic prophets denounced those who cried, " 'Peace, peace,' when there [was] no peace" (Jer. 6:14; 8:11; Ezek. 13:10). Just as they avoided the term *rûᵃḥ* because of its association with the more violent forms of "ecstasy,"[38] so also they hesitated to call themselves *mᵉl'ākîm* because of the ordinary connotations of the title. It is also significant that only one of these prophets refers to the *mal'ak yhwh* (Hos. 12:5—EVV 12:4).

The situation changes in the Exilic and post-Exilic periods, however, when the message *is* "peace." Israel, as the servant of Yahweh, is called "my messenger whom I send."[39] And the prophets themselves are said to be Yahweh's messengers (Isa.

---

[37] The same word or a cognate is often used in the introductions or conclusions to ancient Near Eastern letters; cf. Lachish letters II.2; III.3; VI.2; IX.2; and probably V.2. For similar formulas see ANET, pp. 482-483, 491-492; cf. also the beginnings of Ugaritic letters 18, 21, 54, 95, 101, 117, and 138 (Gordon's numbering).

[38] Sigmund Mowinckel, " 'The Spirit' and 'The Word' in the Pre-Exilic Reforming Prophets," JBL, LIII (1934), pp. 199-227.

[39] Isa. 42:19. Perhaps *mᵉšullām* (RSV "dedicated one"), the parallel to *mal'āk* in this passage, should be interpreted as "the one whose message is perfected, completed," on the basis of *'ᵃṣat māl'ākāw yašlîm* ("performs the counsel of his messengers") in 44:26. This would bring out the chiastic structure of the verse (a-b-b-a: servant-messenger-faithful envoy-servant of Yahweh). For a convenient list of the various interpretations of *mᵉšullām* see Muilenburg, IB, V (1956), p. 476.

44:26); similarly the author of Isa. 61:1 seems to refer to himself, at least in part, when he says,

The Spirit of Adonai Yahweh is upon me,
    because the Lord has anointed me
to bring good tidings to the afflicted;
    he has sent me to bind up the brokenhearted,
to proclaim liberty to the captives,
    and the opening of the prison to those who are bound . . . .

Other specific references to the prophets as messengers are in the third person: "Then Haggai, the messenger of Yahweh, spoke to the people with Yahweh's message. . ."; "Yahweh . . . sent persistently to them by his messengers . . . , but they kept mocking the messengers of God, despising his words, and scoffing at his prophets. . ." (Hag. 1:13; II Chr. 36:15-16). Finally, the editor of an anonymous collection of late prophetic oracles does not hesitate to provide it with the title *mal'ākî*.[40]

Thus the prophets, although they seldom called themselves "messengers," used the form of the *Botenspruch* and claimed that their authority was that of one sent by Yahweh or from his council. They did not identify themselves with the one who sent them; there is no "mystic union" with the divine.[41] Nevertheless, they did not "prophesy the deceit of their own heart" (Jer. 23:26), for they had "stood in the council" of Yahweh. The line is not easy to draw: does a messenger speak only the words of his lord, or are they in some sense his own? Perhaps we say more than we know when we refer to "the message of the prophets."

[40] It is generally held that the title was taken from Mal. 3:1, where Yahweh promises that he will send "my messenger" and/or "the messenger of the covenant" to prepare the way before him; later this messenger was identified with Elijah (3:23—EVV 4:5).

[41] Cf. Pedersen, *op. cit.*, III-IV, pp. 493-494.

VII

Amos and Wisdom

SAMUEL TERRIEN

Parallels between the Book of Amos and the wisdom literature
of the Old Testament have been observed for a long time, but
usually they have been explained as a result of a unilateral influence exercised by the eighth-century prophet on the post-
Exilic sages. Fifty years ago, for instance, William R. Harper
could write:

> The external relation of the book of Amos to the wisdom
> literature is not indicated by anything that has come down to
> us. That its influence was felt can scarcely be doubted, since
> in it we have the first definite formulation of Yahweh's rela-
> tion to the outside world, the idea which lay at the basis of all
> Hebrew wisdom, the assignment of Israel to a place upon a
> level with other nations (cf. the absence of any reference to
> Israel in the book of Proverbs); an example of Oriental learn-
> ing in history, geography, social customs; the very essence of
> wisdom, in the emphasis placed upon honesty, purity, etc.;
> together with an almost total absence of the religious
> sentiment. . . .[1]

For the past decades, both the prophetic literature and the wisdom literature of Israel have appeared in a new light. Scholars
have pointed out especially that the sapiential books, although
edited in their present form at a relatively late date, have preserved many substantial sources of the pre-Exilic period and

[1] William R. Harper, *A Critical and Exegetical Commentary on Amos and
Hosea,* ICC (1910), p. cxxxvii.

belong indeed to the literary movement of international wisdom[2] which seems to have begun in the third millennium B.C.[3] Proper emphasis on the early date of an oral tradition among the wise may reopen the question of the influences which the prophets have received. The investigation of possible contacts between Amos and the *ḥokmic* language, style, and ideas assumes therefore a hitherto unsuspected importance.

Among the many words and expressions of Amos which may reflect an acquaintance with the language and speech habits of the wisemen, only a few will be selected for discussion here.

1. Consecutive numerals are used in pairs. "On account of three transgressions of Damascus, yea, even four . . ." (Am. 1:3; cf. vss. 6, 9, 11, 13; 2:1, 4, 6). There can be little doubt that this formula is a device which is typical of the wisdom style. "In one way, yea, even in two" (Job 33:14); "I have spoken once, and I

[2] A. Causse, "Introduction à l'étude de la sagesse juive," RHPR, I (1921), pp. 45-60; "Les origines étrangères et la tendance humaniste de la sagesse juive," *Congrès d'Histoire des Religions*, II (1923), pp. 45-54; "Sagesse égyptienne et sagesse juive," RHPR, IX (1929), pp. 154 ff.; H. Gressmann, *Israels Spruchweisheit im Zusammenhang der Weltliteratur* (1925); W. O. E. Oesterley, *The Wisdom of Egypt and the Old Testament* (1927); P. Humbert, *Recherches sur les sources égyptiennes de la littérature sapientiale d'Israël* (1929); T. E. Peet, *A Comparative Study of the Literatures of Egypt, Palestine, and Mesopotamia* (1929); W. Baumgartner, *Israelitische und altorientalische Weisheit* (1933); W. Baumgartner, "The Wisdom Literature," in *The Old Testament and Modern Study*, H. H. Rowley, ed. (1951), pp. 210-237; J. Fichtner, *Die altorientalische Weisheit in ihrer israelitisch-jüdischen Ausprägung* (1933); W. Zimmerli, "Zur Struktur der alttestamentlichen Weisheit," ZAW, 51 (1933), pp. 177 ff.; O. S. Rankin, *Israel's Wisdom Literature* (1936); A. Drubbel, *Les livres sapientiaux d'Israël dans leurs sources préexiliques* (1936); "Le conflit entre la sagesse profane et la sagesse religieuse," *Biblica*, XVII (1936), pp. 45-70, 407-428; J. Schmidt, *Studien zur Stilistik der alttestamentlichen Spruchliteratur* (1936); H. Duesberg, *Les scribes inspirés*, 2 vols. (1938-39); A. Dubarle, *Les sages d'Israël* (1946); J. C. Rylaarsdam, *Revelation in Jewish Wisdom Literature* (1946); A. Bentzen, *Introduction to the Old Testament* (1948), I, pp. 167-183; II, pp. 171-179, 188-191; B. Couroyer, "Idéal sapientiel en Egypte et en Israël," RB, LVII (1950), pp. 174-179; W. F. Albright, "Some Canaanite-Phoenician Sources of Hebrew Wisdom," in *Wisdom in Israel and in the Ancient Near East*, M. Noth and D. Winton Thomas, eds. (Suppl. VT, III [1955], pp. 1-15; R. B. Y. Scott, "Solomon and the Beginning of Wisdom in Israel," in *ibid.*, pp. 262-279; G. von Rad, *Theologie des Alten Testaments*, I (1957), pp. 381-457.

[3] J. J. A. vanDijk, *La sagesse suméro-accadienne* (1953); S. N. Kramer, "'Man and His God': A Sumerian Variation on the 'Job' Motif," Suppl. VT, III (1955), pp. 170-182; *From the Tablets of Sumer* (1956), pp. 71-168.

will not answer; twice, but I will proceed no further" (Job
40:5; cf. Ps. 62:12). Other examples with higher numerals are
all found in the wisdom literature: "Two times and three times"
(Sirach 23:16; 26:28; 50:25; cf. Ahiqar vi, Aramaic); "three
times and four times" as in Amos (Pr. 30:15, 18, 21, 29; Sirach
36:5); "four times and five times" (Pr. 6:16; Job 5:19); "seven
times and eight times" (Ec. 11:2); "nine times and ten times"
(Sirach 25:7). It will be observed that such a phrase is employed
by Amos but not by any of the other prophets. The expression
"seven shepherds and eight princes of men" (Mic. 5:5), whatever its precise meaning may be, does not appear to belong to
the same form of numerical gradation with an implication of
indefiniteness. Likewise, the words "three columns and four"
(Jer. 36:23) must be taken literally, and therefore do not constitute a parallel. There is evidence that the numerical pattern
was already common in the second millennium B.C.[4] We are thus
justified in asking the question, Why is it that in the Old Testament only Amos and the wisdom literature show an acquaintance with this form of speaking? Many exegetes recognize that
this formula originated among the wise.[5]

2. In Am. 9:2 Yahweh describes through the mouth of his
prophet the completeness of eschatological retribution. "If they
dig into Sheol, from there shall my hand seize them!" For the
Old Testament in general Sheol remains outside of Yahweh's
realm of activity or jurisdiction. It is a place of horror because
in it the dead are estranged from the Deity (Isa. 38:18; Ps.
88:11; etc.). Either Yahweh has no possibility of access to the
grave or, more probably, he does not concern himself with it.[6]
Outside of Amos, only the wisdom literature (Pr. 15:11; Job

---

[4] In the Ugaritic poem of Keret, the device of numerical gradation appears
under several forms. "One-third, one-fourth, one-fifth, one-sixth, one-seventh"
(col. i, 16-20); "a fifth and a sixth" (col. ii, 83); "in thousands, in myriads; after
two, after three" (col. ii, 92-95); "a fifth and a sixth" (col. iv, 174-175); "a day,
a second, on a third" (col iv, 194-195).

[5] See J. Lindblom, "Wisdom in the Old Testament Prophets," Suppl. VT, III
(1955), p. 203.

[6] See J. Pedersen, Israel, Its Life and Culture, I-II (1926), pp. 453-470; Ch.
Barth, Die Erretung vom Tode in den individuellen Klage- und Dankliedern des
Alten Testaments (1947); von Rad, op. cit., pp. 385-386; E. Jacob, Theology of
the Old Testament (1958), pp. 303-304.

26:6; cf. 7:21?) and a hymnic meditation (Ps. 139:7) of the
sapiential type[7] dare to conceive poetically the imagery of a rap-
port between Yahweh and the sojourn of the dead. It seems
hardly possible that Amos influenced the wisdom poets. The
prophet referred to Sheol incidentally. His purpose was to show
that there was no escape from the reach of divine wrath; it was
not to affirm that Yahweh had access to the underworld. He took
this idea for granted. On the contrary, the *ḥokmic* passages mentioned above state a general truth according to which no limit or
restriction is opposed to God's omnipotence, omniscience, and
omnipresence. The tone of Amos is one of urgency and violence.
That of the wise is one of awe in serenity. While the tenor of
Ps. 139 is much more somber than is generally recognized, since
the psalmist attempts to flee from the presence of Yahweh, no
one will seriously maintain that in this psalm as in Am. 9
Yahweh is said to go to Sheol in order to exercise his retributive
justice. Quite clearly, the wise held cosmological beliefs which
were different from those generally followed by the prophets
and the priests or the reciters of cultic traditions.[8] Amos alone
appears to agree with the wise in accepting the view that the
underworld was completely within the sphere of Yahweh's
influence.

3. In the poetic sequence on prophetic authority (Am. 3:3-8),
the prophet uses the didactic method of appealing to common
sense by running through a series of cause-and-effect relation-

[7] It is difficult to escape the conclusion that Ps. 139 has come from a milieu
strongly influenced by the Joban poetic school (cf. Ps. 139:3 with Job 22:21; Ps.
139:5 with Job 9:33; Ps. 139:6 with Job 11:6; Ps. 139:8 with Job 17:13; Ps. 139:13
with Job 10-11; etc.).

[8] The enigmatic reference of Amos to Yahweh's trial of the great abyss by fire
(7:4) may constitute another evidence of contact with the sapiential beliefs.
The precise meaning of the expression *tᵉhôm rabbâ*, however, is open to question.
If *tᵉhôm* in this passage designates the primeval waters (as in Gen. 1:2; Job
38:16, 30; Ps. 104:6; cf. Ps. 33:7; 36:6; 78:15), the prophet displays a belief in
Yahweh's unopposed sway over the universe in its totality, including the watery
deep. While Amos does not explicitly state that Yahweh has created the *tᵉhôm*,
his reference implies that there is no room in his cosmogonic scheme for the
theme of the dualistic fight or for a belief in the non-created or pre-existent
character of the abyss. If this interpretation is correct, Amos may show once
again a close affinity with the sapiential idea of the creation of the deep (Pr.
8:24, 27-28).

ships in the form of rhetorical questions (cf. also 5:25; 6:2, 12; 9:7). The use of the interrogative maxim is so widespread in the Old Testament in general that it cannot be presented as an argument tending to show points of contact between the wise and Amos. Nevertheless, the fact that the prophet expects to stimulate audience approval in a matter of logical thinking involving assent to the principle of empirically observed causation is strongly reminiscent of the teaching method of the wise.[9]

4. In the climax of the same poetic sequence on prophetic authority, Amos declares, "Surely, Adonay Yahweh will do nothing without revealing his secret to his servants the prophets" (3:7). The use of the word *sôd*, "secret," is not restricted to Amos. The word occurs quite frequently with several different meanings in pericopes of various literary types (Gen. 49:6; Jer. 23:18, 22; Ezek. 13:9; Pss. 25:14; 55:15; 64:3; 83:4; 89:8; 111:1). In the sense of "intimate secret," however, the word appears to be typical of the wisdom literature (Job 15:8, 17; 19:19; 29:4; Pr. 3:32; 11:13; 15:22; 20:19; 25:9; Sirach 8:17; 9:4, 14; 42:12). We may say that the word *sôd* is par excellence a sapiential term, conveying the idea of confidential and intimate exchange in an atmosphere of friendship and mutual trust.[10]

5. Amos accuses Israel of not knowing "how to do what is right" (*nᵉkôḥâ;* 3:10). For a pre-Exilic prophet, this is a most unusual way of speaking. Isaiah alone (30:10) besides Amos in the monarchic period employs the same word (in the plural), but only when he quotes his adversaries, who probably include the party of the royal wise (see Isa. 5:21; 29:14). The other occurrences of the word are confined almost exclusively to the Exilic and post-Exilic passages of the Isaianic school (Isa. 57:2; 59:14; 26:10). Undoubtedly it is a favorite term of wisdom (Pr. 8:9; 24:26; 26:28; Sirach 11:21), and the fact that it was used by Absalom (II Sam. 15:3) is perhaps an indication of its origin in courtly circles. In any case, Amos did not select a term

---

[9] See Pr. 6:27; 17:16; 30:4; Job 8:11; etc. Cf. J. Hempel, *Die althebräische Literatur* (1930), pp. 49-50; Schmidt, *op. cit.,* pp. 56-57.

[10] Even when the sapiential poet speaks of the *sôd* of God, he places the word in parallelism with *ḥokmâ* (Job 15:8). Amos associates the secret of God with the prophetic word, and this idea is taken up by Jeremiah (23:19). See A. Neher, *Amos* (1950), p. 16; cf. A. Weiser, *Die Profetie des Amos* (1929), pp. 127-128.

typical of the covenant traditions or of the legal literature, with which he shows otherwise a close acquaintance.[11]

6. In the indictment of Edom Amos says, "And his anger did tear as a prey continually" (1:11). While a number of exegetes wish to correct the difficult verb *wayyiṭrōp*, "and he tore," on the basis of the Syriac and Vulgate, the MT appears to be supported here by the fact that in Job 16:9, "his anger has found a prey," the same verb occurs with the same subject, *'ap*, "anger," and in Job 18:4, "in his anger he tears himself as a prey," the same verb occurs with the same noun as an indirect object. The double occurrence of the two words together in Job suggests the existence of a sapiential idiom which was familiar to Amos. It will be observed that nowhere else in the Old Testament are the verb and the noun found together.

7. While the prophets never spoke of the nation under the appellation of "Isaac," Amos did so twice (7:9 and 7:16). Such a peculiarity needs to be treated with another, which follows.

8. Only Amos among the prophets referred to Beer-sheba, and he did so in two different passages (5:5 and 8:14). The connection between Isaac and Beer-sheba is well known (see Gen. 21:31-33; 26:15-25). The ethnic group which is related to the patronym "Isaac" included the Israelites and the Edomites (Gen. 25:29, 30), and the two peoples were described as "brothers" (Num. 20:14; Dt. 23:8). The historical affinities which united Judah and Edom, and eventually made their mutual hatred especially virulent, are repeatedly displayed in the Judah traditions. Caleb and Othniel, who played a part in the conquest of what later on became Judah territory (Jos. 15:16, 17; Jg. 1:13-21), were related to Kenaz, an Edomite (Gen. 36:11, 40, 42; cf. Num. 32:12; Jos. 14:6, 14). The Jerahmeelites, who were descendants of a brother of Caleb and Othniel (I Chr. 2:34, 42), came to the tribal territory of Judah from the general vicinity of Edom (I Sam. 27:10; 30:29). The geographical proximity of Teqoa to Beer-sheba on the one hand and to Edom on the other

---

[11] A point which is to be held side by side with the opinion that Amos is acquainted with international customs in law and morality. See Neher, "The Noahidic Berith," *op. cit.*, pp. 49-81; R. Bach, "Gottesrecht und weltliches Recht in der Verkündigung des Propheten Amos," *Festschrift für Günther Dehn* (1957), pp. 23-34.

offers at least the possibility of cultural exchanges between the milieu to which tradition had connected Amos (Am. 1:1; cf. 7:12) and the Edomites themselves. The reputation of Edom for wisdom[12] offers support to the hypothesis that the prophet may have received from the seminomads who lived in the south and the southeast of the Dead Sea an outlook on man and a world view which were generally those of the international wisdom movement.[13]

The above remarks, which deal chiefly with matters of terminology and style, tend to show that peculiar affinities existed between Amos and the wise. A conjecture may therefore be elaborated, according to which the prophet received from the sapiential circles some of his ideas. Like the wise, Amos was uncommonly well versed in Oriental learning, especially in astronomy. He was acquainted with the geography, the history, and the social customs of nations outside of Israel. He thought of the Deity as the ruler of all peoples and he was aware of standards of ethical behavior which were common to all men, independently of a revealed legislation. He was not concerned with the problems of idolatry (in spite of 5:26), and the importance of ritual was subsumed by him under the questions of morality. Unlike the wise, Amos was an eschatologist whose thinking moved within the framework of an interpretation of history which was dominated by the reality of election and cove-

[12] See I Kg. 4:30-31; Jer. 49:7; Baruch 3:22-23. The location of the action in the folk tale of Job should be sought in Edom rather than in Hauran (cf. Job 1:1 and Jer. 25:19 ff.; Lam. 4:21; P. Dhorme, *Le livre de Job* [1926], pp. xix-xxii; R. H. Pfeiffer, "Edomitic Wisdom," ZAW, 44 [1926], pp. 13-25); A. Musil, *Arabia Petraea* (1908), vol. II, pp. 337 and 339, note d: *The Northern Heğāz* (1926), pp. 249-52; J. Simons, *The Geographical and Topographical Texts of the Old Testament* (1959), p. 25 and map III c.

[13] This hypothesis, however, should not include another, according to which Amos himself might have been an Edomite through the clan of Zerah (Gen. 36:13; see G. Hölscher, *Die Profeten* [1914], pp. 189-190, who refers to the discussion of E. Meyer on Teqoa: *Die Israeliten und ihre Nachbarstämme* [1906], p. 435). In any case, one should not affirm too confidently that Amos was a native of Teqoa. The editorial note states that he "was among shepherds from Teqoa" (1:1). The use of the preposition "among" suggests that he was not one of them. The fact that nothing is told about his family, that he has no genealogy, that even the name of his father is unknown, further indicates the obscure origins of the prophet.

nant. He was not a humanistic moralist. He was moved by a sense of prophetic compulsion. Nevertheless, there is in his message the seed of a moralistic conception of salvation. He made repentance a condition of forgiveness rather than considering repentance itself as a fruit of creative grace. His soteriological implications are not far distant from those of the ancient wise of the Babylonian and Egyptian literatures, the poets of the canonical proverbs, and the friends of Job. His utter pessimism concerning the ability of man to repent led him to predict the doom of Israel. Even if the saying, "Perhaps Yahweh God of Hosts will have mercy for the remnant of Joseph" (5:15) is considered authentic, one may remark that this mercy is hypothetical and that it is moreover conditioned by the fulfillment of morality: hate evil, love good, and establish justice at the gate. In other words, like the wise, Amos makes ethical behavior the prerequisite of divine favor.

Such a hypothesis should not be construed as meaning that the prophet was not primarily steeped in the covenant theology of Israel.[14] It rather tends to prevent the overstressing of the separation of classes among the leaders of the eighth century B.C. That various groups, such as priests, prophets, and wisemen, existed should not be denied. At the same time, such groups were not alien one from the others, and they lived in a common and mutually interacting environment.[15]

[14] See E. Würthwein, "Amos-Studien," ZAW, 62 (1950), pp. 10-52, pp. 49 ff.; von Rad, op. cit., II (1960), pp. 141-149.
[15] See A. Robert, "Le Yahwisme de Prov. x, 1–xii, 16; xxv–xxix," Mémorial Lagrange (1940), p. 165.

VIII

"Rejoice Not, O Israel!"

DOROTHEA WARD HARVEY

The emphasis on rejoicing in the religion of Israel has long been recognized. To "rejoice before the LORD" is a characteristic term for the celebration of public worship in Deuteronomy (12:12; 14:26; 16:10-11, 13-15; 27:7), and appears in this same sense in Leviticus (23:40). The hymns in the Book of Psalms again and again call Israel to sing, make music, and shout for joy before the LORD (Pss. 33:1-3; 47:2-8; 95:1-2; 96:1-4; 98:1-6; 100:2-3; 105:1-3; 149:1-5; 150). Joy and happiness play a prominent part in the Hebrew understanding of the goodness of God's creation, as well as in public worship. The ideas of blessedness and happiness are inseparably related in the Old Testament,[1] and the blessings of success, abundance, and prosperity are God's good gifts, rightly and naturally bestowed on his people.[2] There seems to be no reason to doubt the judgment of Ludwig Köhler that "there is hardly a word that is so central in the Old Testament as the word 'joy.' "[3]

In sharp contrast with this emphasis, however, is the statement in Hos. 9:1,

Rejoice not, O Israel!
Exult not like the peoples;[4]

[1] This is seen in the use of both 'ašrê (Dt. 33:29; Pss. 32:1-2; 33:10-23; 34:8-10; 40:5; 41:2; 65:5; 89:16; 94:12; 127:4-6; 128:2-7; 144:12-15; Job 29) and bārûk (Gen. 27:27-29; Dt. 7:14; 28:3-8; Isa. 65:23; Jer. 17:7-8; Pss. 31:22; 115:15).

[2] See Johannes Pedersen, Israel, I-II (1926), pp. 182-212, for his discussion of the content of blessing as seen in the Old Testament.

[3] Ludwig Köhler, Theologie des Alten Testaments (1936), p. 137.

[4] MT: "to exultation like the peoples."

116

for you have played the harlot, forsaking your God.
You have loved a harlot's hire upon all threshing floors.

It should be noted that Hosea does not seem to condemn all rejoicing, or even cultic rejoicing as such. But he does clearly
reject certain aspects of Israel's cultic practice, and in this he is
typical of prophetic thought as a whole. There are differences
among the prophets, of course, but two elements seem to be
consistent in their criticism of Israel's rejoicing in the cult. One
is the condemnation of "rejoicing" as a technical term for specific acts associated with the fertility rituals of Canaanite worship. The other is a polemic against the magical use of even
legitimate forms of public rejoicing in the cult.

Let us deal first with the association of rejoicing with the
Canaanite cult. In calling on Israel not to rejoice, Hosea uses
the root śāmah in combination with gîl. The term gîl does seem
to be associated with Canaanite ritual in the Old Testament.
The meanings of śāmah and gîl can be seen in comparison with
the meanings of two of the other major terms used to express
rejoicing in the Old Testament, ṣāḥaq and hālal. All four of
these roots appear in both Canaanite and Biblical texts.[5] Two of
them, śāmah and hālal, have an official place in the Israelite cult,
both in regulations for public worship[6] and in descriptions of
the people's and Levites' part in worship.[7] Both terms seem to
refer to singing and vocal expressions of joy and praise in the
cult. The praise (hālal) and thanksgiving which is to be sung
to the LORD is specified in I Chr. 16:4-36. Many hymns begin and end with the imperative form "Hallelujah!" urging
the worshiper to join in the praise to God (Pss. 113; 117;
135; 146-150). Declaration to the congregation of the good
which the LORD has done is part of this praise in Pss. 22, 40,
66, 102, 107, and 116. The verb hālal occurs most frequently
with such words as telling (Pss. 22:23-27; 102:22), singing (Pss.
66:2; 146:2; 147:1), letting the sound be heard (Ps. 66:8),

[5] For the occurrence of śmh, gl, ṣhq, and hll in the Ugaritic texts, see G. R.
Driver, Canaanite Myths and Legends (1956), pp. 148, 146, 150, and 137.

[6] śāmah in Dt. 12:12; 14:26; 16:10-11, 13-15; 27:7; Lev. 23:40; I Chr. 15:16; II
Chr. 23:18; hālal in Lev. 19:24-25; I Chr. 16:4; II Chr. 5:13.

[7] śāmah in I Chr. 29:9, 17, 22; II Chr. 15:15; 20:27; 23:18; 24:10; 29:30; 30:21,
23, 26; Ezra 3:12, 13; hālal in I Chr. 29:13; II Chr. 7:6; 29:30; 30:21; Ezra 3:10-11.

uttering (Ps. 106:2), and proclaiming (Jer. 31.7).

The predominantly vocal character of *śāmaḥ* is also clear from the contexts in which this root is found. The most frequent context has to do with "lifting up the voice" (I Chr. 15:16; Ezra 3:12), with words like singing (*śîr*, Gen. 31:27; Isa. 24:7; II Chr. 23:18; Ps. 137:3), singing praise (*zāmar*, Pss. 9:3; 68:4), noise (*qôl*, I Kg. 1:40; Ezra 3:13), uproar (I Kg. 1:41, 45), a loud voice (II Chr. 15:14), "Long live the King!" (I Kg. 1:39), and all kinds of musical instruments. The next most frequent context is that of eating and drinking, with words like sacrifice (I Sam. 11:15; Isa. 56:7), first fruits and tithes (Dt. 12:7, 17; 26:10-11), and so on. Among other words used with *śāmaḥ* are dancing (II Sam. 6:14-16), clapping the hands (Isa. 55:12), stamping the feet (Ezek. 25:6), and giving thanks (Ps. 97:12; Isa. 51:3). The part which the people play in Israel's public worship, in singing, giving thanks, and joining in the feast, comes out plainly in the meanings of *śāmaḥ* and *hālal*.

The other two roots, *ṣāḥaq* and *gîl*, do not seem to be used officially for any legitimate forms of public rejoicing in the Israelite cult. The verb *ṣāḥaq* occurs in official descriptions of Israelite worship only in connection with acts mentioned with disapproval. It appears in Ex. 32:6 to describe the people's "play" (that is, their dancing; cf. 32:19) in the worship of the calf. This passage seems clearly to be intended as a polemic against the Canaanite cult.[8] The root occurs also in the form *śāḥaq* in the description of David's dancing uncovered before the Ark (II Sam. 6:5, 16-21).[9] In both of these passages licentious

---

[8] See Pedersen, *op. cit.*, III-IV (1940), p. 192; J. Coert Rylaarsdam, "The Book of Exodus," IB, I (1952), pp. 1065-1067.

[9] *ṣāḥaq* and *śāḥaq* are generally accepted as spelling or dialect variations of the same root. See Hans Bauer and Pontus Leander, *Historische Grammatik der hebräischen Sprache des alten Testaments* (1922), p. 28; Carl Brockelmann, *Grundriss der vergleichenden Grammatik der semitischen Sprachen*, I (1907-8), pp. 156, 238-239. The various meanings associated with *ṣāḥaq* occur also in connection with *śāḥaq* (dancing, Ex. 32:6; cf. Jer. 31:4; laughing, Gen. 18:12-15; cf. Ec. 3:4; joking, Gen. 19:14; cf. Pr. 26:19; mocking, Ezek. 23:32; cf. Ps. 2:4; playing, Gen. 21:9; cf. Zech. 8:5). The name Isaac is spelled *yiṣḥāq* in J, E, P, Joshua, Kings, and Chronicles, and *yiśḥāq* in Jer. 33:26; Ps. 105:9; and Am. 7:9, 16. A spelling variation also appears in Ugaritic texts in connection with this root (Driver, *op. cit.*, pp. 128, 150).

dance seems to be involved, although here disapproval is expressed only by Michal, while David defends his action. Elsewhere in passages connected with cultic usage in the Old Testament, śāḥaq describes the merriment of women as they sang and danced to celebrate a victory (I Sam. 18:7), and appears with timbrels, dancing, and planting and enjoying vineyards (Jer. 31:4) and the tears and laughter associated with successful sowing and reaping in Ps. 126. Ecstatic dance around the bull sacrifice is connected with the prophets of Baal in I Kg. 18:26-28. Ṣāḥaq is condemned in the E source (Ex. 32:6) as dance in honor of the bull. It is elsewhere associated with dance and uncovered dance, and with planting, sowing, and reaping in cultic usage in the Old Testament. It is omitted in all official descriptions of the legitimate Israelite cult but used popularly in Ps. 126 and Jer. 31:4 for practices connected with planting and reaping.

The earliest[10] use of the root gîl in the Old Testament is in Hos. 9:1. This verse refers to the Canaanite type of worship.

> For you have played the harlot, forsaking your God.
> You have loved a harlot's hire upon all threshing floors.

The root appears also in the Hebrew text of Hos. 10:5, where it describes the idolatrous mourning and exulting over the bull of Bethaven.[11] Elsewhere in the prophetic books, gîl appears most frequently in connection with harvest and fertility,[12] and occasionally with the language of warfare or victory.[13] The root appears in the Song of Songs (1:4) of rejoicing in the beloved. It appears with high frequency in the Book of Psalms (twenty-one out of a total of fifty-three occurrences in the Old Testament). The remaining instances are in Proverbs (four times) and in Job (3:22) once. Gîl is a normal literary parallel of śāmaḥ in

[10] This statement omits consideration of Psalms and Proverbs as far as chronological evidence is concerned.

[11] Procksch and most commentators read yêlîlû (or yēlîlû) at this point. Cf. W. R. Harper, Commentary on Amos and Hosea (ICC [1905]), p. 347; W. Nowack, Die Kleinen Propheten (1922), p. 54; and RSV. This correction has no textual support and seems unnecessary in the context. See F. Fleming Hvidberg, "Vom Weinen und Lachen im Alten Testament," ZAW, 57 (1939), pp. 150-151.

[12] Isa. 16:10 (cf. Jer. 48:33); 25:9; 29:19; 35:1-2; 41:16; 49:13; 61:10; 65:18-19; 66:10; Joel 1:16; 2:21, 23; Hab. 3:18.

[13] Isa. 9:2; Hab. 1:15; Zeph. 3:17; Zech. 9:9, 10:7.

both Old Testament and Ugaritic texts.[14] In these cases no distinctive associations for the term can be observed. The only negative use of *gîl* seems to be that in Hosea. With the exception of the MT of Hos. 10:5, there is no explicit meaning of *gîl* which does not appear also in connection with *śāmaḥ* in the Old Testament.

In spite of these similarities, there is a distinct difference in the way these two roots are used in the Old Testament. We have seen that *śāmaḥ* appears as a technical term in D and P for the actual celebration of the festival in the cult. *Gîl* alone never receives this technical meaning. *Śāmaḥ* occurs in JE, D, P, Chronicles, Ezra, Nehemiah, and Esther, with high frequency in Deuteronomy and the writings of the Chronicler. *Gîl* appears in none of these, but only in poetry and Proverbs. The writings, then, which give the regulations for the Israelite cult do not mention *gîl*, although the Psalms, and especially the hymns (Pss. 48:12; 65:13; 96:11; 97:1, 8; 149:2) and psalms of individual thanksgiving (9:15; 32:11; 118:24),[15] suggest that the term was in popular use in the cult.

There is considerable difference also in the verbal contexts in which *śāmaḥ* and *gîl* appear. We noted above the vocal character of *śāmaḥ* and *hālal*. The kinds of words with which *gîl* is used give no such clear association with vocal rejoicing. In addition to the two contexts in which *gîl* is condemned by Hosea, the root appears in connection with grain and flocks (Ps. 65:12-13), planting and enjoying the produce (Isa. 65:18-23), fruitful fields (Isa. 16:10), green pastures (Joel 2:21-23), food (Joel 1:16), rain (Ps. 65:9-13; Joel 2:23), threshing (Isa. 41:15-16), the desert blossoming (Isa. 35:1-2), bones flourishing or rejoicing (Isa. 66:10-14; Ps. 51:8), singing as on a day of festival (Zeph. 3:17), procession in the Temple (Ps. 118:24-27), dancing (Ps. 149:2-3), the sea roaring (Ps. 96:11), the sound of weeping and distress (Isa. 65:18-19), dividing spoil (Isa. 9:2), and God as Warrior (Zeph. 3:17). The association with the enjoyment of fertility and abundance is clear. The kind of rejoicing is not specified, however.

[14] Keret II i 14; ii 37; Isa. 29:19; Zech. 10:7; Pss. 14:7 (53:7) ; 16:9; 21:2; 48:12; 51:10; 96:11; 97:1, 8; Pr. 2:14; 23:24-25; 24:17.

[15] See Hermann Gunkel, *Einleitung in die Psalmen* (1933) , pp. 32, 265.

Paul Humbert, in a study of these two roots,[16] notes that both are associated with harvest festivals and with the Canaanite cult. He points out the differences in usage noted above and the condemnation of *gîl* by Hosea, and concludes that the term was omitted deliberately from the official cultic vocabulary of Israel because of an original connection with the objectionable elements of the Canaanite cult. The etymology of *gîl* tends to support this conclusion. There is general agreement that the root meaning of *gîl* has to do with moving in a circle.[17] *Ṣāḥaq*, with similar popular use, and similar omission from official cultic language in the Old Testament, is connected with cultic dance and with the worship of the bull. The etymology of *gîl* and the MT of Hos. 10:5 suggest a similar connection for this root. When the meaning, association, and usage of these four terms is considered, it seems probable that *śāmaḥ* and *hālal* represent the form of popular participation accepted officially in the Israelite cult: the singing of praise, rendering of thanks, and joining in the feasts and processions, while *ṣāḥaq* and *gîl* were omitted because of a more specific association with the techniques of Canaanite cultic dance. It is suggested, therefore, that Hosea's command to Israel that she not exult (*gîl*) "like the peoples," is at least in part a condemnation of a "rejoicing" too closely connected with specific acts of the fertility ritual of Canaanite worship.

A part of the reason for this condemnation is certainly the foreign worship involved. The worship of Baal is attacked in other passages in the Book of Hosea (2:5-17 [EVV]; 3:1; 4:12-14; 7:14; 10:1-2, 5). The demand for faithfulness to the LORD alone is typical of prophetic thought, and the condemnation of Canaanite elements appears in connection with other prophets (I Kg. 18; Mic. 5:12-14; Jer. 2:20-27; 3:6-11; 7:9; Ezek. 6:13; 20:28). The demand for faithful worship is one element in Hos. 9:1.

If we are right in our analysis of *gîl*, it seems probable that

---

[16] "'Laetari et exultare' dans le vocabulaire religieux de l'Ancien Testament," RHPR, XXII (1942), pp. 185-214.

[17] Theodor Nöldeke, in his *Beiträge zur semitischen Sprachwissenschaft* (1904), p. 43, Gesenius-Buhl, Brown-Driver-Briggs, and Köhler-Baumgartner all give this basic meaning and refer to the Arabic *jal* to "go around or about."

the polemic against the magical use of forms of rejoicing in the cult is also involved in this verse. Clearly, many of the ritual practices of the ancient Near East were based on the idea of sympathetic magic. The person could take the role of the god and, by doing himself what he wanted the god to do, compel the god to act in the same way. Or by representing the desired event, and performing it himself, he could bring the event about. G. E. Wright cites Jacobsen on this point: "By identifying himself with Dumuzi, the king is Dumuzi; and similarly the priestess is Inanna—our texts clearly state this. Their marriage is the marriage of creative powers in the spring." Wright goes on to describe the Babylonian New Year festival as "the means by which society secured its life for the year ahead."[18] Cyrus Gordon takes the Ugaritic text, "The Birth of the Gods," as "the libretto of a religious drama" performed at the beginning of a new growing cycle. He says that the "purpose of the performance is to assure that the new cycle will be one of abundance with bread to eat and wine to drink."[19] There seems to be no doubt that the Canaanite fertility ritual was for the purpose of causing the gods to bring about fertility of the land and of the flocks.[20] And it is precisely those terms which seem to have been associated with a specific Canaanite ritual (ṣāḥaq and gîl) that are omitted from the official language of the Israelite cult.

The prophetic criticism of rejoicing in the cult seems to involve more than a protest against the magical use of specific rituals, however. Probably the people's rejoicing in even the legitimate ceremonies of the cult was thought to have a magical effect of insuring the favor of God, in a way somewhat similar to the effect of a specific technique. This attitude seems to have been present both in Israel and in the wider background of the ancient Near East. In Akkadian as well as in Hebrew texts, the celebration of public worship is called "rejoicing" (in Hebrew śāmah, in Akkadian ḥadû or ḥidatu). The society of the gods in

[18] G. E. Wright, *The Old Testament Against Its Environment* (1950), pp. 93-94.

[19] Cyrus Gordon, *Ugaritic Literature* (1949), p. 57.

[20] Compare Baal III ii 30-35; iii I* 5-9; and see Driver, *op. cit.*, pp. 18-21, and T. Worden, "The Literary Influence of the Ugaritic Fertility Myths on the OT," VT, II (1952), p. 277.

Mesopotamia was apparently the counterpart of human society.[21] Jeremias cites a Babylonian text to the effect that "musicians rejoice (*ḫadû*) the heart of the gods" as well as of men, and refers to the parallelism between divine and human harmony.[22]

The purpose expressed again and again in Akkadian hymns is to make the god feel happy, so that he will be favorable and grant the request. The usual motif for the end of a lamentation or a hymn to a god is

> May thy heart be at rest,
> may thy mind be pacified.[23]

Calmness of heart and happiness seem to be interchangeable in many of these texts. In a hymn to Marduk the prayer is made that when he enters into his temple, the temple will say to him, "Be tranquil."[24] In many other hymns the prayer is that the god may enter a temple with joy (*ḫadiš*), and so be favorable.[25] Often joy and tranquillity are mentioned together. To be happy seems to mean the same thing as to be calm or favorable in a *Beschwörung* tablet asking that Ea's heart may be glad and his mood happy (*libba-ka li-ṭib ka-bit-ta-ka liḫ-du*).[26] Friedrich Stummer describes "*šamû liḫduka*," rejoicing the name of the god, as a typical motif of Babylonian hymns, comparable to the praising of the name of God in the Old Testament.[27] To make the gods feel happy seems to be one important element in Babylonian and Assyrian religion.

[21] See Thorkild Jacobsen, *The Intellectual Adventure of Ancient Man* (1946), pp. 135 ff., and Isaac Mendelsohn, ed., *Religions of the Ancient Near East*, Vol. IV of *The Library of Religion* (1955), p. ix.

[22] A. Jeremias, *Handbuch der altorientalischen Geisteskultur* (2nd ed., 1929), pp. 82-83.

[23] Stephen Langdon, *Sumerian and Babylonian Psalms* (1909), p. 282.

[24] Peter Jensen, *Texte zur assyrisch-babylonischen Religion* (Vol. VI, Part 2: *Keilinschriftliche Bibliothek*, E. Schrader, ed. [1915]), pp. 36-37, lines 40-41; cf. the same phrase in a hymn to Sin, *ibid.*, pp. 94-95, Rev. lines 22, 24.

[25] Charles J. Ball, "Inscriptions of Nebuchadrezzar II," PSBA, X (1888), pp. 299, 368.

[26] H. Zimmern, *Beiträge zur Kenntnis der babylonischen Religion* (1901), pp. 140-141, line 30.

[27] Friedrich Stummer, *Sumerisch-akkadische Parallelen zum Aufbau alttestamentlicher Psalmen* (1922), pp. 120-121.

Sacrifices and rebuilt and redecorated temples are one obvious way to do this. Nebuchadrezzar put up a cylinder to say that he had rebuilt the temple Ebarra with "rejoicings and festivities" (*ḫi-da-a-ti u ri-ša-tim*), and to ask Shamash to enter with joy (*ḫadiš*) and let good things be in store for Nebuchadrezzar.[28] This kind of statement is common in the royal inscriptions. But it also seems to be true that the rejoicing of the worshiper is a part of the effort to make the god rejoice. The worshiper's eating of the sacrifice means the god's eating of it, and the worshiper's joy in the eating and drinking and music means the god's joy in these, according to the principle of sympathetic magic. In some passages the joy of the gods and of the people seems to merge in this way. In a description of a festival to Ishtar, all lands are to join in the joy of the festival, Ishtar and all the gods of the heavens are to rejoice, Ea is to rejoice in the sea, the goddesses of the land are to be glad, the offerers of the sacrifice are to dance and rejoice their heart with song, the chief offerer (Ashurnasirpal) is to be glad, and Ishtar is to grant him long life and protection.[29] The joy of gods and men seems to be part of the same experience, all apparently aimed at increasing the joy, and so the favor, of Ishtar in this case. The description of the ritual as rejoicing in Akkadian texts and the care to mention the joy of the human participants seem to relate to the purpose of bringing the gods into a happy frame of mind.

Similarly, in the Old Testament *šāmaḥ* is used for the actual celebration of the festival as well as for the experience of joy. The joy of eating and drinking in the sacrificial meal is of course present in the Biblical as in the Akkadian accounts (Dt. 12:7, 12, 18; 14:26; 16:11, 14, 15). In Israel too there seems to have been the idea that the celebration of the festival had a magical force. The prophets specifically and repeatedly condemn the view that performance of ritual secures the favor and protection of God (Am. 4:4-6; 5:18-24; Isa. 1:12-20; Mic. 3:11; Jer. 7:3-11). D makes this same point in connection with rejoicing. Rejoic-

[28] C. J. Ball, "Inscriptions of Nebuchadrezzar the Great," PSBA, XI (1889), pp. 127-128.
[29] Erich Ebeling, "Quellen zur Kenntnis der babylonischen Religion," *Mitteilungen der vorderasiatischen Gesellschaft*, I (1918), pp. 58-62.

ing in the harvest is strictly for "the good which the LORD your God has given you" in past history, and for the fruit of the ground which has just been given (Dt. 26:11). Because God has already shown his love for you and delivered you from Egypt, you are to keep his commandments and celebrate his festivals (Dt. 10:22-11:1; 11:7-8; 16:12). D's insistence on this order seems to be a polemic against the idea of forcing God by any ritual, moral, or psychological magic. Rejoicing is connected with keeping the festival, as it is in the Akkadian sources. But you are to rejoice because God has made you joyful, and not to force his favor. In the protest against the magical use of both specific ritual acts as ways of technical "rejoicing," and in the emphasis upon the actual joy in the celebration of the festival, the prophetic and the official attitude in Israel seems to differ from the usual attitude toward cultic joy in the Near East.

It is probable, however, that this statement of difference must be qualified somewhat if we are to give a true picture of even the official Israelite attitude toward public rejoicing. A magical element does appear to be involved to the extent that the cultic response to a benefit which God has bestowed seems in a sense to consolidate the benefit and to lead to further blessing. The use of Israel's warcry, the *terû'â*, seems to be an example of this. When employed against the enemy in ancient times, it had the awesome effect of producing a divine panic and confusion in the enemy (Jg. 7:20-23; cf. Ex. 23:27; I Sam. 14:15).[30] The utmost care seems to have been taken before the battle to make sure that the LORD was actually with his people, and that the battle followed his timing and plan (I Sam. 14:18, 37; 22:5). But when it was sure that the LORD was with the army for victory, the *terû'â* seems to have been used to send, or perhaps to focus, his terror against the enemy. It is this ancient battle shout which then appears in the Psalms, and particularly in the hymns, as Israel's characteristic way of praising God in public worship (see especially Ps. 89:16, and compare Pss. 33:3; 65:14; 66:1; 81:2; 95:1-2; 100:1; 150:5). Possibly the use of this response in worship was again thought to focus the successful power of God

[30] See Paul Humbert, *La "Terou'a"* (1946), p. 7; F. Schwally, *Semitische Kriegsaltertümer* (1901), p. 27.

and encourage further blessing. This usage would be in line with the power of the spoken blessing. To call someone happy seems to be almost identical with making him happy.[31] Mowinckel speaks of the Hebrew concept of blessing as "a prophecy which creates the future."[32] Caspari makes a similar suggestion with regard to the rejoicing (śāmaḥ) on the occasion of the moving of the Ark to Jerusalem. He says that this rejoicing was not a psychological state but a cultic action comparable to the blessing, action which would have a power in itself to encourage further evidence of God's grace.[33] Perhaps the t*rû'â shouted aloud in the cult was thought to have a similar effect of confirming the blessing and giving it power to continue. Weiser speaks of the use of hymns in the Old Testament not only to make the appropriate response of thanksgiving to God for his salvation but also to preserve and extend the salvation which God has given.[34] Rejoicing in the cult seems to have been a significant act, with a power of its own in the Biblical view. If this is true, the temptation to find magical power in ritual rejoicing is strong, and the prophetic criticism, the condemnation of any attempt to use this power to force God's favor, is important.

There is no indication that the prophets made any consistent attack on rejoicing as such in Israel. Joy is clearly out of place as a response to a prophetic declaration of God's judgment, as in Amos (5:18-20) or Isaiah (22:12-14). But the prophets do not condemn rejoicing as such. On the contrary, an objection in Hos. 2:8 (EVV) is that Israel did not realize that it was the LORD who gave her the blessings of harvest. The prophet Joel mourns the loss of Israel's festival "joy and gladness" (śāmaḥ and gîl) when the "grain has failed" (Joel 1:16-17), and calls on her to rejoice when the rain has come again (2:21-27). Second Isaiah calls Israel to go forth with singing (48:20; 54:1) and speaks frequently of singing for joy in wording similar to that of the Psalms (52:7-10; cf. 51:11; 55:12). Rejoicing in the

[31] See Pedersen, op. cit., I-II, p. 167.

[32] Sigmund Mowinckel, He That Cometh (1955), p. 90.

[33] Wilhelm Caspari, Die Samuelbücher (Kommentar zum alten Testament), E. Sellin, ed. (1926), p. 467.

[34] Artur Weiser, Die Psalmen, ATD (1950), p. 31.

mighty acts of God, and declaring this aloud to the ends of the earth, is a praise and service acceptable to God (Isa. 42:10-13; 43:19-21; 44:23; 48:20; 49:13). Even the doing of symbolic acts, if done to further the will of God, was possible for the prophets (Isa. 20:2; Jer. 13:1-11; Ezek. 4:1-15; 5:1-14). But "rejoicing" as magic, either in terms of specific techniques of Canaanite fertility ritual or in terms of using the legitimate significant acts of Israelite worship to compel God's action or to force his favor, is condemned.

IX

Essentials of the Theology of Isaiah

TH. C. VRIEZEN

It is not easy to define the mutual relations between the different parts of the message of Isaiah. Certainly he was not systematic, although one can clearly find theological perspectives in his writings. To understand him one has to be concerned with three different factors: the tradition of his people, his call, and his life experiences.

I

Isaiah is solidly rooted in the religious tradition of Israel. For him, as for other prophets, Israel is the people of God. As in the writings of other contemporaries, Amos, Hosea, and Micah, through his prophet God frequently speaks of Israel as "my people" (1:3; 3:12, 15; 5:13; 10:2 [24]; 22:4; 32:13, 18). This is even more evident when the prophet on many occasions speaks of Israel as "this people" (6:10; 8:6, 11, 12; 9:15; 28:11, 14; 29:13, 14). Thus Isaiah creates a sense of distance between God and his people. Belief in the fellowship between God and man is the foundation of the prophet's religious ideas; at the same time, he knows that God removes himself from his people, criticizing them as an object, standing at a distance before them. This already indicates how Isaiah is aware of the crisis which threatens his people.

One of the peculiar things that one finds when inquiring into the prophet's relation to the tradition of his people is the scarc-

128

ity, if not total absence, of an appeal or reference to the Exodus from Egypt. The other prophets refer to the Exodus repeatedly, whether as a standpoint for their warnings or as a basis of their prophecy of salvation, but Isaiah does not. The only passage which can be construed in this manner is Isa. 10:24-26, but its authenticity is very uncertain.[1] Even if this reference were considered authentic, the way the remembrance of Egypt is used cannot be regarded as the starting point of Isaiah's preaching.

Why Isaiah is such an exception among his contemporaries, Amos, Hosea, and Micah, and also in comparison with the later, great citizens of Jerusalem, Jeremiah and Ezekiel, is not an easy question to answer. Besides Isaiah, Zephaniah should be noted, but owing to the small size of his book an adequate comparison cannot be made. Of course, it is impossible to conclude that Isaiah did not know the tradition of the Exodus; but we can say that generally history does not play an important part in his prophecies. Reminiscences of historical traditions we find only in the mention of such names as Sodom and Gomorrah (1:9; 3:9),[2] in the allusion to the story of Gideon (9:3; [10:26?]), and in hints of events in the life of David (28:21; 29:1).[3]

While there are in fact only few connections with the later history of Israel in Isaiah, the ancient history of the people, which other prophets made the basis of Israel's dependence on Yahweh and responsibility to him, does not play any part at all.

In Isaiah the relation between God and his people is concentrated in the name Zion. Attention has often been focused on the importance of Zion in the theology of Isaiah. Of the twenty-nine times that the name is used in the first thirty-nine

[1] 11:16 is not Isaianic. The pāsōaḥ in 31:5 can hardly be considered as a reference to the feast of Passover, for the relation is not clear enough. Also 4:5, in which can be seen a reminiscence of the tradition of the cloud by day and the appearance of fire by night, is probably not Isaianic. See, among others, E. Rohland, *Die Bedeutung der Erwählungstraditionen Israels für die Eschatologie der alttestamentlichen Propheten*, Diss. Heidelberg (1956), pp. 112-116.

[2] Abraham is mentioned only in a later passage (29:22). Isaiah frequently mentions Jacob for the people of Israel, without alluding to the traditions in the life of the ancestor (chs. 2, 8, 10, 27, and 29).

[3] Three times the house of David is mentioned (7:2, 13; 22:22) and once the throne of David is spoken of (9:6 [and the tent of David, 16:5]). In 37:35 David is called "my servant" and in 38:5 Yahweh is called "the God of your father David," but these passages possibly are not authentic.

chapters of the book, eleven are from the prophet himself. Zion is the place which Yahweh founded (14:32), where he dwells (8:18; 31:9), and where he reveals himself (2:3; cf. 6:1; 28:16).

From this one cannot conclude, without more information, that Isaiah's "interest and *horizon* are restricted to Jerusalem,"[4] in which case the prophet could be thought of as a narrow-minded nationalist. In Isaiah the idea of Zion obviously has a religious character. With Rohland,[5] I am convinced that one must distinguish between the Zion tradition and the David tradition. It is not true that Zion plays a part as the political center of power for David; rather, it is only the abode of God. The house of David is mentioned as the ruling dynasty (chs. 8, 22), and twice his throne is mentioned in the messianic expectation (16:5; 9:6); but the house of David will first of all collapse, at any rate in the later prophecies (11:1), before it can play that part.

Something is expected for Jerusalem, not on the basis of the view that the house of David politically should be of eternal importance, but because God has entered into relation with his people. In the Book of Isaiah the idea of salvation is not based on the cultic element or on the existence of the Temple as such. The sanctuary plays a part (ch. 6), but for Isaiah it is never a basis for the existence of the people of Israel. The *hêkāl* is mentioned only once, in 6:1; and, further, the Temple is referred to as *bêt Yahweh* and *bet 'aelōhîm* only twice, in ch. 2. The name Ariel seems to imply that the presence of the altar in Jerusalem is a privilege granted by Yahweh to Israel, but this is a dubious privilege since it may also be the cause of the destruction of the city by fire (29:1-9). The altar itself is mentioned only once (6:6). In Isaiah the cult as such does not bring assurance of salvation; one cannot appeal to him for support in that false security which says: "We are safe; the temple of the Lord is here" (cf. 1:13 ff.!).

The Temple of God in Jerusalem is indeed a great privilege, but it is still more a cause for great responsibility; for it means that the living, holy God dwells in Jerusalem. This is the reason

---

[4] Johannes Pedersen, *Israel*, III-IV (1940), p. 551. The italics are mine.
[5] Rohland, *op. cit.*, p. 267.

for the importance of Zion: its value is founded in him only. In Isaiah it is neither the political situation nor the pretension of the cult that dominates his spiritual life, but the certitude of the real presence of God. This gives his prophecy its "actuality." The past is scarcely employed in it; the future is appealed to only slightly and then as a personal message to his disciples. In fact his prophecy is completely focused on the present, on his own time, or, to say it in a much better manner, on what God is doing in Isaiah's own day. From this point of view he sees his time in the light of the living God.

II

In studying Isaiah's prophecies one gets the impression that through his call new light was thrown upon his life and world, which did not alienate him from the tradition of the people but caused him to find his place in the world of his time. At that moment he met God, not face to face but separated from his sight by the Seraphim. Nevertheless he saw so much of his glory and his holiness that it remained in his mind during his whole life and dominated his existence completely. In this experience he came to know himself and his people truly, and he came to understand something of the nature of sin. He himself was purified from sin by an angel, with fire that was taken from the altar. As a result he placed himself at the disposal of God. It was at this moment that God revealed himself to him in his Being as the Holy One, unapproachable by angels, yet at the same time as the One whose glory is spread over the whole earth. He transcends the reality of the world, while the radiance of his glory fills the earth. As such, both transcendent and immanent, he is *Yahweh Ṣᵉbā'ôt* (6:3) and the King (6:5). The descriptive allusions to the majesty of God, which arose out of Isaiah's inaugural vision, dominate his thoughts and words from this moment. They occur frequently in his subsequent prophecies, from his earliest to his latest. "Yahweh, the Holy One of Israel," the expression he created, becomes characteristic and almost a stereotype for him (1:4; 5:19, 24; 10:17, 20, [24], 33; [29:19, 23;] 30:11, [12], 15; 31:1; [37:23]).

Also one should compare the "Holy God" as a parallel to *Yahweh Ṣᵉbā'ôt* in 5:16, and further 2:10, 11, 17b, 19; 8:13, where Yahweh is characterized as the high and dreadful.

In Isaiah the holiness of Yahweh emerges, as it were, out of the cultic sphere of the sanctuary where it had been confined and appears in the world, filling the whole earth with its glory. Thus Yahweh as the Holy One goes out to rule the world and its history. In this way his work acquires its decisive character for mankind.

Therefore Yahweh is almost always called *Yahweh Ṣᵉbā'ôt*, that is, the One who unites in himself all the powers of heaven and earth[6] (1:9, 24; 2:12; 3:1, 15; 5:7, 9, 16, 24; 6:3, 5; 8:13, 18; 9:6 [12], 18; 10:16, [23, 24, 26], 33; 14:24, 27; 17:3; 18:7; 19:12; 22:5, [14]; 28:5, 22, 29; 29:6; 31:4, 5; [37:32]).

H. A. Brongers' conclusion[7] that the expression *Yahweh Ṣᵉbā'ôt* occurs for the first time in Isaiah and that he may be recognized as its *auctor intellectualis* seems to be very plausible. The unity of God's holiness and God's majesty has been apprehended as a fact by Isaiah.

Isaiah also calls Yahweh the King, *hammélek* (6:5; [30:33?]);[8] and this expression may be considered as one coined by Isaiah. Besides this, God is called *hā'ādón* (1:24; 3:1; 10:[16], 33; [19:4]), an expression found exclusively in Isaiah with the exception of two instances in Exodus (chs. 23 and 24) and in Malachi. Here we may perhaps point to the occurrence of *'ᵃdônāy* as a distinctive title for God in Isaiah, although on this particular point the old manuscripts and/or translations deviate considerably from the Masoretic text (6:1, 8, 11; 3:17 f.; 7:14, 20; 8:7; 9:7, 16; [10:12]; 21:16; 29:13; [30:20]; [37:24]).

To this series of terms we can also add *'ᵃbîr Yiśrā'él*, the Mighty One of Israel (1:24). Apart from Isaiah this term is found only in Gen. 49:24 and Ps. 132:2, 5. The power of Yahweh stems from the fact that the whole world belongs to him;

---

[6] See Th. C. Vriezen, *An Outline of Old Testament Theology* (1958), p. 150, and O. Eissfeldt, "Yahwe Zebaoth," in *Miscellanea Academica Berolinensia* II, 2 (1950), pp. 128 ff. Compare also the Greek translation *pantokrator*.

[7] *De scheppingstradities bij de profeten*, Diss. Leiden (1945), pp. 117 ff.

[8] With the exception of this text, according to Köhler's Lexicon, the title occurs only in Jer., Pss. 9 and 145.

the nations are subjected to him. He whistles and the Assyrians come (5:26; 7:18); the mighty king is a rod in his hand (10:5 ff.; cf. 17:12 f.).

Yahweh's holiness, which causes the angels to cover themselves; his glory, which fills the whole earth; and his unique power in general make him absolute in his Being. In the thinking of Isaiah these three qualities belong together; and he was the first to grasp this unity as absolute. It was out of this experience of God that his conscience was awakened to his time.

The first thing that comes from this experience is the sense of being lost[9] and sinful, both of which are absolutely the same for Isaiah.[10] One of the profoundest elements in 6:5 seems to be that along with the awakening awareness of his sin before God comes the consciousness of the guilt of his people before God. A collective consciousness of guilt becomes manifest, under which the prophet suffers personally. He becomes conscious of living in the midst of a people of unclean lips and he shares with them their impurity.

By purification with the fire from the altar, his sins are forgiven and thus he is prepared for his vocation—a vocation which puts him at the side of God, over against his people. Twice God speaks to him of "this people." This creates a distance between the prophet and his people, so that his action becomes a judgment on them.

In his preaching, the judgment remains the point at issue. This is the paramount fact for Isaiah. At the beginning of his ministry there is, in my estimation, no possibility of the restoration either of the nation as a whole or of a remnant thereof. The latter ideas, which we find in Isaiah more than once, are not yet found in ch. 6, although the idea of a remnant is added to it by way of *gloss* (6:13).[11] Nevertheless the absolute certainty

[9] In spite of Köhler's Lexicon, the more symbolic meaning "to perish" seems to me more correct than "to be put to silence" (compare 15:1, 2). In the Old Testament seeing God is usually connected with the impression of having to die. For a parallel development compare also the meaning of the verb *š-m-m*. Further, the sound of the words of lament (the continuously repeated *i*) is an imitation of the sound of someone in agony; only Jer. 15:10 has the same sounds.

[10] Cf. R Otto, *Das Heilige* (English: *The Idea of the Holy*, 2nd ed., 1950).

[11] For this matter, I refer to my contribution in Suppl. VT, I (1953).

of divine judgment pervades the preaching of Isaiah. It is varied in his later prophecy but is not changed essentially.

The knowledge of the holiness, glory, and majesty of God informs the third characteristic note of his later preaching, one that was not yet explicit in the inaugural vision. This note is the demand to have faith and wait for God, and the assurance of the rest which God gives.

For each of these three emphases—guilt, judgment, and the demand for faith—further references in the preaching of Isaiah will be cited. In the first place we note the guilt of the people. Isaiah underlines this so emphatically that he does not hesitate to call the people "Sodom and Gomorrah" (1:10) and to compare them in another passage with Sodom (3:9). Amos (4:11), on the other hand, had only compared the punishment of Israel with that of Sodom and Gomorrah (as Isaiah does also in 1:9). Only Jeremiah (23:14) and Ezekiel (ch. 16) are as severe in their judgment as Isaiah.[12]

Still more important than noticing the severity of Isaiah's message of judgment is the consideration of what is for him the essence of sin. It may be said without hesitation that the conception of sin is purely religious in Isaiah. On closer examination, sin proves to be essentially revolt against Yahweh (1:2; 1:4), contempt for Yahweh (3:8 f.; 5:4 f., 24; 8:6; 28:12; 29:15 f.; 30:9-13, 15), and derision of Yahweh (5:18 f.). With the words *sārar* (1:23; 30:1) and *sārâ* (1:5; [31:6]), "rebellion" and "being rebellious," he characterizes the attitude of his people. Other charges are: neglecting Yahweh (17:10; 22:11), pride (2:7 ff.; 3:16 ff.; 9:8 ff.; 10:5 ff.; 22:15 ff.; 28:1 ff., 14 ff. [*lāşôn*, boasting]), not having faith in God, not believing (7:9; 22:11; 31:1), and not being willing to be obedient (28:12; 30:9, 15; [1:19]). Isaiah is the only pre-Exilic prophet who emphasizes the last of these charges; after him Ezekiel is the only prophet who makes use of this idea. Isaiah continues his accusations: Israel is wise in its own eyes (5:21; 28:14 ff.); it is a godless people (*hānēp*, twice only in Isaiah: 9:16; 10:6, but also in Jeremiah) and is defiant of Yahweh (3:8 f.).

---

[12] The reference to Sodom is found once more in the Old Testament after the destruction of Jerusalem: Lam. 4:6; in later prophecies it is used only in connection with foreign countries [Zeph. 2:9], Isa. 13:19; Jer. 49:18; 50:40.

Just as there is in fact only one great sin for Isaiah, the contempt of the *tôrâ*, the Word of God (5:24; cf. 8:16, 20), so there is also only one message for the salvation of the world and that is the *tôrâ*, the Word of God (2:3), which radiates throughout the nations. In this preaching there is no nationalistic or naturalistic emphasis.[13] Indeed, in Isaiah only a few specific sins of a cultic or civil character are mentioned. Among other things, magical practices (2:6), idolatry (2:8, 20), as well as fornication (2:8, 20) under holy trees and in gardens (1:29-31; cf. Hos. 4:13 ff.; Jer. 3:6), are condemned. But equally wrong, if not worse, is serving Yahweh with only empty, hypocritical offerings (1:13), sacrificing to him and at the same time doing injustice (29:13), praying with hands full of blood (1:15 ff.), or serving him only outwardly (29:13). In ch. 1 the specific sin of the oppression of the poor by the rich is mentioned; but in the same context Isaiah condemns in a general manner the doing of evil while at the same time championing the doing of good. Good and evil are determined by the *tôrâ* of God, which is to say by the direction of God. More than once he returns to the sin of injustice toward the poor (1:2 ff.; 3:14 ff.; 5:7 ff.), as well as to corruption, generally thought to refer to corrupt judges (1:23; 5:23; 10:1 ff.). Besides this, the desire for luxury (3:16 ff.), intemperance, and dissolute living are exposed (5:11 ff., 22; 28:7 ff.).

The prophet resists foreign alliances because he sees in them neglect of Yahweh (ch. 7; 30:2). The same is true with regard to the nation's confidence in military institutions (ch. 7; 22:7 ff.; 30:15 ff.).

In fact for Isaiah all sins are rooted in failure to recognize God, failure to believe, and the willful rejection of him. These failures Isaiah sees in all spheres of life, military and civil, profane and cultic; among the high and the low, priest and prophet. By these people God is not known as the living God who is the Holy, Glorious, and Mighty One. Therefore they wander into all sorts of ways but they do not choose the only way, the way of revelation. Proud and defiant, their lives come into conflict with God, and therefore they shall perish.

[13] To identify the claims of Yahweh, as these are expressed in the theology of Isaiah, with the *nature of Israel* (Pedersen, *op. cit.*, III-IV, p. 551) is to falsify the religion of Isaiah and to use terminology which is absolutely not Israelitic.

The previously mentioned third aspect of Isaiah's message (the demand to have faith) should be treated here in the light of the foregoing. Since God is the absolute starting point in Isaiah's thought, the true service of God is to know him (1:2), to be faithful to him (1:21, 26) and so to accomplish righteousness and justice. In the whole corpus of prophetic literature the stem *'āmēn* is mentioned for the first time in Isaiah, and there it appears frequently in important places (7:9 [two times]; 28:16; 11:5). Both times when the verb is used in a general sense (7:28) the translation "to believe" conveys the idea of trusting in God faithfully, that is, regarding God as steadfast.

The holy might of God demands belief, in the absolute sense of the word, and this entails waiting and hope, quietness and rest. Isaiah presents a great number of words like these which express the relation between God and man. Besides *'āmēn* the stem *bāṭaḥ* is used for belief in God (30:15), although it occurs more often for false confidence (30:12; 31:1; 32:9-11). This is the case also with *šā'an*, which is used in the unfavorable sense of reliance on man (10:20; 30:12; 31:1) and only once in the favorable sense of putting one's trust in Yahweh (10:20). It seems that these verbs cannot express, as well as the stem *'āmēn*, the idea of self-consecrated devotion to God.

Furthermore, *qiwwâ*, "to hope" (8:17; [5:2, 4, 7, of Yahweh]), *ḥikkâ*, "to wait for" (8:17; 30:18; [also once, 30:18, of Yahweh]), *šāqaṭ* (7:4; 30:15; [18:4 of Yahweh]), *nûªḥ, nāḥat, mᵉnûḥâ* (28:12 [two times]; 30:15), "not to be in haste" ([5:19]; 28:16; [30:16], all evidence Isaiah's message of trust in Yahweh.

The confidence which Isaiah has in God forms the background of his political attitude, which can be expressed in two words: spiritual rearmament. The emphasis is on the spiritual, the religious aspect: on belief and its result, righteousness and justice. This means that Isaiah, in the chaotic time in which he lives, knows that the lost little country of Judah really has to give up every attempt to play the part of a big political power.[14] If one is disposed to characterize Isaiah as "a quietist or as a religious fanatic,"[15] he gives too little attention, in my opinion,

[14] Cf., among others, H.-J. Kraus, *Prophetie und Politik* (1952), pp. 56 ff.
[15] C. A. Keller, "Das quietistische Element in der Botschaft des Jesaja," *Theologische Zeitschrift* (1954), pp. 81-97.

to the fact that Judah, being a very small country, had little or no political influence for the prophet and had, rather, only a religious task. It seems to me that Isaiah had a more realistic view of the politics of his time than even the best politicians of Judah. On the basis of his religious conviction he saw clearly the position of Judah in regard to its military and political role in the world. Therefore he pleaded for Judah to follow the wiser course of political isolation, instead of attempting to play off contemporary military powers against one another so that Judah thereby could preserve itself. At any rate, Isaiah's call for faith had a completely different purpose from that which motivated the false prophets again and again. Isaiah did not appeal to the history of Israel or to the Temple as the basis upon which Israel could build its confidence; he appealed only to the living God who rules the present and whom he met in his inaugural vision.

At this juncture we must take up a matter previously omitted, namely, the question of the absolute judgment which Isaiah expects after his vision (6:11). As far as Judah is concerned, Isaiah sees that the movement of the nations is instigated by Yahweh as a punishment for his people. This punishment is a result of the revolt against God of a people who do not recognize him (1:2 f.; 22:11) but follow their own way in every area, political, moral, and social.

So the judgment which Isaiah expects is an absolute one. His people deserve nothing better. Had the people been punished in proportion to their sin they would have been destroyed completely; but in the Old Testament Yahweh is not like the Babylonian assembly of gods in the story of the deluge, who wanted to destroy the whole human race. Yahweh, the threefold Holy One, never decided—even according to Isaiah—on a collective destruction without creating new life and without leaving a remnant to witness to it. Although the close of 6:13 is a gloss, it is, seen from the whole of Isaiah's theology, essentially a correct addition. Yet actually the idea of the remnant's conversion has an origin independent of the idea of absolute punishment. It is a datum in itself which becomes a certainty for Isaiah on another occasion, namely, after his call (possibly at the birth of his first son). Although we lack any report of a particular revelation which prompts this name-giving, we can make this supposition. It is a misconception to consider the main theme of the prophet's message of judgment as a real dogma for him, which he wanted to maintain à tout et à travers. The prophet not only knows of exceptions to the rule (the remnant that is converted) but he is convinced that Yahweh turns his full wrath against certain culprits (1:21-26). In statements like this it is not the whole people who come under judgment—as in other prophecies in which Yahweh keeps the whole people at a distance (hā'ām hazzê)—but only the guilty part of the nation.

Still another modification of the severe message of judgment in Isaiah appears in the idea of conversion, for example, in 1:10-20, where "the people of Gomorrah" are called to repentance. The word šûb does not play the important part in the utterances of Isaiah which one might expect on the basis of the name š⁰'ār yāšûb. Twice the conversion of the people is denied (6:10; 9:12); once the hope of repentance is expressed in a clear allusion to the name of Isaiah's son (10:21, if authentic); and once the fact is pointed out that the salvation of Israel lies in conversion (30:15).[16] Thus in spite of the fact that Isaiah affirms the judgment, he still calls his people to contrition. One could say here in the words of St. Paul: Love believes all things, hopes all things. Isaiah is obviously not a rationalist but a man who knows his spiritual responsibility, although his people answer his call only with derision and so prepare the way for the imminent judgment.

Concerning his message of judgment, there are more problems, particularly the problem of his expectation with regard to Jerusalem. On the one hand we get the impression (especially from the narratives in chs. 36 ff.) that Isaiah excludes Jerusalem from the judgment. Yet nowhere in his prophecies is this said expressis verbis, just as he does not say—as Micah his contemporary does expressly in his message—that Jerusalem will perish

[16] Cf. among others W. L. Holladay, The root šubh in the Old Testament, Diss. Leiden (1958), pp. 124 ff. Contrary to Holladay (p. 146), I think that the name of Isaiah's son has to be interpreted as meaning "a remnant will repent." The exile is mentioned only once, in 5:13 (gālā). The stem šûb is never used, nor is the word gālût.

with the Temple and all else. It seems that Isaiah has no direct message about it but alternates between fear and hope, notwithstanding the fact that ch. 6 and 1:21 ff. and 3:8 ff., 16 ff. suggest that he actually expects the punishment and conquest of the city.

In my opinion it seems unlikely, all things considered, that Isaiah maintains that Jerusalem would be saved because it was the dwelling-place of God.[17] The fact that he nowhere preached the destruction of the Temple provides only an *argumentum e silentio* upon which we should not build too much;[18] for the Temple as such plays only a small part in his book, as already mentioned. Indeed *Yahweh Ṣᵉbā'ôt* dwells on Zion (8:18); but if on this account Zion is holy, it is indeed made holy only by Yahweh himself (8:12 f.).[19] The degree to which Yahweh himself transcends the Temple in the mind of the prophet appears from his description in 6:1: Yahweh's train filled the Temple. A prophet who can speak as he does in ch. 1 about sacrifices and prayers would not have claimed inviolability for the place of the cult. Remember that in the same discourse he dared to call this "holy" Jerusalem Sodom (1:10).

Still, it is undeniable that a tension exists between Isaiah's prediction of absolute judgment and his behavior as reflected in the historical sections and in some utterances made by the prophet himself. First of all we point to his manner of acting in two stories, one from his own confessions (ch. 7) and the other from the biographical account of him (chs. 36 ff.). On the basis of this Pedersen says, "In two historical situations Isaiah showed that his belief in Zion was unshakable."[20] It seems to me that we should be cautioned against drawing this conclusion from both of the *capita* mentioned (7 and 37). When Isaiah says in 7:3, 4 that Ahaz has only to trust in God and "it shall not stand, and it shall not come to pass" (7:7), namely, that the two kings of Israel and Syria will endanger Jerusalem, that does not mean

[17] Pedersen, *op. cit.*, III-IV, pp. 552 ff.; O. Procksch, *Theologie des Alten Testaments* (1950), p. 189.

[18] Against Procksch.

[19] In 8:12 the reading qādôš is preferable: 8:11 ff. may be connected with vs. 19 f.

[20] Pedersen, *op. cit.*, III-IV, p. 553.

that he believes Jerusalem never will get into danger; nor does it mean that Isaiah refers to or is convinced of the inviolability of Jerusalem. On the contrary, he points out to the king in the words of chs. 7 and 8 that he, by his behavior, is ruining the country (especially 8:6 ff.) and consequently provokes the judgment!

In regard to the narrative in chs. 36-37 one can indeed recognize, whatever he thinks about the authenticity of the miraculous deliverance of Jerusalem,[21] that many words are originally Isaianic; but the question remains as to how far one can accept all the words of that context as authentic. For our consideration 37:32 is important because here it is said emphatically that "out of Jerusalem goes forth a remnant." It is a question whether this manner of relating the remnant with Jerusalem is really Isaianic or whether Isaiah actually would have connected his eschatological expectation with the historical Jerusalem as directly as is the case here. At any rate, we have no such word in his prophecies that have been handed down to us. I doubt, with some scholars, the authenticity of this verse,[22] as well as those found in 10:24-27.[23]

When, in the authentic prophecy of Isaiah, Yahweh calls Assyria to a halt, in Isaiah's view it is not because Jerusalem was inviolable but because this "rod of God" had turned against him, and he was the one who called Assyria to fulfill his judgment (10:5 ff.).

In my opinion Isaiah has not precluded a priori the downfall of Jerusalem on the ground of national-religious or religious-cultic motives. And he has not spiritually retreated to Jerusalem as a last refuge which would be saved at all events. Even when he refers to Zion as an asylum established by Yahweh for the misery of his people (14:32), he does not maintain that Jerusalem is an eternal city. The case of 14:32 is like that of 28:16,

[21] Cf., among others, Procksch, *Jesaja I* (1939) on this chapter; for the view of A. Alt, see especially his article "Hiskia" in RGG² (1935-36), and PJB (1929), pp. 80-88 (= *Kleine Schriften*, II (1953), pp. 272 ff.).

[22] Among others, Duhm; cf. R. B. Y. Scott in IB, V (1956). The verse is a parallel to 2:3d. Compare now the reading given in the Isaiah scroll of the Dead Sea manuscripts.

[23] Among others: Gray (ICC), Duhm, Marti, and Eichrodt.

where the word about the cornerstone in Zion points to Zion itself as the starting point of the holy congregation of the future,[24] not to the notion of the inviolability of the Jerusalem of Isaiah's day. Here the prophet speaks only of the poor[25] who find refuge there, not of citizens, priests, and so on who would be saved in Jerusalem! It cannot be concluded from 14:32 that Isaiah is certain about the deliverance of the holy city from the fire of judgment. The same is true with the messianic expectation of 16:5.

From all this only one conclusion can be drawn, namely, that Isaiah, though preaching the destruction of Israel and Judah, did not start with this idea as a fixed dogma. It seems to me that Isaiah watches with a fearful amazement for the signs of his time and looks for the manner in which God will fulfill his judgment. He knows that God wages a deadly war against Israel but many things remain unclear for the prophet. This is, in my opinion, a sign of his greatness, that he is cautious not to say too much about divine interference in the world. At every turn one gets the impression that Isaiah during the course of his life is faced with great surprises. For him the fate of the historical Jerusalem was unknown and open ended.

In this connection it is remarkable to find an authentic Isaianic word in which Isaiah obviously makes a pronouncement upon the future of Moab in a manner other than that of an earlier prophecy.[26] From this it appears that for a prophet like Isaiah life can be as full of unknown and unexpected things as for any other person. As a prophet Isaiah is completely dependent on the Word of God which he "receives." How much this is the case appears from the narrative in 8:1-4, where he has to write down at first some words whose meaning apparently was not revealed to him until about a year later.[27]

[24] Among others, J. Hempel, *Gott und Mensch*² (1936), p. 138; cf. also J. Lindblom, "Der Eckstein in Jes. ch. 28:16," in *Festschrift Mowinckel*, pp. 123ff., who explains it as referring to the religion of Yahweh.

[25] In the book of Isaiah the *ʿaniyyim* are the oppressed (3:14, 15; 10:2). In emphasizing their deliverance the verse has an eschatological ring.

[26] Isa. 16:13 f.; cf. 21:16 f. See, among others, E. Jenni, *Die politischen Voraussagen der Propheten* (1956), p. 19.

[27] Cf. my "Prophecy and Eschatology," Suppl. VT, I (1953), p. 209, n. 1.

Also, when God initiates the prophet into the work which he performs, many mysteries still continue to exist for him. A prophet is not, in spite of Am. 3:7, initiated into everything. We could say that precisely because, or in the degree that, one learns to understand something of the great work of God in the world, he always faces more enigmas. At any rate this was the case with Isaiah.

III

We have reached the third point, namely, Isaiah's experience of life. More and more Isaiah is amazed at the acts of God in the world. For him two things came to be established facts: on the one hand, God has a design[28] for the world, a design which he knows and follows; on the other hand, this divine design is and remains wonderful. Increasingly, particularly in his latest prophecies, this occupies Isaiah's thinking.

The idea of the counsel of God is connected with the representation of Yahweh as king[29] and is one of the prophet's early established convictions. A counsel is a preparation for action and in many cases decides the future;[30] at any rate this is so with regard to the decree of God. Quite often Isaiah uses the stem *yā'aṣ* both for the action of men[31] and for the action of Yahweh (14:24, 26, 27; 19:12; *'ēṣâ*, 5:19; 14:26; 28:29; [30:1]), as well as for the savior whom he expects and who is characterized by his counsel (9:5; 11:2).[32] The counsel of God does not result in a program that is fixed in detail but in the radical assertion of God's holiness and in the realization of his claim to sovereignty.[33]

[28] Cf. Fichtner, "Jahves Plan in der Botschaft des Jesaja," ZAW, 63 (1951), pp. 16 ff.

[29] Compare the parallel in Mic. 4:9. See further, among others, P. A. H. de Boer, "The Counselor," Suppl. VT, III (1955), p. 55.

[30] De Boer (pp. 44, 56) goes too far, in my opinion, by putting counsel in the Old Testament on a par with the decision which determines the future.

[31] So also in Hosea and Micah; once Micah uses the *nomen* (4:9) in connection with Yahweh, but the authenticity of this passage is not certain. However, it is not used of Yahweh by the contemporaries of Isaiah.

[32] *Ḥāšab* and *dimmâ* are not used of Yahweh.

[33] Fichtner, *op. cit.*, pp. 27 f.

In the later preaching of Isaiah the wonder of Yahweh's plan comes more to the fore (cf. 28:29; 29:14). Divine insight is revealed in acts that are very different in character and at the same time disclose great wisdom—in a manner comparable to the farmer who acts in different ways, sowing and cultivating the different fruits. Thus on the basis of his wisdom God acts in diverse ways in his world and toward his people, to the speechless amazement of man.

By his marvelous acts Yahweh will put to shame not only the common people but even the wise in their wisdom (28:13-16). He acts in this marvelous way because, in fact, the people do not reckon with him but only do his will outwardly. In this way, however, Yahweh will teach them to recognize who he is. Vss. 28:29 and 29:14, already mentioned, are dominated by the word "wonderful" (*péle'*; verb *pālâ*, Hi.). This term implies a positive element, namely, the idea that the decree, the work of God, exceeds all human comprehension. One may compare 9:5 where the child, whose birth is prophesied, is described as *péle' yô'ēṣ* "wonderful counsellor." With this verse we may also compare 11:2, the shoot from the stump of Jesse upon whom the spirit of wisdom and understanding rests; the child, endowed with this spirit, is represented as especially qualified to reign.

The divine manner of action is wonderful because it involves destruction as well as salvation. As evidence for this, note that after 29:14 there follows a prophecy both of disaster and of salvation (29:15-24). Thus these two prophecies, taken together, form the content of the marvelous work of God. With 29:17-24 one can also compare 32:1-5.

In the passage that precedes 28:23-29 the wonderful character of God's work is expressed in still another way: Isaiah describes Yahweh's action against Jerusalem as strange and alien because now Yahweh himself threatens the very city which he once gave to David. He acts contrary to his own former deed, doing something absolutely absurd (*zār*, *nokrî*).

In these last words the inconceivable—one can say the paradoxical—character of Yahweh's work stands out very clearly.[34]

---

[34] See my "Prophecy and Eschatology," Suppl. VT, I (1953), pp. 208 f.

Isaiah includes this also in his hope in God, whose work is wonderful. This is the more striking in his prophecies (in contrast to the later Isaiah narratives), since nowhere in them can anything of a miraculous type of thinking be found. The word *môpēt* has a symbolic meaning[35] and is used by Isaiah only with regard to himself and his children. The word *'ôt* is found only in 7:11, 14 (Isaiah's talk with Ahaz), in which he provokes Ahaz to "ask a sign deep as Sheol and high as heaven." It should not be thought that Isaiah, when speaking about the birth of the child Immanuel of the *'almâ*, the young woman, intends to prophesy a miracle. The birth itself, along with what happens during the first years of youth, is, in my view, the actualization of the sign predicted by the prophet. For Isaiah the point at issue is not to prove by wonders either the glory of God or his own reliability as a prophet. Certainly, however, he is so absolutely convinced of the majesty of Yahweh's action that he knows it goes far beyond human understanding and expectation, and he wants to induce the king to acknowledge this.

The "wonderfulness" of God is manifest in the double character of his judgment and his deliverance, expressed ambiguously in the name and life history of Immanuel. This is evident from the beginning of Isaiah's ministry and continues throughout his preaching. He preaches the coming ruin of his people as a fact but nevertheless expects the ultimate salvation of Israel.

Although convinced on the basis of the knowledge of God's holiness that his people are ripe for judgment, Isaiah is nonetheless sure on the basis of the same might and glory of the holy God that after the day of judgment a new life for Israel and a new creation will be manifest. Therefore he likes to use paradoxical expressions: deliverance comes from rest, and strength from quietness (30:15); the people who walked in darkness shall see a great light (9:1); when the house of David is completely destroyed, a shoot will come forth from the stump of Jesse (11:1); in the picture of the new life in the Kingdom of God the contrasts of the wild and tame animals and children living together are integrated perfectly (11:5 ff.). Likewise it is only the real knowledge of Yahweh that creates universal peace

[35] Isa. 8:18; 20:3.

(2:1-4). Peace (*šālôm*), salvation, is the culminating point in 9:5, 6, in 11:1-9, and also in 2:1-4.[36] The fact that Isaiah, when portraying this salvation, employed features borrowed from mythological representations outside the Bible indicates how much the expected salvation exceeded the limits of his own imaginative faculty. On the other hand, however, the salvation which he expects is connected with historical places and figures known to him, such as the holy mountain (11:9; [the connection is not with the existing Temple!]; 2:2-3) and Jesse (11:1; but the connection is not with David!). It cannot be said that Isaiah's expectations arise out of the existing holy place and the traditional institutions of his people; nevertheless, even in his loftiest expectations he does not lose sight of historical time and place.

On the one hand Isaiah's expectation of the day of judgment, while having an ambiguous character too, is just as definitive as that announced in Am. 5 and therefore bears an eschatological stamp; on the other hand, it is considered to be realized in the sphere of history. Compare his announcement of the *yôm laYahweh* in 2:12 and also 2:11, 17.[37] The historical aspect, in my opinion, does not need to stand in the way of the eschatological character of Isaiah's prophecy, as I attempted to demonstrate in my essay "Prophecy and Eschatology," referred to above. Isaiah applied to Judah and Jerusalem Amos' expectation in regard to Israel and stamped it with such a definite character that the eschatological dimension cannot be left out of consideration. The ruin which Isaiah prophesies for Judah he sees extending to the nations of the world; Assyria and the neighboring nations cannot escape it.

At the same time this is matched by his expectation of salvation, which also has a definite character. On the basis of his faith in the holy majesty of the living Lord, Isaiah is absolutely certain of both judgment and salvation. He understands his

[36] Cf. H. Wildberger, "Die Völkerwallfahrt zum Zion, Isaiah 2:1-5," VT, VII (1957), pp. 62 ff., and J. J. Stamm and H. Bietenhard, *Der Weltfriede im Lichte der Bibel* (1959), pp. 34-46.

[37] See the essay by A. Lefèvre, "L'expression 'en ce jour là' dans le livre d'Isaie," in *Mélanges Bibliques rédiges en l'honneur de André Robert* (1957), pp. 174-179. Lefèvre, probably rightly, puts 22:5, 8, 12 parallel to the above-mentioned texts.

time to be a time of crisis, in which the old world is perishing and the new is about to be born. Everything is enacted before his mental eye, within the limits of time. At this crucial moment the Assyrians in particular play a role that is decisive for Judah and for the whole world. Just as Isaiah's own life is exposed to the eyes of the Holy One, so he sees his people in their world *sub specie sanctitatis Dei.* The prophet's confrontation of the history of his own time with God himself accentuates the certainty of judgment and renewal. Although from the beginning of his preaching this judgment is definite, it is not defined precisely. It seems to be interrupted in its course owing to the fact that the very "staff of God's fury" (10:5) must itself be chastised. Even the prophecy of renewal remains essentially within the sphere of history and sometimes includes the historical Jerusalem (1:24-26); more and more, however, Jerusalem is inescapably involved in the judgment (22:14).

While at first Isaiah's hope for the future seems to center in Jerusalem (1:24-25; 16:5; and perhaps also 9:1 ff.), increasingly salvation is portrayed in new forms and in a universal perspective (chs. 11 and 2).

Although we do not know much about the inner life of Isaiah, apart from what we read in chs. 6-8, he must have been a man of immovably strong faith (one may think of the word *gᵉbûrâ*, used by him more than once: 30:15; 11:12; cf. 9:5; 10:21) but at the same time a man of inner conflict and growth. He knows of the holy, glorious, divine majesty,[38] and so he knows of waiting, hoping, and resting in the darkness; of struggle and righteousness, of justice and truth, of faith and victory. The judgment, of which he is absolutely sure, he sees coming nearer and nearer but his faith in Yahweh provides the source of a new hope for the regeneration of his people. They will be saved as a small remnant from the old Israel. And this remnant will become the foundation of the new Jerusalem, from which the renewal of the world by the Word of God will become a reality.

[38] The word *ḥésed* is used by Isaiah only once (in relation to the kingdom, 16:5, not to God); the word *bᵉrît* in its religious meaning is lacking also in Isaiah (used only twice in a profane sense: 28:15, 18).

X

Nonroyal Motifs in the Royal Eschatology

WALTER HARRELSON

The comprehensive study of Israelite eschatology and messianism by Sigmund Mowinckel[1] has shown once again that Old Testament eschatology must be understood in relation to ancient Near Eastern conceptions of "divine kingship." Mowinckel has acknowledged, however, that early ideas of election and covenant have contributed to and modified the understanding of the king's function, both historically and in the eschatological passages in which royal imagery is evident. The author has done little more than refer to these older ideas;[2] he has not sought to determine just how significant such early understandings of the rule of Yahweh over Israel may have been in the shaping and recasting of the royal motifs taken over by the community from its neighbors. It is the purpose of this essay to analyze certain eschatological passages in which royal imagery is prominent, in order to determine whether this general statement of Mowinckel can be amplified and shown to be defensible. My thesis is that even in those texts which are replete with the imagery of "divine kingship," terms and images drawn from the period prior to the establishment of the kingship are also in evidence. If the thesis can be supported, it should be evident that this fact needs to be taken into account more seriously than is the case in the above-mentioned work of Mowinckel—not to mention the works of

[1] *He That Cometh* (1954); English translation of *Han som kommer* (1951), translated by G. W. Anderson.
[2] See pp. 60-62 and *passim*.

147

others who have ignored entirely these terms and images from early Israelite culture and religion.

The term "royal eschatology" is used to designate those eschatological passages in which the future king from the line of David is portrayed as the "last" representative of the line. Texts which appear to have in view the coming of the "next" Davidic king and which lack the universal scope and characterization of the ruler as "divine" are left out of account. This procedure is recognized to be somewhat arbitrary; I have adopted it only because of the desire to test the thesis by reference to the most explicitly royal eschatological passages, those which seem most to be under the influence of the ideology of "divine kingship." This eschatology is royal in that a royal figure occupies the dominant position (alongside that of Yahweh). It is eschatology, not merely a depiction of a better day or epoch. The agent of the Deity in the royal eschatology is described in such fashion as to show that he has the authority and the power to accomplish the world-wide task assigned to him by Yahweh.

The passages in which these characteristics are most clearly present are the following: Isa. 8:23-9:6 (EVV 9:1-7); 11:1-9; Mic. 4:14-5:4a*a*; (EVV 5:1-5a*a*); and Zech. 9:9-10. Numerous other eschatological passages in the Old Testament have affinities with these particular ones, but they seem to lack one or more of the features singled out as characteristic of the "royal eschatology" to be examined here.

In a brief study it is not possible to deal with all the critical questions raised by an analysis of these texts. The authorship of the passages need not concern us, since we are not attempting to indicate the particular features of the royal eschatology of the prophets in whose works the texts are located. We wish only to examine the passages to determine whether within them other elements of the Israelite tradition, in addition to the royal motifs, are discernible. For our purposes it is not necessary to attempt to date the texts precisely, nor do we need to evaluate Mowinckel's thesis that eschatology is a phenomenon of the Exilic and post-Exilic periods. We are concerned only with an analysis of motifs.

It should be pointed out, nonetheless, that there are weighty arguments against the view that Israelite ideas of divine rule were virtually identical with those of Israel's neighbors. Martin Noth has shown very clearly[3] that the situation within Israel would seem to have prohibited the simple adoption of divine kingship ideology into Israel, even if it be granted that the "pattern" of the ideology of divine kingship had been as uniform throughout the ancient world as is sometimes supposed. The Israelite community remembered that once there *was* no king in Israel. Israel was a community consisting of twelve tribes; the tribal system was never abandoned. Ezekiel's vision of the reconstitution of Israel reveals the tenacity with which the community held to this ideal. The laws of Israel are all associated with the Mosaic period; no laws are reported to have been promulgated by the kings. The king was subject to challenge and outright attack by the prophetic spokesmen of the community. The capital city of Judah was known to have been a Canaanite town, captured by David and made the political and religious center of Israel. David's own ascendancy to the throne of Israel is portrayed as the work of an extraordinarily clever man, not the result of an investiture with divine authority and prerogatives by the God of Israel. These qualifications of the "divine kingship" thesis are important; they make it all the more appropriate for Mowinckel to acknowledge in his recent work that the old ideas of election and covenant have played their part in the development of Israel's understanding of the place of the king in life and cult. The same qualifications may be applied to the royal eschatology. It would not be surprising in the least to find that the Israelite prophets have drawn upon the older traditions in their portrayal of the royal representative of David's line who is to arise in the "last day."

I

The first passage to be studied is Isa. 8:23-9:6. Albrecht Alt's masterful examination of the text offers adequate reason for the inclusion of 8:23 as the opening strophe of the oracle.[4] Alt's treatment of the passage is well known, but it may be useful to

[3] *Gesammelte Studien zum Alten Testament* (1957), pp. 188-229.
[4] *Kleine Schriften zur Geschichte des Volkes Israel*, II (1953), pp. 206-225. Alt considers 8:23aa to be a gloss.

summarize his interpretation here. The text is considered to come from Isaiah of Jerusalem. It originated sometime within the period from 732 to 722 B.C. The occasion of the oracle was the conquest of the Galilean portion of North Israel by Tiglath-pileser III in the years 734-732. The oracle, which was not intended for public proclamation in Judah, is in the form of a message to be proclaimed by a herald in the "land of Zebulun and Naphtali" as the Assyrian forces are destroyed by Yahweh and as a new descendant of David comes to the throne of Judah. The prophet is looking into the future of Israel and tells of a day to come on which a new king of Judah will be installed at precisely the same time that the Assyrian forces are driven out of the land they have occupied. The lands of Zebulun and Naphtali are expected to see in the occurrence of the two events a sign that Yahweh is restoring the old united kingdom of Israel under a ruler whose reign will endure. The destruction of the Assyrians and the adoption of the new king as Yahweh's son, together with the investiture of this king with royal authority and the conferral upon him of the manifold name, constitute one magnificent act of Yahweh. Confronted by this portrayal of the "zeal of Yahweh of hosts," the people are expected to return in fidelity to Yahweh their God.

Alt suggests that the passage has been appended to the "Book of Testimony" (6:1-8:18) not long after the latter was collected (after 734 B.C.). Although this oracle has no precise analogue in the other prophecies of Isaiah, it is in all essential respects consistent with the prophet's message and with his view of Yahweh's use of and lordship over Assyria.

This interpretation of the passage is quite convincing to the present writer. The oracle is provided with a specific historical locus, which is not the case with the other texts to be examined below. At the same time, it is still an example of the royal eschatology, in the sense of the term stated above. The king who is to come will arise in the "latter days." His rule is to extend "from this time forth and for evermore" (vs. 6).[5] He is, accord-

---

[5] Alt notes that the designation of the kingship as eternal, like the manifold name given to the king, is probably borrowed from the titles assigned to the kings of Egypt; *op. cit.*, pp. 219-222 and notes.

ingly, the "last" king, not merely the next in succession to the throne of David.

The oracle is replete with the imagery of kingship, although the title *mélek* is not employed. Alt has suggested that the omission of this title may be due to the process of transformation which the borrowings from Egypt have undergone.[6] It is remarkable, however, that this most appropriate title should not have been used, even though its equivalent is found in the Egyptian texts. Furthermore, only two of the titles ("Mighty God" and "Everlasting Father") appear to be closely akin to the presumed Egyptian titles. It would appear that the prophet is deliberately avoiding the designation of the future king as king. Yahweh of hosts is Israel's true king (6:5). The term *śar* is employed most frequently not of kings but of military or political leaders under the authority of a monarch. The words *miśrâ* ("dominion") and *śar* are derived from the same or related roots (*śārar* or *śārâ*). Isaiah's choice of the term *miśrâ*, which occurs only in this passage in the entire Old Testament, may be an instance of his deliberately avoiding the imagery of kingship; the coming ruler is to have an "office" under Yahweh's rule. The word *yô'ēṣ* ("counselor") is used in parallelism with the term "king" (Job 3:14, etc.); the king is of course a counselor in his own right in Israel. Nonetheless, this is an office in Israel distinct from that of king, and the prophet in this instance also may be seeking terms which do not explicitly identify the coming ruler as a king.

Does the passage also contain references which are not only nonroyal but also related to the period prior to the establishment of the monarchy? I am convinced that it does. It is difficult to be certain whether the employment of this imagery from early Israelite life is deliberate or accidental. When the several instances are viewed together, however, the choice of the terms does appear to be deliberate.

The use of the fate of Zebulun and Naphtali for the purpose of introducing the oracle of the coming ruler is noteworthy in itself. We are reminded of the Blessing of Jacob (Gen. 49) and that of Moses (Dt. 33). Ps. 68, which is dependent upon these

---

[6] *Ibid.*, p. 219, n. 3.

two Blessings, also comes to mind, as does Jg. 5. In Gen. 49:15, Issachar (not Zebulun or Naphtali) is to "bow his shoulder to bear [burdens]"; the terms are identical with those found in Isa. 9:3a. Benjamin is characterized as one who "divides the spoil" (Gen. 49:27), an expression found in 9:2c. In Ps. 68, and in Jg. 5, the dividing of spoil is a prominent motif (Jg. 5:30; Ps. 68:13). It is noteworthy also that the princes of Zebulun and Naphtali, along with those of Judah, are described in the psalm as marching in triumphal procession into Yahweh's sanctuary in Zion (vs. 28). Zebulun and Naphtali were fierce combatants on the side of Deborah and Barak in the battle against Sisera. Barak was from the tribe of Naphtali, and his intial forces were drawn from Zebulun and Naphtali (Jg. 4:6, 10; 5:14, 15, 18). It is possible that Kedesh, the North Israelite refuge city (Jos. 20:7; 21:32) and cult center (the name is related to the root for "holiness"), was the cite of a small confederation of tribes prior to the Conquest—as were Shechem and Hebron.[7] Thus, despite the probable connection of the oracle with the conquest of the territory of these tribes by Tiglath-pileser III, the prophet may also be alluding to the "former" days of darkness and oppression under the king of Hazor (Jg. 4:1-3) and to these tribes' turn of fortune as a result of the great victory won by Barak of Naphtali. These motifs which appear in the old blessings and hymns of early Israel might be considered stock materials employed by Isaiah in the shaping of his oracle. Their occurrence would not be significant, perhaps, were it not for the fact that one particular motif in the oracle is drawn unquestionably from the period of the Judges: the "day of Midian" (9:3).

Alt has called attention to this term and has suggested that the prophet is thinking of an act of deliverance which, like the battle of Gideon against the Midianites, is to be completed in a single night—apart from mopping-up operations on the next day (Jg. 7:19 ff.).[8] In my judgment, the prophet has done more than make a passing allusion to Gideon's victory. He is describing the coming ruler of Israel by means of terms and images taken from the early poems, narratives, and traditions of the

[7] M. Noth, *Das System der zwölf Stämme Israels* (1930), pp. 79-81; 107-108.
[8] Alt, *op. cit.*, p. 215.

period prior to the monarchy. He wishes to indicate that God is providing a ruler in the "latter days" for whom the best analogy is to be found in the old charismatic leaders of Israel, and particularly in Gideon. In the story of the appearance of the angel of Yahweh to Gideon, additional possible connections with Isaiah's oracle may be found. Gideon is from the clan of Abiezer (Jg. 6:11; the term means "the divine father is a helper"). The title of the coming ruler, *'ªbî 'ad* ("Everlasting Father"), although of course a different term, might possibly be an allusion to the name of the clan of Gideon. Gideon is declared by the angel to be a *gibbôr heḥáyil* ("mighty man of valor"—Jg. 6:12); the term *'El Gibbôr* ("Mighty God") comes to mind. The cult center established by Gideon is given the name *Yahweh šālôm* ("Yahweh is peace"; 6:24). The designation of the ruler as *Śar Šālôm* ("Prince of Peace") could also have the Gideon cult center in mind. We have no analogy in the Gideon tradition for the term *Péle' Yô'ēs* ("Wonderful Counselor"); a kind of analogy does suggest itself in the story of the appearance of the angel to Manoah and his wife (Jg. 13). The formula "Behold, you shall conceive and bear a son" (13:7) is nearly identical with that found in Isa. 7:14 (see also Gen. 16:11), a passage which is almost certainly related to the oracle of Isaiah in our passage. And in Jg. 13:17-20, Manoah's request to know the name of the angel is refused with the question, "Why do you ask my name, seeing it is wonderful (*pil'î*)?" The term *yô'ēs* ("Counselor") does not occur in the Judges traditions; Isaiah himself refers, however, to the coming restoration of Israel's "judges and counselors" as at the first (1:26). Although the prophet is addressing the city of Jerusalem, he has in mind the people of Israel. Thus Isaiah has brought into direct association the office of judge and that of counselor. It appears that *he* looks to the early Israelite period for a norm both for true judgment and for true counsel. Each of the four titles of the ruler may be said, then, to bear reminiscences of the stories of the judges and of Gideon in particular. Alt's suggestion that the titles are borrowed from Egypt may stand; it might be modified to indicate only that the transformation of the titles has been carried through with the early Israelite period in mind.

II

The second of the texts representing the royal eschatology is found in Isa. 11:1-9. Here again it must be pointed out that we are not attempting to do more than determine whether or not imagery of both the royal and the non-royal type is to be found. The passage does not designate the coming ruler as king, but it clearly indicates that he comes from the family of David. The use of the uncommon terms *ḥōṭer* ("shoot"), *gézaʿ* ("stump"), and *nēṣer* ("branch"), all of which have their earliest occurrence here, is probably a deliberate device for indicating that no "next" successor to David's throne is intended. The reference to "Jesse" rather than to David may point in the same direction. At the least, it seems evident that the prophet is seeking to indicate some break in the genealogical chain, even though the Davidic lineage of the ruler is unmistakable.[9]

Only minor possible connections with the early traditions of Israel are observable. The Spirit of Yahweh is to rest (*nûªḥ*) upon the ruler in extraordinary abundance (11:2). We are reminded of the connection between the Spirit of Yahweh and the judges of Israel (Jg. 3:10; 6:34; 11:29; 13:25; 14:6, 19; 15:14, 19), although the verb *nûªḥ* is not used in the Judges passages. Yet the Spirit of Yahweh has also been connected with the kings of Israel (I Sam. 10:6, 10; 11:6; 16:13, 14; 19:9, 20, 23; and especially II Sam. 23:2). Mowinckel is probably right in identifying the nonroyal sort of motifs with the work of the great prophets, particularly the references to the "Spirit of knowledge and fear of Yahweh" (vs. 2) and the king's righteous judgments in behalf of the poor and the weak, as well as the judgment of the wicked (vs. 4).[10] The use of the term *šāpaṭ* (vs. 4) is not at all alien to the royal duties, but it is more closely identified with the "judges" of Israel, if we deal only with the Old Testament. The exercise of judgment by the kings of the surrounding cultures is a well-known motif in the available literature. The ruler is to slay the wicked with the rod (*šébeṭ*) of his

---

[9] See Alt's comments on this point; *op. cit.*, p. 224, n. 3. Mowinckel insists that the terms imply that the Judean monarchy has ceased to exist; *op. cit.*, p. 17 and n. 2.

[10] Mowinckel, *op. cit.*, pp. 179-181.

mouth. The same term is employed for the tribes of Israel and for the staff or scepter borne by the tribal leaders (see Gen. 49:10; Num. 24:17). The establishment of peace in the natural order is also reminiscent of Gen. 49:10-12. It must be admitted, however, that the non-royal motifs in this text are more closely akin to the prophetic tradition than to that of early Israel.

III

In Mic. 4:14-5:4aa, we have a text similar both in form and in content to Isa. 8:23–9:6. The opening line almost certainly provides the context and setting for the oracle, as is true of Isa. 8:23 for the analogous oracle. The verse depicts the city—doubtless Jerusalem—in mourning and under heavy siege. An invader is humiliating Judah and her ruler. We propose that the verse be translated as follows: "Now you are in mourning, besieged one; siege is laid against us. With a rod they smite the cheek of the judge of Israel."[11] The prophet (Micah himself, in all probability) sees the city of Jerusalem besieged and depicts its humiliation by means of a (probable) allusion to Gen. 49:19. In the latter passage, the tribe of Gad is promised that although a raiding band (gᵉdûd) will plunder its territory, Gad will drive the raiders out of its land. The use of the terms šēbeṭ and šôpēṭ are to be understood, we suggest, as further instances of the prophet's employment of imagery from the tribal period and his avoidance of the term mélek.

Jerusalem is referred to as "daughter of siege" (bat gᵉdûd) in 4:14, we have suggested; the old city of Bethlehem, traditional home of David, is then designated by the term "Bethlehem Ephrathah." It is possible that the author wishes to draw a contrast between the mourning city under siege—and thus facing starvation—and Bethlehem Ephrathah, for which he may have in mind a popular etymology, "House of bread [and] fruitfulness" (léhem, "bread"; 'eprātâ, from pārâ, "to be fruitful")![12] Although Bethlehem Ephrathah (Ru. 4:11) is a small town

---

[11] The Masoretic text is not as difficult as it has been thought to be. The term bat gᵉdûd simply means "daughter of a raid" and is a substitute name for bat ṣiyyôn, "daughter of Zion."

[12] The fact that the etymology would be incorrect constitutes no argument against the suggestion; popular etymologies are generally incorrect.

(and region) to be among the "thousands" of Judah, it will yet produce the leader who will rule over Israel. The term *'élep* designates a portion of a tribe; it occurs in the Gideon story (Jg. 6:15) with the precise meaning which seems to be intended here: Gideon tells the angel of Yahweh, "Behold, my clan (*'alpî*) is the weakest in Manasseh, and I am the least (*haṣṣā'îr*) in my family." The expression "little (*ṣā'îr*) to be among the clans (*'alpê*) of Judah" thus appears to be a conscious use of the phraseology of the Gideon story, to which other elements of the oracle seem also to allude (see below).[13]

The term used to designate the ruler from Bethlehem Ephrathah is *môšēl*. This word has its associations with kingship (see in particular II Sam. 23:3), but it is also used to refer to one who exercises authority in behalf of another. Joseph is *môšēl* over the house of the Pharaoh (Gen. 45:8, 26). Abraham's servant is *môšēl* over his master's household (Gen. 24:2). The word (in the verbal form) is found also in the earliest passage in which kingship is dealt with directly: Jg. 8:22-23. The men of Israel invited Gideon to rule (*māšal*) over them and to establish a dynasty which would continue this rule. Gideon refused, saying that Yahweh was to (continue to) rule over them. Thus once more we have a possible connection of the oracle with the Gideon cycle of traditions.

The origin of this ruler is from of old (*miqqédem*), from ancient times (5:1). It is difficult to see how this characterization of the ruler can well be applied to David directly. Should the passage be from the period of the Exile, or even from post-Exilic times, it is a strange way to refer to David; David was still very much a living part of the Israelite tradition. In fact, it was precisely during and after the period of the Exile that the figure of David assumed such massive proportions in Israel's life and cult (see, e.g., the treatment of David by the Chronicler). A personality from early Israelite history must be intended—and the most appropriate person to think of is Gideon.

---

[13] Some worth-while observations on the relation between our passage and the Gideon narrative may be found in A. Bruno, *Micha und der Herrscher aus der Vorzeit* (1923), despite the curious and untenable thesis of the book and the cavalier way in which the text is emended.

As in the dark days of Midianite oppression Yahweh raised up a deliverer for Israel who destroyed the forces of the Midianites in a single night (see above), so also in this day of siege and deprivation Yahweh will raise up a *môšēl* for his people. Even though Gideon refused the position of a *môšēl* (according to 8:23), he ruled over the central Palestinian area (Jg. 9:2, 7-21). A new Gideon, not from Manasseh but from Judah, is shortly to arise. The prophet is by no means repudiating the continuity of the line of David in Judah; he is, however, pointing to a break in the regular genealogical chain, it would appear (a fact which seemed also to be evident in Isa. 8:23-9:6 and in 11:1; see above). The best analogy for this *môšēl* is found, not in the tradition of Israelite kings, but in the career of Israel's famous judge, Gideon.

If this reference to a ruler from ancient times is in any way connected with the myth of the first man (primeval man, the *Urmensch*), the connection is very remote indeed.[14] Mowinckel also has suggested that the term *môṣā'ôt* in 5:1 refers to the "rising" of the sun-god and is thus a part of the mythological trappings of the oracle.[15] The verb *yāṣā'* is employed for the rising of the sun (Gen. 19:23; Ps. 19:6; etc.) and the causative form of the verb (found in our passage) is used of Yahweh's causing the heavenly bodies to come forth (Isa. 40:26; cf. Job 38:32). I doubt, however, that any such allusion is present. The term is best understood to refer simply to the origin of the deliverer (see Gen. 15:4; 25:26, etc., for this usage), his connection with a personality of the past. The chief point concerning the origin of the deliverer is that his coming is not without analogy; such deliverers have been sent by Yahweh of old, and he is fully prepared to bring the hoped-for deliverer in this new and decisive time of crisis.

In 5:2 the prophet declares that the time of oppression of the people will shortly be over. Yahweh is handing the people over

---

[14] Mowinckel argues against any widespread influence of the myth of the primeval man in the Old Testament, although he finds more allusions to this myth in the present passage than seem to me to be supportable; *op. cit.*, pp. 181-185 and *passim*.

[15] *Ibid.*

(*nātan*) to the enemy only until a woman, who even now is preparing to give birth, has brought forth a son. The verse is reminiscent of Isa. 7:14 and 9:5. Yahweh is preparing a child, to be born to an unnamed woman of Israel. The birth of the wonder-child is a common motif in the ancient world. Here (as in the Isaiah passages) the prophet is making clear that the deliverance of Israel is imminent. A "mother in Israel" (Jg. 5:7) even now bears in her body the long-awaited savior of Israel.

The ruler who is to appear will see the people of Israel reunited as one people. It is not indicated what part, if any, the ruler will play in this reunification of the nation. Here, as in other portions of the royal eschatology, it is Yahweh who establishes the divine rule on earth. The term *yéter* ("rest, remainder") has been used to support the view that the passage is from Exilic times. Israel is scattered among the nations. When the ruler arises, his appearance will signal the time of return of Israel's sons to their homeland. This interpretation has much to commend it. It should not be overlooked, however, that the term *yéter* simply means that additional portion of a given entity not included in the portion referred to. It may mean, therefore, that all Israel will be reconstituted as in the former days; those who are now on hand to greet the coming ruler will be joined by those who are absent. The prophet may have in mind the reunification of Judah and North Israel, not the return of exiles after the fall of Judah. For the prophets, the true Israel is one people of God; the division of the kingdom could not be considered by them to be a part of the continuing purpose of Yahweh.[16]

The ruler will stand and feed the flock in Yahweh's strength, in the majesty of Yahweh's name. The terms used would apply equally well to a king or to one of the leaders of the people at almost any time within Israel's history. The shepherd motif is widely used of kings in the ancient world (Hammurabi, etc.), and in Israel (Jer. 23; Ezek. 34); it is also used for princes and other lesser leaders of the community. The other terms employed in the verse are equally general. The strength (*'ōz*) and

[16] See G. A. Danell, *Studies in the Name Israel in the Old Testament* (1946), *passim*.

pride (gā'ôn) of Yahweh are conferred upon the ruler. Comparable endowments are said to have been bestowed upon the early tribal leaders (cf. Gen. 49:3, where the term *yéter*, "preeminence," and '*ōz* occur; see also Jg. 5:21).

The oracle in its original form probably ended with the phrase *wᵉhāyâ zê šālôm*, which should be translated: "And this one [or: he] is Peace."[17] Here once more we are reminded of Jg. 6:24, the cult place named Yahweh Shalom, and of Isa. 9:5, *śar šālôm*. The responsibility of kings for the maintenance of peace is well attested (Pedersen). But is it not odd that the king should be given the name "Peace"? Here, as in 5:2a, the prophet seems to have in mind Isa. 8:23-9:6, and especially one of the four titles of the ruler whose coming was prophesied by Isaiah. And behind the Isaiah passage we have seen possible allusions to the traditions of the judges.

Again, we must acknowledge that many of the allusions to early Israelite situations and motifs may bear little weight, considered individually. It does appear to me, however, that when they are viewed as a whole they support the probability that the author of the oracle wishes explicitly to describe the expected ruler by means of analogies drawn from the period of Israel's charismatic leadership under Yahweh, prior to the establishment of the kingship.

IV

The last text to be examined is Zech. 9:9-10. In this passage, the coming ruler is specifically designated as Jerusalem's king (*mélek*, vs. 9). Perhaps the term need no longer be avoided inasmuch as the Judean kingship has long since come to an end. The king is given the epithets *ṣaddîq* and *nôšā'*. The latter term, if accepted as it stands in the received text, is unusual for a royal figure. It means "one who has been delivered (from trouble or oppression or the like)." Karl Elliger holds that the word need not be amended; both *ṣaddîq* and *nôšā'* depict Yahweh's having

---

[17] Cf. *zê sina* (Jg. 5:5 and Ps. 68:9). See Mowinckel, *op. cit.*, p. 176, and H. Birkeland, "Hebrew *zae* and Arabic *du*," ST, II (1948), pp. 210 f., for a discussion of the meaning of the expression.

vindicated the coming king (declared him to be in the right—
one meaning of *ṣaddîq*) and raised him up from oppression and
humiliation. Elliger thus has a picture of a monarch whose humility and lowliness may be portrayed very appropriately as
"humble and riding on an ass."[18]

Most interpreters of the oracle find it difficult to accept the
term *nôšā'* as correct. The word *ṣaddîq* might better be translated "victorious," by analogy with the meaning of the term in
Second Isaiah (see Jg. 5:11, the "*ṣidqôt* Yahweh," Yahweh's
glorious deeds of salvation). The law of parallelism would then
suggest that instead of *nôšā'* we should read *môšîa'*, "victor, one
who is triumphant." This term is frequently used to describe
Yahweh's deliverance through the judges of old Israel (Jg. 3:9,
15; 6:36; Neh. 9:27; cf. I Sam. 11:3). The word also occurs often
as a designation of Yahweh as Savior (Isa. 43:3, 11; 45:15, 21;
47:15; 49:26; 60:16, etc.). The kings of Israel and of Judah, re-
markably enough, are seldom referred to by this term (II Kg.
13:5; Isa. 19:20; cf. I Sam. 14:39). In fact, not one occurrence of
the word is directly connected with a military conflict waged by
an Israelite king. (The parenthetical reference to deliverance
from the Syrians in the days of Jehoahaz is followed by an indication that this king's forces were almost entirely obliterated by
the Syrians; II Kg. 13:5 is no more than a general reference by
the Deuteronomistic historian, who is using the stereotyped formula found in the Book of Judges.)

The passage has affinities with Isa. 8:23-9:6 and Mic. 4:14-
5:4aα, as is clear from the opening line. The summons to Jerusalem to rejoice (*gîl*) at the coming of her king calls to mind the
rejoicing of Isa. 9:2 (*gîlâ*). The *bat gᵉdûd* of Mic. 4:14 (where
Jerusalem almost certainly is meant) may have its counterpart
in "daughter of Zion," "daughter of Jerusalem" (9:9). The
motif of peace and the removal of signs and weapons of warfare
also suggest that the passages belong together.

Jerusalem's king is to ride into the city upon a young ass
(*ḥᵃmôr, 'áyir ben 'ᵃtōnôt*). From this designation of the royal
mount, various conclusions have been drawn as to the character

[18] K. Elliger, *Die Bücher der zwölf kleinen Propheten*, ATD, II, 25 (1950),
in loc.

of the king's entry into Jerusalem. The ass is said to be the regular mount of kings: thus the passage appropriately depicts the entrance of the messianic king. Others have held that the horse is the normal mount of a king and that the choice of this beast is a deliberate effort to describe the *peaceful* character of the king's rule; it is also suggested that riding upon an ass portrays the humility of the king. The former judgment gains support from the fact that the ass is the mount of Danil in the Ugaritic text of Aqhat,[19] as pointed out by Mowinckel (with reference to Engnell). Mowinckel also argues that "the ass or mule is the royal mount of ancient times."[20] But the references given by him do not support the point made (Jg. 5:10; 10:4, etc.). The references from the Book of Judges have in mind the heads of tribes rather than kings. The mount most closely associated with ceremonial acts of kings is the mule (*péred, pirdâ*). This is clear especially from I Kg. 1:33, 38, 44, where Solomon rides the "king's mule" to and from the site of the ceremony of coronation—the Gihon spring outside Jerusalem's walls (see also II Sam. 13:29; 18:9).

Albright[21] and Noth,[22] among others, have drawn attention to certain Mari texts containing the expression *ḥayarum TUR atānim,* which refers to an ass slain in connection with the making of a covenant. The term is the exact equivalent of the Hebrew expression in Zech. 9:9 which is usually translated "a colt, the foal of an ass": *'áyir ben 'ªtōnôt.* Noth understands the expression to mean an ass of pure blood, as distinguished from one of mixed blood (a mule, or an ass produced through crossbreeding). It is assumed that the animal to be sacrificed must be declared to be of pure blood.

Once more we are led back to Gen. 49. In vs. 11 is found the only other occurrence of this term in the Old Testament. The reference is to the ruler who is to arise in Judah and whose appearance will be marked by peace and extraordinary fertility of the soil. The coming one in Gen. 49 is portrayed more by

[19] J. B. Pritchard, ed., ANET (² 1955), p. 153 (lines 50-60).
[20] Mowinckel, *op. cit.,* p. 176.
[21] In Pritchard, *op. cit.,* p. 482, n. 6.
[22] *Gesammelte Studien zum Alten Testament,* pp. 142-149.

analogy with the leader of the tribal system than with the later
kings. Note, for example, the reference to *šébeṭ* ("staff," "rod,"
"tribe") and *meḥōqēq* ("commander," "commander's staff"; see
Jg. 5:14; Num. 21:18; Ps. 60:9; 108:9), terms which are much
more closely connected with the period of the confederacy and
with tribal leadership than with the kingship and its rulers. It
is entirely likely, in my judgment, that the author of Zech.
9:9-10 is consciously employing the term for the pure-blooded
ass, in dependence upon Gen. 49:10-12. It is not evident, but it
is possible, that the expression occurs in both cases to indicate
that the rider of the pure-blooded ass has come to fulfill the
covenant between Yahweh and Israel. If this should be the case,
the term would be no more than a reminiscence of old north-
west Mesopotamian acts of covenant making, since the slaughter
of an ass is nowhere directly attested in Israel in connection
with covenant making. Attention might be called, however, to
the *beṇê ḥᵃmôr* of Shechem (Gen. 33:19; cf. Gen. 34). The
Shechemites and the family of Jacob are represented to have
made an agreement with one another (a general connubium).
Although the term "covenant" is not used, the fact is that the
deity worshiped at Shechem is known by the Israelites under the
name El-berith or Baal-berith (Jg. 8:33; 9:4, 46). The expression *beṇê ḥᵃmôr* ("sons of the ass") is perhaps equivalent to
"sons of the covenant." Furthermore, the slaughter of animals
(not an ass) is connected with acts of covenant making (Gen.
15:9-10; Jer. 34:18).[23]

The humble king of Jerusalem thus rides into the city upon
an animal associated with the old tradition of premonarchical
times, rather than upon a war horse. Yahweh himself will set
aside (*hikrátti*, vs. 10) the weapons of warfare available to
Ephraim and Jerusalem (unless the text is changed, with LXX,
to *hikrît*, "he will cut off"). The king will speak peace to the
nations, i.e., he will declare peace as other nations declare war.
He will be active in the maintenance of peace, through his
exercising of dominion (*môšēl*) over the whole earth. Baby-

[23] It is possible that Zech. 9:11-12 continues the oracle found in 9:9-10. If this is
true, the oracle itself contains a covenant reference—the covenant between
Yahweh and Jerusalem (Zion).

lonian imagery is contained in the specification of the universal
rule of the king. The same expression (vs. 10c) is found in Ps.
72:8, with the exception of the term *môšēl*. In the psalm the
term used is from the verb *rādâ*, "to rule, to exercise dominion
over someone." This variation in the two texts may or may not
be significant. Since, however, Ps. 72 is a part of the royal
hymnody of Israel used in connection with the coronation of
Israelite kings, its phraseology is likely to have become fixed and
standard. In Num. 24:15-19, an oracle portraying the coming
of a ruler to Israel who is a warlike figure (in contrast with the
ruler of Gen. 49:10-12), the verb *rādâ* is used: "By Jacob shall
dominion be exercised, and the survivors of cities be destroyed"
(vs. 19). We have noted above that the term *môšēl* often refers
to one in a position of authority under a higher authority and
that it has its parallels in the early Israelite traditions, particularly in the Gideon story. Its use here may perhaps be a
deliberate alteration of the royal imagery, for the sake of portraying the peaceful character of the king's rule, and a further
instance of the prophet's choosing a term from the early Israelite
period. Thus, in the midst of phraseology which is unmistakably royal and which comes from the cultic practices associated
with Israelite and non-Israelite kingship, a term is used which
appears to express the author's qualification of the character of
"divine kingship."

The declaration of *šālôm* to the nations is analogous to the
peaceful rule of the royal figure in the other passages. The
maintenance of peace is a central responsibility of Israel's kings
and chieftains. Yet here and in the other texts as well (exclud-
ing Isa. 11:1-9; see vs. 4) it is Yahweh who establishes peace;
the royal figure seems to be, at most, the preserver of the peace
established by Yahweh. The Gideon story is a classical example
of peace established by Yahweh (as the story is related). In a
number of ways, the story is designed to show that the victory
belongs not to Gideon, but to Yahweh (the reduction of the
number of warriors, the strategy which led to the rout of the
Midianites, the speed with which the host of Midian was over-
thrown, etc.; see above). And the phrase "Yahweh is peace"
(Jg. 6:24) once more comes to mind.

V

The royal eschatology of the Israelite prophetic tradition is thus seen to have been constructed in close dependence upon the ideology of "divine kingship" in the ancient Near Eastern world. Some of the terms used seem to reflect Mesopotamian influences; others are more closely analogous to Egyptian terms and conceptions. Syrian-Phoenician-Canaanite influences may also be traced at some points. Israelite eschatology is clearly dependent upon the royal imagery used to describe the character and function of kingship outside of Israel and within Israel. Yet we have seen that interwoven into this body of imagery from the royal cult are other terms and images reminiscent of Israel's early history under Yahweh's guidance, prior to the establishment of the kingship. The terms and images are found in ancient hymns and blessings and in the old narratives as well. The period of the judges, the charismatic leaders of Israel, seems to have been of particular importance to the prophets as a source for the portrayal of the coming of the royal figure of the "latter days" and for understanding the function of this leader.

The prophets have been required to do battle with the kings of Israel and Judah. They have been forced to attack despotism, injustice, corruption of the cult and the social structure of Israel. It is not surprising, therefore, that they turned back to the early period in order to interpret what lay ahead for Yahweh's people. The period of the wilderness and of the charismatic leadership has served as a kind of prototype for the shaping of their eschatology, even the royal eschatology. They have anticipated the coming of a king, raised up by Yahweh, who would rule over the entire earth under Yahweh's sovereignty. But they had no adequate analogy in the history of the kingship by means of which to portray the coming of the king and the nature of his rule. Not even the reign of David could serve as a prototype. They turned, naturally enough, to the time of the tribal confederacy when Israel was one people of Yahweh, ruled by Yahweh alone, and was provided with earthly leaders as occasion required.

Even so, the prophets have not spoken of a "return" to the period of the tribal confederacy in their royal eschatology. Their anticipated ruler will do more than any judge or king has done. The eyes of the prophets are fixed not upon the past but upon the future. The past provides analogies for the future, but not more than analogies. They look for the coming of a king—yet he is not to be a king "like those of all the nations" (I Sam. 8:5).

One final question must be raised. In what form have these non-royal motifs from early Israel been accessible to the framers of the royal eschatology? The early Israelite narratives ("J" and "E") have been available to them, of course, but it would appear that the Israelite cult would have been a more appropriate bearer of these motifs. The annual celebration of the festivals, the festival of Tabernacles in particular, provides the most obvious cultic setting. The Tabernacles festival must be understood, in my judgment, as the occasion for the reaffirmation of the covenant between Yahweh and Israel and also as the occasion for the reinvestiture of the kings with authority from Yahweh. Thus the celebration of Israel's equivalent for a New Year's Day festival may have preserved and developed both the imagery of "divine kingship" and that from the period prior to the kingship. Descriptions of the coming king of the last days, then, would have been drawn from the cultic source which had been used by the community to celebrate the New Year's Day-Covenant Renewal festival during the period of the kingship. Recent studies of the character of this festival support the view that pre-monarchical traditions of Israel were of considerable importance in its celebration, despite many later changes in the community's understanding of the festival.[24]

[24] In addition to Mowinckel's work referred to above, see especially Hans-Joachim Kraus, *Die Königsherrschaft Gottes im Alten Testament* (1951), pp. 82-99; *Gottesdienst in Israel* (1954), pp. 49-66 and *passim; Psalmen,* Biblischer Kommentar, Altes Testament XV (1958-60), pp. 197-205; Edzard Rohland, *Die Bedeutung der Erwählungstraditionen Israels für die Eschatologie der alttestamentlichen Propheten* (Heidelberg Dissertation, 1956), pp. 209-283; George Widengren, "King and Covenant"; *JSS* II, 1 (1957), pp. 1-32.

XI

The King in the Garden of Eden: A Study of Ezekiel 28:12-19

HERBERT G. MAY

The language of a literary composition must be understood in the light of its cultural milieu, for words and phrases carry significant overtones that are missed if one interprets them exclusively in terms of what their translated equivalents mean in a contemporary setting. With his interest in language and literary forms, Professor Muilenburg has appreciated this fact. His literary discernment is illustrated in his recognition of the background scene of the council of Yahweh in Isa. 40[1] and in his conclusion that the pervasive cultic language and imagery of Ps. 47 and its association with the king indicate some connection with the enthronement and coronation of Yahweh.[2] Whatever the faults of the so-called "myth and ritual" school, it has endeavored to place ancient literature in its ancient setting. Many of its opponents fail to do this.

There have been numerous attempts to interpret the garden of Eden motif used by the prophet in Ezek. 28:12-19, in the oracle against the king of Tyre. The endeavor is hampered by lack of adequate parallels and by uncertainty about the extent to which the author adapted the myth to his immediate purposes. The ramifications of the studies take one in many directions, involving among other things the concepts of primeval or First Man (*Urmensch*) and the Son of Man and difficult ques-

---

[1] J. Muilenburg, *Isaiah 40-66*, IB, V (1956), pp. 422 ff.
[2] J. Muilenburg, "Psalm 47," JBL, LXIII (1944), pp. 235-256.

tions of possible foreign influences. A Pandora's box of problems is immediately opened.

A more immediate issue is the relationship of this oracle to the one in the first part of the chapter. The two oracles have often been interpreted as essentially a unit; recently this has been done most effectively by Marvin Pope in terms of Ugaritic analogies.[3] They are presented by Ezekiel as separate oracles, and they may not have been uttered on the same occasion. In vss. 12-19 the figure changes, presenting no longer a god fallen from his throne in the recesses of the seas, but First Man in Eden, a perfect and wise mortal, driven from his paradise because of his sin. This suggests that the primary antecedents of Ezekiel's Eden are not to be found in myths of deities, even though there may be common elements in such myths. The Canaanite Eden or First Man myth is yet to be recovered. This is not to deny that there are certain definite parallels between vss. 2-10, where the prince of Tyre is represented as a god, and vss. 12-19.

The closest plausible analogies to Ugaritic literature are not in vss. 12-19 but in vss. 2-10, although it is dubious whether Daniel (*Dn'l*) in vs. 3 is one of them, contrary to almost unanimous opinion. Elsewhere the writer has maintained that the Daniel mentioned in Ezek. 14:12, 20, in a passage from the post-Exilic redactor, is an allusion to the traditional hero of the Exile, rather than to the Ugaritic Danel.[4] Here also the reference accords better with the Daniel of Hebrew tradition than with the Ugaritic Danel, who appears in no known texts after the fourteenth century. It is the Jew Daniel, not the Ugaritic Danel, who was noted for his wisdom and from whom no secret thing was hidden (compare Dan. 2:19-23; 4:7, 8; 5:13, 14, etc.).[5] It is not improbable that this seemingly parenthetic (prose?)

---

[3] M. Pope, *El in the Ugaritic Texts,* Suppl. VT, II (1955), pp. 97-104; cf. J. Morgenstern, "The King God among the Western Semites and the Meaning of Epiphanes"; VT, X (1960), pp. 152 ff.

[4] H. G. May, *Ezekiel,* IB, VI (1956), p. 137.

[5] One might presume that Ezekiel's picture of a Phoenician Danel, variant from the Ugaritic Danel in this respect, influenced the tradition of the Daniel of the Exile, but this smacks of circular reasoning; see A. Feuillet, "Le Fils de l'homme de Daniel," RB, LX (1953), p. 185.

reference to Daniel is a later addition to Ezekiel's oracle, suggested by vs. 4a. It is evident from the Qumrân Nabonidus fragment[6] that the Daniel traditions, in variant form yet with much the same phraseology and ideology, circulated before the composition of the present book of Daniel, for this fragment represents an earlier form of the story of the king's madness than that which now appears in Dan. 4. The Ezekiel allusions to Daniel may come from the early Persian period.

Although the garden of God (vs. 13) is paralleled by the seat of the gods in the heart of the seas (vs. 2), and the wisdom motif appears in both oracles, the figure in vss. 12-19 (in contrast with vss. 2-10) is evidently not a more than human one,[7] despite the fact that one scholar has rendered vs. 14, "You were a cherub . . . a god you were, in the midst of the stones of fire you walked."[8] Unfortunately this verse, which might have provided the key to the interpretation of the imagery, has been corrupted; the LXX rendition "with the cherub" and "holy mountain of God,"[9] suggests a reading more consonant with the imagery and symbolism familiar elsewhere. Kings and gods sat on cherub thrones[10] but were not identified with cherubs. There is in vss. 2-10 no suggestion of the Eden myth of fallen man, so clear in vss. 12-19. The parallels to the former are the myths of fallen or deposed gods, reflected also in Isa. 14:12 ff.;[11] Ps. 82,[12] and elsewhere. In vss. 12-19 the prophet draws on an Eden story which, while it has enough in common with the Gen. 2-3 narrative for its character to be recognized, is obviously a variant.[13] Here there is no naked figure, serpent, woman, or tree of knowledge, although the scene is Eden, a garden of God, and the

[6] J. T. Milik, "Prière de Nabonide," RB, LXIII (1956), pp. 406-415.
[7] J. L. McKenzie, "Mythological Allusions in Ezek. 28:12-18," JBL, LXXV (1956), pp. 323-324; see also TS, XV (1954), p. 552.
[8] G. Widengren, Sacrales Königtum im Alten Testamentum und im Judentum (1955), p. 27.
[9] Compare the Hebrew construction in Dan. 9:20.
[10] See W. F. Albright, "What Were the Cherubim?" BA, I (1938), pp. 1-3; M. Haran, "The Ark and the Cherubim," IEJ, IX (1959), pp. 35-38.
[11] Cf. Pope, op. cit., pp. 102-103.
[12] J. Morgenstern, "The Mythological Background of Ps. 82," HUCA, XIV (1939), pp. 29-126.
[13] McKenzie, op. cit., pp. 326-327.

"hero" is a blameless figure before he falls and is cast out. In contrast with Gen. 2-3, he is before his fall "full of wisdom." As we shall see, the basic underlying pattern of Ezekiel's Eden myth provides a more adequate background for the creation theme in Pr. 8:22 ff. and certain other passages than does Gen. 2-3.

Ezekiel's allegory seems to have been based on a story of a royal First Man, an "Adam" who was king, and this makes its application to the king of Tyre more appropriate. The description of Ezekiel's Eden figure as "a signet of perfection" (or better, "a finely wrought signet," read *ḥôtām*) in vs. 12 points in this direction; compare the signet as symbol of the king in Jer. 22:24 (Coniah, the signet on Yahweh's right hand) and in Hag. 2:23 (the "messianic" king-to-be, Zerubbabel), and the royal seals and signet rings found in the excavations. In the garden First Man wears what is probably a royal pectoral or breastplate on which are twelve jewels (so LXX), comparable to that worn by the high priests according to post-Exilic sources (*ḥōšen,* only in the P source); cf. Ex. 28:17-20; 39:10-12. Widengren suggests that Israelite kings wore the sacred breastplate and were bearers of the urim and thummim.[14] It is not improbable that some connection exists between the breastplate of the priestly head of the post-Exilic theocracy and the royal pectoral of the politico-religious head of the pre-Exilic monarchy. The precious stones in 28:13 have been associated with the obscure "stones of fire" in vs. 14 and interpreted as the materials from which the dwelling of the king of Tyre was made; according to this view, the stones of fire (*'abnê 'ēš*), like the *abn brq* of Ugarit, refer to the notion that the lightning is the flashing of the precious metals and jewels from which the heavenly dwelling was made.[15] The hypothesis, which presumes a motif in a myth about the gods, is attractive, but the problem cannot be said to be solved and the stones of fire remain obscure. The stones of fire and the Ugaritic *abn brq* have been interpreted as firestones or flint, connected with the thunder god and his lightning.[16] It would be tempting

[14] Widengren, *op. cit.,* pp. 27-28.
[15] Pope, *op. cit.,* pp. 101-102; cf. McKenzie, *op. cit.,* pp. 324-325.
[16] C. Fensham, "Thunder Stones in Ugarit," JNES, XVIII (1959), pp. 273-274.

to accept the common emendation to "sons of fire" or "sons of God," which implies a reference to the stars—the sons of God as they appear in the creation allusion in Job 38:4-7, where Job is perhaps being asked if he thinks himself primordial First Man, who was present at the creation of the world when the morning stars sang together and the sons of God shouted for joy. One would then have a picture of First Man walking among the sons of God, parallel to Job 15:7, 8 where Job is asked if he is First Man, brought forth before the hills and having access to the council of God (the sons of God); in this Job passage the image significantly implies a First Man of wisdom (vs. 8b). Although many make this emendation,[17] the expression "stones of fire" in Ezekiel, despite its obscurity, has too many parallels in Near Eastern literature to make the emendation plausible. The bejeweled garb, however, does suggest kingship, and there are other hints of a royal First Man in the Old Testament. While this motif is not apparent in Gen. 1-3, some scholars find it there. Bentzen, for instance, interprets First Man as first ruler of the world in Gen. 1:26-28, and holds the same for Gen. 2.[18] If this is correct, the motif lies so distantly in the background as to be no longer obvious.

More probable is the hint of a conception of a royal First Man in Ps. 8, which has often been called to witness in this connection. The psalm may be pre-Exilic and may reflect an earlier form of the creation story than that now found in Gen. 1.[19] In the psalm the nature of man is described in creation imagery. "Man" and "son of man" (vs. 4) do not mean First Man, but man in general (see Num. 23:19; Isa. 51:12, and particularly Job 25:1-6, which is perhaps influenced by Ps. 8); but in the total symbolism man in general is thought of in terms of First Man, who was of the nature of every man,[20]

[17] See J. Steinmann, *Le prophète Ézékiel et les débuts de l'exil* (1953), pp. 146-148, who so amends and compares the flame of the sword in Gen. 3:24 and the fiery seraphim of Isa. 6:2, 6.

[18] A. Bentzen, *King and Messiah* (1955), p. 18; also his article "King Ideology-Urmensch-Troonbestijginsfeest," ST, II (1950), p. 152. Compare S. Mowinckel, "Urmensch und Königsideologie," ST, II (1949), p. 83.

[19] H. G. May, "The Creation of Light in Gen. 1-3," JBL, LVIII (1939), p. 205.

[20] Cf. J. Pedersen's statement that Adam is primeval man, and at the same time first man, and the genus man; *Israel, I-II* (1926), p. 491.

created a little lower than God (but not a god), crowned with glory and honor (cf. Pss. 96:6; 145:12), and at the time of creation given dominion over all the creatures. The royal terminology is evident and a kingly First Man at least implicit. Bentzen finds First Man here to be First King.[21] It is suggested that the words in vss. 4, 5, which seem to refer to man in general, were perhaps originally said about the king, and further, that the creative acts of God and man's dominion over creation were actualized in the annual festival when the king played the role of Adam as the representative of mankind.[22] To interpret this psalm as essentially a royal psalm does not seem to be justified by the context, but it does seem to contain echoes of a First King concept. Note also vs. 6b, "Thou hast put all things under his feet," and compare Ps. 110:1 and II Sam. 22:39; I Kg. 5:3, etc.

A royal First Man may also be implied in the crucial creation passage, Pr. 8:22 ff., where wisdom is personified in terms of primordial First Man; we recall, obversely, that the figure in Ezekiel's allegory is "full of wisdom."[23] A. Feuillet has argued for the influence of the prophetic messianic oracles on the wisdom tradition, this tradition in turn reacting on the classical conception of the Messiah to give us the Danielic Son of Man figure.[24] That there is a relationship between certain pictures of the Messiah, the wisdom tradition, and the Son of Man conception is more than probable. The origin of the latter should be sought, in so far as possible, within Israelite culture rather than in Babylonian or Iranian influences, although the direct lines of the development of the Son of Man concept may not be precisely as Feuillet has indicated. Among other things, the relative dating of the messianic passages in the prophets and the wisdom literature is uncertain; some or all of the prophetic passages involved may be post-Exilic. Likewise, the derivation of the idea of a pre-existent Messiah from the canonical prophetic literature is based on passages too obscure in their import; this view re-

[21] *King and Messiah*, pp. 18, 43.
[22] H. Ringgren, *The Messiah in the Old Testament* (1956), pp. 19, 20; A. Bentzen, ST, II, p. 150.
[23] H. Ringgren, *Word and Wisdom* (1947), pp. 90 ff.
[24] Feuillet, *op. cit.*, pp. 170 ff., 321 ff.

mains only a questionable probability, despite the strong convictions of some scholars on the subject.

In Ezek. 28:12-19 there is no hint of the motif of a cosmic First Man, created before the earth and mountains,[25] although the concept is presupposed in Pr. 8:22 ff. Wisdom was the first of the Lord's creation: "Ages ago I was set up (*nissakti*), at the first, before the beginning of the earth" (vs. 23). With reason Feuillet also finds in these words a suggestion of royal investiture, in view of the striking parallel in Ps. 2:6:[26] "I have set up (*nāsakti*) my king on Zion, my holy hill." Like Ps. 8, this may imply a royal First Man motif. In the same vein, the creation of wisdom is described in birth symbolism: "When there were no depths I was brought forth" (vs. 24, *ḥôlalti*). The Hebrew means to be born in travail, as in Ps. 51:5 (H 6) and particularly in Job 15:7: "Are you the first man that was born? Were you brought forth before the hills?" Both the Proverbs and the Job passages recall Ps. 2:7 and Ps. 110:3 (many mss. LXX, Syr.) where the words "I have begotten you" are spoken to the king on his coronation. Incidentally, the cherub motif in Ezek. 28:12-19 may also point in the direction of kingship, for the cherub was commonly associated with the enthroned king (god or man).

As seen from the above quotation, the motif of First Man, created before the earth, appears in Job 15:7, 8 and is also found in Job 38:4-7.[27] The wisdom theme appears in both passages and perhaps reflects the parent myth, as in Ezek. 28; wisdom may well have been regarded as a natural kingly virtue (cf. I Kg. 3:9-13; 4:29-34; Isa. 11:2). Widengren suggests that the spirit of God received by the king through anointing was the spirit of wisdom (see Isa. 11:2).[28] In Job 15:8b the question "Do you limit wisdom to yourself?" is paralleled with "Have you listened in the council of God?" In Job 38 the theme is wisdom and knowledge which Job, in contrast with God, does not have; he was not there (as First Man was there) when God laid the

[25] Mowinckel, *op. cit.*, pp. 71 ff.
[26] Feuillet, *op. cit.*, pp. 323-324.
[27] Cf. G. Hölscher, *Das Buch Hiob* (1939), pp. 37-38. Not all scholars agree; see S. Terrien, *Job*, IB, III (1954), pp. 1017-1018.
[28] Widengren, *op. cit.*, p. 31.

foundations of the earth and the members of God's council (the morning stars, the sons of God) rejoiced. Possibly in some deliberate contradiction to the form of the myth in which First Man possessed wisdom, Gen. 2-3 reckons it a sin that man should eat of the fruit of the tree which was desired "to make one wise" (Gen. 3:6). Compare how Gen. 1 stands in deliberate (?) contrast with the view that God created with his hands and fingers (cf. Gen. 2:19; Pss. 8:3; 19:1).

Although representing a later development, the "one like a son of man" who came in the clouds of heaven (Dan. 7) is, to judge from the manner of his coming, a figure based on the motif of a pre-existent being. He is a human and not a divine image, and he is identified with the saints of the Most High. The motif of a royal figure is basic to his description, for his function is to rule over the earth; to him is given dominion, glory, and kingdom (7:14, 27). In vs. 13 we read: "And he was presented before him" (i.e., before God), and this has been interpreted in terms of the Semitic ritual for the proclamation of a king (Hempel) and an Achaemenid ceremonial of investiture (Herzfeld).[29] The promise (vs. 14) that all nations will serve him recalls the coronation promise in Ps. 2:8, and the words "everlasting dominion" may echo in an eschatological context the theme of Pss. 72:5; 89:29, etc. Many strands have gone into the making of the Son of Man figure in Dan. 7, among them elements from the milieu of the myth with which we are concerned here.

Obversely, whether the king was identified with First Man is a controversial issue. We have noted above affirmative scholarly opinion. Of the messianic oracles Mic. 5:2 (H 1) is taken to imply the primeval election and birth of the king: "His origin was from of old, from ancient days." This may refer only to the origins of the Davidic dynasty. Compare also the messianic title "Father of Eternity" (?) in Isa. 9:6 (H 5), which may mean only that the messianic king will be a "Father forever."[30] Isa. 49:2 refers not to the pre-existent Messiah but to Israel called before birth (cf. Jer. 1:5). Ps. 110:3, tantalizingly

[29] A. Jeffery, Daniel, IB, VI (1956), pp. 389, 461.
[30] R. B. Y. Scott, Isaiah, IB, V (1956), p. 233.

and admittedly obscure, is thought to point to the same belief; and Ps. 2:7, perhaps more closely related to Ps. 110:3 than is apparent, is taken as an allusion to the election and enthrone-ment of the king in primeval time, at the time of creation (as also Ps. 89:19 [H 20]).[31] See the comments above on the theory that the king played the role of First Man in the enthronement ritual, or, in the view of Bentzen, in the annual festival which was a re-creation of the *Urzeit*.[32] It is demonstrable that the en-thronement of Yahweh, the enthronement of the king, and creation and chaos-conflict motifs were often inextricably bound together, but despite this fact the actual representation of the king as First Man, as a pre-existent figure, is difficult to show convincingly.

That the royal First Man concept lies behind the later messi-anic Son of Man ideology is most probable, especially since it is found in Enoch (the Similitudes) and IV Esdras, where it ap-pears to be particularly influenced by the motif of the pre-creation royal First Man in the wisdom literature. One of the most thoroughgoing attempts to explain the Danielic Son of Man concept in terms of native Israelite culture is that of Feuillet, who finds a primary influence of Ezekiel and the wis-dom tradition. For him, Daniel's Son of Man is a messianic figure; his Davidic nature and origins are to be assumed but are not mentioned because the persecuted Jews did not await the coming of the messianic kingdom merely as an expansion of the kingdom of Israel.[33] Feuillet has uncovered many legitimate possible lines of influence and parallels; it is contrary to the seemingly obvious meaning of the context, however, to identify the Son of Man in Dan. 7 not as a symbol of the saints of the Most High but as a representative of the messianic people in the same way as is the Davidic Messiah, albeit not explicitly. The eschatology of the Book of Daniel is consistently theo-cratic, not messianic. An effort to explain the Son of Man imagery in Daniel in terms of a Baal-Yahweh figure, with pri-

[31] Bentzen, *King and Messiah*, pp. 17, 18. See also Ps. 80:17 (H 18), which is interpreted as an allusion to the pre-existent Messiah.

[32] Bentzen, ST, II, p. 150.

[33] Feuillet, *op. cit.*, pp. 180 ff., 321 ff.

mary origins in Canaanite motifs, is less successful,[34] despite recognized analogies to Canaanite themes in the chapter and in the later messianic Son of Man contexts. There is really no suggestion in Dan. 7 that the Son of Man, in the role of a Baal figure, killed the fourth beast, even though vs. 21 mentions the war of the little horn against the saints of the Most High. In Daniel, the Son of Man is not a savior and he accomplishes no saving acts. God is the savior and judge. This is not to say that in the current efforts to discover Canaanite-Phoenician, Canaanite-Babylonian,[35] or native Israelite origins of the Son of Man conception, the probabilities of Iranian influence should be ignored.[36] But even as the use of Greek gnostic materials to explain elements of New Testament ideology and diction has had to give way in considerable measure to a recognition of pregnostic Jewish parallels and influences as a result of the Qumrân disclosures, so here also elements of native Israelite cultural origins must now be given greater recognition.

The idea of the Son of Man, however, is not the primary problem of this study, although the First Man motif became an important aspect of that concept. As reflected in the wisdom tradition, the Son of Man was named (had existence) before the sun and stars were created; he was hidden and chosen before the creation of the world (Enoch 48:3, and note the wisdom associations, recalling the allusions to wisdom in Ezek. 28). He is a royal figure, seated on a throne (Enoch 62:1-3). In Enoch 51:3 the Elect One (the Son of Man) is seated on his throne and his mouth pours forth wisdom and counsel (cf. 48:1).

The Son of Man concept in the New Testament is also not the concern of this essay. We may note that the concept does not occur in the Qumrân literature. This is understandable in the light of the Qumrân sect's belief in two Messiahs: the Messiah of Israel and the Messiah of Aaron. The Qumrân community did not expect a savior from heaven but a royal Davidic Messiah who would command the troops in the final war against

[34] J. A. Emerton, "The Origin of the Son of Man Imagery," JTS, IX (1958), pp. 225 ff.

[35] See G. Fohrer, Ezechiel, HAT (1955), pp. 162-164.

[36] See especially C. H. Kraeling, Anthropos and Son of Man (1927).

the sons of darkness. It is understandable that the Similitudes of Enoch are not found in the Qumrân library. Some have supposed this to indicate that this part of the Enoch cycle is post-Essene in date, but more plausibly, in view of the immediate antecedents of the Enochic Son of Man concepts in the Old Testament, the Son of Man in Enoch represents a contemporary and parallel apocalyptic tradition, as Christianity represents still another.

Additional note. Professor Muilenburg's important perspicuous study, "The Son of Man in Daniel and the Ethiopic Apocalypse of Enoch," JBL, LXXIX (1960), pp. 197 ff., appeared after this essay had been submitted to the Editors, too late for his helpful insights to be incorporated in it. The same is true of the relevant, fruitful discussion of "Wisdom in Creation; the *'āmôn* of Proverbs 8:30," by R. B. Y. Scott in VT, X (1960), pp. 213 ff.

XII

Exodus Typology in Second Isaiah

BERNHARD W. ANDERSON

Recent discussions of Biblical hermeneutics have displayed a new, although cautious, interest in typology as a means to express the Biblical understanding of history.[1] Usually typology is regarded as a way to understand the dramatic unity of the Scriptures, on the supposition that events of the Old Testament, seen from the angle of Christian faith, foreshadow and point beyond to the decisive event of God's revelation in Jesus Christ. Just as every stage of a drama moves toward the final denouement, so the events of the Old Testament are held to be types or images which anticipate the greater fulfillment in the time of the new covenant, when the sacred history of God's dealings with men reaches its climax. From the early centuries of the Church typology has been used to interpret the Old Testament; and this kind of interpretation is deeply rooted in the New Testament itself, as shown by Leonhard Goppelt in his study *Typos: die typologische Deutung des Alten Testaments im Neuen* (1939). Whether this ancient interpretive method is relevant today, when historical criticism has thrown new light on the original significance of Biblical passages, is a moot question. Typology is regarded, even by those who stress the unity of the Bible, as a

[1] See the summary in H.-J. Kraus, *Geschichte der historisch-kritischen Erforschung des Alten Testaments von der Reformation bis zur Gegenwart* (1956), pp. 432-440. For a perspicacious re-evaluation of typology, see the article by Walther Eichrodt, "Ist die typologische Exegese sachgemässe Exegese?" in Suppl. VT, IV (Volume du Congrès, Strasbourg, 1956), pp. 161-180. Also G. W. H. Lampe and K. J. Woollcombe, *Essays in Typology; SBT, 22* (1952).

"dangerous exercise."[2] When employed to show the Christo-
centric unity of the Bible, it may—and often does—impose an
artificial unity upon Scripture and frequently results in an over-
interpretation of the Old Testament.)

It may be helpful to take another look at this question by
turning away from the problem of the unity of the Bible. This
fact deserves emphasis: typology is fundamentally a mode of
historical understanding. It does not deal in the first instance
with the relation between the canons of the Old and the New
Testaments. Whether it is suitable to the New Testament depends upon the prior question of the relevance of this mode of
interpretation to the Christian proclamation of God's historical
action in Jesus Christ. Therefore, I propose to reconsider typology as a mode of historical interpretation by concentrating
on a small area of Scripture which has had a profound influence
upon the New Testament, namely, the poems of Second Isaiah
found in Isa. 40-55.

I

To begin with, it is necessary to draw a distinction between
allegory and typology, particularly with regard to the ontology
which each presupposes. To be sure, neither of these terms is
found in the Old Testament; but the possibilities of historical
understanding for which each term stands were available to
Israel, as evidenced by the long struggle between the prophetic
(or "historical") and pagan (or "mythological") views of existence. Allegory presupposes a view of existence which depreci-
ates, if not abolishes, the meaningfulness of concrete, historical
time. According to this view, man encounters reality by freeing
himself from time and history and relating himself to that which
is timeless and eternal. Concrete history is not the realm of
reality; therefore, there is no remembrance of a past which
shapes the present or no hope for a future of fulfillment. His-

---

[2] G. E. Wright, God Who Acts, SBT, 8 (1952), p. 66. In his Theologie des Alten
Testaments, Vol. II (1960), Gerhard von Rad gives an excellent discussion of the
relations between the Testaments (pp. 329-424), including a fresh treatment of
typological interpretation (pp. 375-387).

torical events move in a cycle of eternal recurrence and, at best, are only temporal embodiments of timeless truths. This historical understanding is summed up in Goethe's words: *"Alles Vergängliche ist nur ein Gleichnis."*[3] It is not surprising that allegory flourished in Greek culture, especially under the influence of Plato, who provided philosophical sanction for the ontology presupposed in the ancient mythological view of existence.[4]

Under Hellenistic influence the Church has resorted to allegory from time to time in order to find scriptural similitudes for the eternal meaning of Christian doctrines, held to be timelessly true even though revealed at a point in time. Thus the allegorist moves away quickly from the literal meaning of a passage to the spiritual meaning that is articulated in the doctrines guarded by the Church. By and large, the Reformers rejected allegory as a hermeneutical method and returned to typology, with its emphasis upon the historical pattern of God's saving deeds. But since the Enlightenment, allegory has returned through the back door, so to speak—disguised in the interpretation of the Bible as the record of man's discovery of "timeless truths" and "abiding values." To be sure, this modern view is characterized by a greater historical realism and relativism than prevailed in Hellenistic times. It is important for the critic to recover the historical matrix of ideas and to understand the social and personal dynamic which brought them to birth; but "the historical occasion, once it is past, is more or less irrelevant *except for the purposes of illustration*."[5] Here we find ourselves on Goethe's ground: Biblical teachings are similitudes of rational truths. From this standpoint, Second Isaiah may be regarded as "a thinker and a poet, rather than a prophet," who "formulated religious and theological principles of universal

---

[3] "Everything temporal is only a similitude." The opening lines of the final ode of *Faust* (Part II, Act V). I am indebted to my colleague Will Herberg for this quotation and for helping to sharpen in my mind the distinction between allegory and typology, as set forth in these paragraphs.

[4] See Mircea Eliade, *Cosmos and History: The Myth of the Eternal Return* (Harper Torchbook, 1954), pp. 34-35.

[5] The quotation is from C. R. North, *The Old Testament Interpretation of History* (1946), pp. 153-154. North vigorously criticizes the presuppositions of this approach. Italics are mine.

validity" and thereby "endowed his words with permanent significance."[6] So regarded, his contribution was that he freed Israel's religion from the particularities of Israel's history and set forth ideas and principles whose validity is independent of the historical circumstances through which they were mediated.

Typology, on the other hand, is primarily concerned with history. Events are not symbolic of eternal truths or timeless principles but disclose in their concreteness and temporality that which is ultimately real. (According to this view, man's concern is not to free himself from time and history but rather to realize the meaning of history, through the remembrance of the past, participation in history's drama in the present, and facing the future in hope.) Specifically, man understands himself in relation to a "crucial event," the significance of which he shares and confesses as a member of a community of faith (cf. Dt. 26:5-10). Viewed from this point of vantage, previous events are seen to be an anticipation of the decisive event; and subsequent events are understood as the consequences which flow from it, pointing toward an even greater fulfillment.

Typological thinking is not a peculiarity of the Biblical faith. It may be found in any historical community, such as the American, within which men remember a decisive event whose meaning was anticipated by a previous history and is being fulfilled in the course of subsequent history. This kind of thinking, however is peculiarly intense in the Bible owing to the witness that the ultimate meaning of human life is bound up with events in which God has revealed himself and has formed a special community for the realization of his historical purpose. And such thinking is found pre-eminently in Second Isaiah. For him, history was not the matrix of ideas which the interpreter can separate from their historical occasion, as the husk is removed from the pure grain; rather, Israel's history, with its center in crucial historical moments like the Exodus from Egypt, was the sphere of the action of God to inaugurate a new age which would include Israel and the nations.

[6] R. H. Pfeiffer, *Introduction to the Old Testament* (rev. ed., 1948), p. 471.

II

In the development of Second Isaiah's eschatological message, one of the dominant themes is that of the new exodus. Previous prophets, to be sure, had appealed to the memory of the Exodus.[7] But it was Second Isaiah who, more than any of his prophetic predecessors, perceived the meaning of the Exodus in an eschatological dimension. "The conception of the new exodus," writes Professor James Muilenburg in his superb commentary, "is the most profound and most prominent of the motifs in the tradition which Second Isaiah employs to portray the eschatological finale."[8] In this respect he goes beyond Isaiah of Jerusalem, with whom he shares the themes of the New Jerusalem, the covenant with the Davidic dynasty, and the kingly rule of the Holy One of Israel, although transforming these themes in his own way. To this royal theology he adds the Exodus traditions, almost wholly ignored by Isaiah of Jerusalem. His expectation of Yahweh's coming to inaugurate his eschatological rule was shaped according to the pattern of the Exodus from Egypt, the crucial event of Israel's past.

While there are numerous linguistic echoes of the Exodus tradition throughout the poems of Second Isaiah, the theme of the new exodus is the specific subject in several passages.[9]

1. 40:3-5   The highway in the wilderness.
2. 41:17-20   The transformation of the wilderness.
3. 42:14-16   Yahweh leads his people in a way they know not.
4. 43:1-3   Passing through the waters and the fire.[10]
5. 43:14-21   A way in the wilderness.

[7] Hos. 2:14-15 [H 2:16-17]; 11:1; 12:9, 1 3 [H 12:10, 14]; 13:4-5; Am. 2:9-10; 3:1-2; 9:7; Mic. 6:4; Isa. 10:24, 26; 11:15-16; Jer. 2:6-7; 7:22, 25; 11:4, 7; 23:7-8 = 16:14-15; 31:32; 32:20-22; 34:13-14; Ezek. 20:5-10.
[8] IB, V (1956), p. 602.
[9] See Johann Fischer, "Das Problem des neuen Exodus in Isaias c. 40-55," TQ, 110 (1929), pp. 111-130; also Alfred Zillessen, "Der alte und der neue Exodus," ARW, VI, 4 (1903), pp. 289-304.
[10] The allusion to the Exodus is more indirect in 43:1-3 than any other passage listed above (but cf. Ps. 66:12); 52:3-6 is listed by Zillessen (op. cit., pp. 291-292), but this passage has difficulties and is probably an insertion. Ch. 35, whose theme is the new exodus, has strong affinities with Second Isaiah.

  6. 48:20-21   The exodus from Babylon.
  7. 49:8-12   The new entry into the Promised Land.
  8. 51:9-10   The new victory at the sea.
  9. 52:11-12   The new exodus.
  10. 55:12-13 Israel shall go out in joy and peace.

The historical setting of Second Isaiah's prophecy is the Babylonian Exile—Israel's captivity, which the prophet likens to the oppression in Egypt. But already, with the rise of Cyrus of Persia, events with far-reaching implications were taking place. Behind and within these events the prophet perceived the activity of Yahweh, the Creator of the ends of the earth and the sole director of the course of human history, who was revealing himself in a glorious theophany. He had chosen Cyrus as the instrument of his purpose (44:28; 45:1) in order to overthrow Babylon and to set Israel free. The fall of Babylon would be followed by a new exodus, more marvelous than the Exodus under Moses, and by the restoration of Zion. This new event would prompt the whole world to recognize that Yahweh is God alone and that his salvation extends to the ends of the earth. It is significant that Second Isaiah's prophecy begins (40:3-5) and ends (55:12-13) with the theme of the new exodus. Indeed, the poems as a whole are largely variations on the Exodus tradition.

The Exodus, of course, was not an isolated event in Second Isaiah's memory and imagination but, as in the early confessions of Israelite faith (e.g., Dt. 26:5-9; cf. Jos. 24:2-13), was part of a sacred tradition or *Heilsgeschichte* which extended from the patriarchal period to the occupation of the Promised Land. The following outline summarizes the motifs of the sacred history which Second Isaiah reinterpreted eschatologically:

a. The promises to the fathers.
  1. The birth of Israel is traced back to Abraham whom, when he was but one, Yahweh called and blessed (41:8; 51:1-2).
  2. Even though Israel's subsequent history was marred by the sin of Jacob, the "first father" (43:27; cf. Hos. 12:3), the blessings given to the patriarchs will be continued in his descendants. These blessings, which Israel had forfeited

(48:18-19), include the gift of the land, the miraculous fertility of "barren" Israel (49:19-21; 54:1-3; cf. Gen. 28: 14), and the mediation of saving benefits to other nations (42:6-7; cf. Gen. 12:2-3).

b. The deliverance from Egypt.

 1. Yahweh delivered his people from bondage "with a mighty hand and an outstretched arm" (cf. 40:10; 51:9; 52:10). His "glory" (kābôd), seen only by Israel in the old exodus (Ex. 16:7 etc. in P), will ultimately be seen by all flesh (40:5), for all nations will behold the miracles of the new exodus.

   (a) There is no specific allusion to the plagues on Egypt, nor any reference to the Passover (but see the statement in 52:12 that Israel shall not go out "in haste"; cf. Dt. 16:3; Ex. 12:11).

 2. During the Exodus Yahweh was Israel's "rear guard" and "went before" his people (52:12)—an allusion to the protecting and guiding pillar of fire and cloud (cf. Ex. 13:21-22; 14:19-20).

 3. Like a man of war (42:13; cf. Ex. 15:3), Yahweh fought for his people (Ex. 14:25) and won the decisive victory at the Sea of Reeds (51:9-10). He caused "chariot and horse" to lie down, never to rise again (43:16-17; cf. Ex. 14:28; 15:10, 21) and in a like fashion he will overcome all of Israel's oppressors (49:24-26; 51:22-23; cf. 52:3-6).

 4. The new exodus will be accompanied by a victory song, like Miriam's song after the deliverance at the sea (42:10-13; cf. Ex. 15:21).

c. The journey through the wilderness.

 1. Yahweh prepared a way (dérek) through the wilderness and led his people toward their destination (40:3-5; 42: 16; 43:19; cf. 11:16; 35:8-10).

 2. Along the way he supplied his people with food and drink (41:17-20; 43:19-21; 49:10); he made water to flow from the rock (48:21; cf. Ex. 17:2-7; Num. 20:8). In the time of the new exodus the wilderness will be marvelously transformed (49:9-11; 55:13; cf. 35:6-7).

 3. Second Isaiah does not mention the journey toward Sinai, but the revelation of the law is presupposed (42:21, 24; 48:17-18; cf. 51:7). The new exodus also is accompanied

by a new covenant, although different from the Mosaic covenant (55:3; cf. 54:10); 55:1-2 echoes the tradition of the covenant meal (cf. Ex. 24:11).
d. The re-entry into the Promised Land.
  1. Yahweh guided his people through the wilderness to Zion, where the land was apportioned among the tribes (49:8).
  2. The New Israel will consist of a tribal confederation, gathered together from Babylon and the Dispersion to Zion, the "holy city" (52:1).[11]

From the above summary it is clear that Second Isaiah's eschatological perspective is profoundly shaped by the main outline of Israel's *Heilsgeschichte* although, as indicated above, this has been been supplemented with the theology of the Davidic tradition (cf. 55:3). The prophet's historical retrospect, however, reaches back before the patriarchal period and, like the Yahwist, includes the *Urgeschichte*. He remembers "the days of Noah" when Yahweh established an everlasting covenant after the divine judgment of the Flood (54:9-10; cf. Gen. 8:21-22; 9:11-17). He alludes to the tradition of the marvelous fertility of Eden to depict the eschatological transformation of nature (51:3; cf. Ezek. 28:13). And above all he harks back to the time of the Creation, when Yahweh stretched out the heavens and laid the foundations of the earth (40:12-31; 42:5; 44:24; 45:9-13, 18; 48:13; 51:13, 16). In an apparent reference to priestly tradition concerning creation out of chaos (45:18-19), he declares that it is not Yahweh's purpose to allow the earth to lapse back again to precreation chaos (*tōhû*, as in Gen. 1:2).

Thus Second Isaiah knew a historical tradition which reached back before the patriarchal period to the Creation. In every case, however, the primeval traditions have been drawn into the prophet's eschatological perspective. This is true, for instance, in his references to Yahweh's sovereignty as Creator. Never does the prophet think of Creation out of relation to history. Frequently he appeals to Yahweh's creation to support faith in his power to redeem his people and to accomplish his world-em-

---

[11] Gerhard von Rad suggests that the reference to the restoration of the tribes (49:5-6) may mean a reconstitution of the old tribal confederacy, i.e., the formation of a new Israel after the ancient model.

bracing purpose (40:21-31; 44:24-28; 45:12-13). But more significantly, in some places he links creation and redemption so closely together that one is involved in the other. Yahweh's creative acts belong to the history of salvation, whether performed in the *Urzeit* (51:9) or at the time of the new creation (45:8; 48:7; cf. 42:9). His redemptive acts are acts of creation; and his creative acts are acts of history.[12] Thus in Second Isaiah's prophecy the *Urgeschichte*, especially the Creation, is inseparably bound to *Heilsgeschichte*, the crucial event of which was the Exodus. The new exodus, which he regards as the counterpart of the old exodus, is portrayed in the mythopoeic colors of creation (51:9-10). Of these eschatological events he can say: "they are created (*nibr^e'û*) now, not long ago" (48:7; cf. 41:20).

III

Prophetic eschatology is based upon the premise: *Endzeit gleich Urzeit*.[13] The end-time will correspond to and parallel the beginning-time, even though it will be far more wonderful. Second Isaiah, of course, did not devise this eschatological pattern. He inherited it from prophetic tradition, although transforming it according to his own insights and the historical situation of his time. In particular, he viewed the events of his day— the rise of Cyrus, the imminent fall of Babylon, and the expected release of exiles—as a new exodus, corresponding to the exodus under Moses. The emphasis upon a parallelism between the old and the new exodus, anticipated as early as Hosea (2: 14-18 [H 16-20]), was one of his major contributions to eschatology.[14]

In the first part of Second Isaiah's prophecy (chs. 40-48) the prophet often juxtaposes the "first things" (*ri'šōnôt*) and the

[12] See Gerhard von Rad, "Das theologische Problem der alttestamentlichen Schöpfungsglaubens," *Werden und Wesen des Alten Testaments*, BZAW 66 (1936), pp. 140-142; also *Theologie des Alten Testaments*, I (1957), pp. 144-157.

[13] Cf. Hermann Gunkel, *Schöpfung und Chaos in Urzeit und Endzeit* (2nd ed., 1921).

[14] Cf. Joachim Begrich, *Studien zu Deuterojesaja*, BWANT, 25 (1938), pp. 101-102. For a general discussion of this eschatological perspective, including the new exodus, see N. A. Dahl, *Das Volk Gottes* (1941), pp. 38-42.

"new things" (*haḏāšôṯ*) or the "things to come" (*bā'ôṯ, 'ōṯiyyôṯ*).[15]
The following passages develop this theme: (a) 41:21-29; (b)
42:6-9; (c) 43:8-13; (d) 43:14-21; (e) 44:6-8; (f) 45:20-21; (g)
46:8-11; (h) 48:3-8; (i) 48:14-16 (45:9-13 could be included
also, but the text of vs. 11 is uncertain). What does the prophet
mean by the "former things" and the "new things"?

Before venturing an answer to this question, it is important
to consider the theological context within which these passages
are placed, namely, Second Isaiah's argument from prophecy.
He scorns the idols of the nations because they cannot foretell
an event and bring it to pass, that is, they have no sovereignty
in history. Products of men's artifice, they are imprisoned within
the change and transcience of the times. They lack the two
major traits of deity: wisdom which fathoms the past and the
future, and power to realize their will and purpose. In a great
rîḇ or legal proceeding (cf. Mic. 6:1) they are brought to trial,
and the verdict is rendered that they are not gods at all (41:
21-29; cf. 43:8-13; 45:20-21). Yahweh, on the other hand, is the
true and only God, the Creator of heaven and earth and the
ruler of history. His deity is shown by his wisdom, which com-
prehends times past and times to come, and by his power to
bring to pass the purpose which he has announced to his prophetic servants. While the idols can produce no witnesses, the
people of Israel, out of their historical experience, stand as witnesses to Yahweh's sovereign wisdom and power, to his sole and
absolute deity (43:8-13).[16]

In accordance with ancient cosmology, Second Isaiah can
speak of divine transcendence in spatial imagery (40:22); but
more effectively and significantly he speaks of transcendence in
temporal terms. Yahweh is the "first" (*rī'šôn*) and the "last"
(*'aḥarôn*) (44:6; 48:12; cf. 41:4); before him there was no god,
neither shall any come after him (43:10). As the only, eternal
God, incomparable in majesty, he declares "the end (*'aḥarîṯ*)

[15] Cf. Franz Feldmann, "Das Frühere und das Neue," *Festschrift for Eduard Zachau* (1915), pp. 162-169; C. R. North, "The 'Former Things' and the 'New Things' in Deutero-Isaiah," *Studies in Old Testament Prophecy*, H. H. Rowley, ed. (1950), pp. 111-126.

[16] On the motif of the witness, see James Muilenburg, "The Form and Structure of the Covenantal Formulations," *VT*, IX (1959), pp. 347-365, especially pp. 354, 359-360, 363-364.

from the beginning (*mērē'šît*)," and "from ancient times" (*miqqédem*) things not yet done (46:10). History, therefore, is not capricious. The rise of Cyrus was not an accident or an unexpected event; it was part of the plan of Yahweh, who calls the generations "from the beginning" (*mērō'š*) (41:4). According to Second Isaiah the whole course of history, from beginning to end, is set within the purpose of the eternal God, the Creator and Sovereign.

Clearly the "new things" are the tremendous events that are about to take place in the wake of the rise of Cyrus: the overthrow of Babylon, Israel's return from exile, and the restoration of Zion—in a word, the new exodus. It is more difficult, however, to determine the "former things." At the very least it is clear that they were events that had been foretold and had already come to pass (42:9; 48:3, 5). But when did they occur? It has been argued that in some cases they were events of the relatively recent past, namely, the early victories of Cyrus, and that these fulfilled prophecies were made by Second Isaiah himself.[17] Admittedly, the time indications do not in themselves settle the question, and their meaning must be determined by the context. For instance, the expression *mē'āz* in 48:3, 5, 7 does not necessarily have to refer to events of remote antiquity; and in its immediate context vs. 16 apparently intends to emphasize that Yahweh's purpose had attended and prospered Cyrus from the moment he appeared on the world scene: "From the beginning (*mērō'š*) I have not spoken in secret, from the time it came to be (*mē'ēt heeyôtāh*) I have been there" (cf. also 41:25-27). Yet the passages concerning the "former things" must also be interpreted in the light of Second Isaiah's argument from prophecy which dominates all of these contexts. No mere appeal to the immediate past would support the prophet's proclamation that Yahweh alone is the sovereign of history and that his purpose embraces the times from beginning to end. He announced his purpose "long ago" (*miqqédem*), declared it "of old"

---

[17] This view is challenged by Feldmann, *op. cit.*, pp. 165-169, and is reaffirmed by North, *Studies in Old Testament Prophecy, loc. cit.* The latter believes that 41:21 ff., 43:8 ff., and 48:3 ff. refer to the victories of Cyrus before the fall of Sardis in 547 B.C., although he admits that other passages refer to a more distant past.

(*mē'āz*) (45:21). Israel is to remember "the former things of old" (*ri'šōnôt mē'ôlām*), for Yahweh is the only God, declaring "from ancient times" (*miqqédem*) things not yet done (46:9, 10).[18] Indeed, the prophet, speaking to a generation that experienced the claim of the nations' gods, insists that Yahweh foretold the "former things" long ago, when there was no "strange god" among the people (43:12), lest they should say: "My idol did them" (48:5). Even though Israel has been blind and deaf, the people are called as witnesses to a sacred history which reaches back to the beginning when Yahweh first announced his purpose and fulfilled it in decisive deeds. Probably the announcement "from of old" is to be identified with the promises to the patriarchs (so Muilenburg on 44:7); the "former things," then, are the events of Israel's *Heilsgeschichte,* pre-eminently the old exodus.

In one passage it is eminently clear that "the former things" belong to the *Urzeit.* In 43:16-19 the prophet harks back to the decisive moment in the Exodus story: the miracle at the Sea of Reeds. Even this dramatic event, however, will be overshadowed by the greater wonder of the new exodus, for Yahweh is about to do a "new thing." The prophet says, "Remember not the former things (*ri'šōnôt*), nor consider the things of old (*qadmōniyyôt*)." These "things of old" were Yahweh's saving acts, performed long ago when Israel "went down at the first (*bāri'šōnâ*) into Egypt" (52:4). In the prophet's mind the Exodus, the classical instance of Yahweh's act of redemption, is typical of the deliverance from Babylon, "the furnace of affliction" (48:10)—a phrase often applied to bondage in Egypt. It is significant that mention of the "former things" occurs in contexts dominated by the motif of the new exodus.

IV

Thus Second Isaiah interpreted what was happening in his day in the light of a historical memory which focused upon the

---

[18] In the emended text of 44:7 (followed by RSV), it is said that Yahweh announced "from of old" (*mē'ôlām*) the things to come; cf. vs. 8: "from of old" (*mē'āz*) he declared it.

events of Israel's sacred history. From the "crucial event" of the Exodus flowed consequences which, in his eschatological faith, were on the verge of reaching their consummation.

Two elements of this historical typology deserve special attention. First, the prophet discerns a correspondence between the events of the *Urzeit* and the *Endzeit,* between the "former things" and the "new things." There is a meaning common to the old exodus and the new. This parallelism, however, is not based upon mere poetic analogy: it is an expression of the unity and continuity of history in Yahweh's purposive and dynamic will. For this reason the gods of the nations are challenged to make known the "former things" so that men may know their meaning (lit. "take them to heart"; 41:22b), may know their *'aḥ°rît* or outcome; for the goal of history is understood in the light of the crucial events of the past in which the divine purpose was disclosed.

Moreover, the Exodus is a guarantee that Yahweh will redeem his people, for that event demonstrates that he has the wisdom and power to accomplish what he purposes. Second Isaiah spoke to a people in exile, in despair about the meaningfulness of their history and about Yahweh's power to give them a future. The prophet's intention is to awaken their confidence by proclaiming that Yahweh is the only Lord of history, for he accomplishes what he announces. Israel's redemption will surely come, for Yahweh's historical purpose runs consistently from the remote past to the present and on to the future which is yet to be. Just as in olden times he announced events before they happened and his word accomplished his purpose, so now his word accomplishes that which he purposes (55:10-11). Past prophecies which have already been fulfilled guarantee that Yahweh's announcement of the new exodus will become a historical reality; indeed, the first signs of the new era are already evident, like the streaks of dawn that herald a new day (43:19; 48:7). The rise of Cyrus, when viewed in the perspective of the events of the old exodus, is evidence that Yahweh has spoken: "My counsel shall stand, and I will accomplish all my purpose" (46:10; cf. 41:25-27; 48:14-16).[19]

[19] Cf. Feldmann, *op. cit.,* pp. 166-167.

According to ancient mythological thought, a correspondence existed between terrestrial and celestial things. Babylonian cities had their celestial archetypes and temples were constructed after models believed to exist in heaven. The Old Testament preserves an echo of this pagan typology in the instructions to Moses (P) that he should construct the tabernacle and its paraphernalia according to the "pattern" (*tabnît;* the LXX renders *tupos*) shown to him on the sacred mountain (Ex. 25:9, 40; cf. I Chr. 28:19). In Israel's tradition, however, a radical change took place: typology was shifted from a vertical celestial-earthly plane to a horizontal historical one.[20] Here the correspondence is between two temporal termini: the first things and the last things, protology and eschatology. From the standpoint of faith, a consistent purpose runs through history from first to last, undergirding the present with meaning. Thus Second Isaiah, in whom this theology of history is most profoundly articulate, shapes his vision of the eschatological finale according to the imagery of the old exodus.

Secondly, in Second Isaiah's typology of the old exodus and the new there is a *Steigerung* or heightening, like the shift of music into a new key as it crescendoes to a climax. It is erroneous to assume that the new exodus is the same as the old, as though the end-time were a return to primeval time. The prophet is conscious of a heightening of historical meaning. During the old exodus and wilderness journey Yahweh delivered his people with a mighty hand, drove back the waters of the Reed Sea, led his people through the trackless wilderness, and sustained them with food and water. But in the new exodus, historical conditions will be marvelously transformed: Yahweh will bare his holy arm before all the nations, will conquer the waters of the Deep as at the time of creation, will prepare a supernatural highway through the wilderness, and will convert the desert into a garden like Eden. To be sure, the traditions of the old exodus had already been heightened in the process of transmission and cultic usage, so that a *doxa* or glory enhanced the original events. Ex. 1-15, for instance, may reflect a cultic

---

[20] Cf. Gerhard von Rad, "Typologische Auslegung des Alten Testaments," EVT, XII (1952-53) , pp. 17-33; also Eliade, *op. cit.,* pp. 6-11.

legend which is concerned not with recounting the factual events of the Exodus but with reciting and reliving the sacred history which is the basis of Israel's relation to God. In the repetition of this cultic legend through the ages, the tradition was given an ever new meaning, surpassing the original historical experiences.[21] Second Isaiah, however, does not merely heighten the tradition a few degrees more: he transposes the whole sacred story into a higher key as he announces the good tidings of salvation. The new exodus will be a radically *new* event. It will surpass the old exodus not only in wonder but also in soteriological meaning, as evidenced by the theme of divine forgiveness which runs through the whole of his prophecy, or by the extension of salvation to include all nations.

The new event not only surpasses the old; it supersedes it in many respects. Thus the prophet traces elements of contrast between the old and the new exodus. In Moses' time the fugitives had to celebrate the Passover in haste (Dt. 16:3: $b^ehippāzôn$ $yāṣā'tā$; cf. Ex. 12:11), but of the new exodus it is said: "you shall not go out in haste" ($lō'$ $b^ehippāzôn$ $tēṣē'û$, Isa. 52:12); for Israel shall go out in joy and be led forth in peace (55:12). Unlike the old exodus, there will be no terrors or dangers along the way, and the people, instead of murmuring, will march with a faith that breaks forth into hymns of praise, the music of which will be taken up by the mountains and the hills. The new exodus will be accompanied by a new covenant, but not like the old contractual covenant of Moses. Second Isaiah avoids mention of the Mosaic covenant (cf. Jer. 31:31-34) and instead, with a theocentric emphasis, turns to the "everlasting covenant" ($b^erît$ '$ôlām$) made with David (II Sam. 23:5; cf. Ps. 89:29), a covenant of grace with no conditions required. Here, however, the $b^erît$ '$ôlām$ is not made with a member of the house of David, but with Israel (55:3), and is analogous to the permanent covenant made with Noah after the Flood (54:9-10).[22] The discontinuity between the old exodus and the new is so signifi-

---

[21] Cf. Johannes Pedersen, *Israel: Its Life and Culture*, III-IV (1940), pp. 401-415. This view is accepted with modification by Martin Noth, *Ueberlieferungsgeschichte des Pentateuch* (1948), pp. 70-77.

[22] Cf. Begrich, *op. cit.*, pp. 101-102.

cant that in one place (43:18-19), speaking with necessary paradox (cf. 46:8-11), the prophet urges the people not to remember the "former things," for Yahweh is doing a "new thing" which will overshadow and supersede the old.)

In this typology, then, there are elements of both continuity and discontinuity, of tradition and novelty. It is a misunderstanding to regard this kind of thinking as an expression of the pattern of cyclical repetition current in the ancient Near East.[23] Although there is a correspondence of meaning between the first things and the last things, the new exodus is not a return to the old in a great historical cycle. It is a new event, a new creation.

> From this time forth I make you hear new things,
>   hidden things which you have not known.
> They are created now, not long ago;
>   before today you have never heard them,
>   lest you should say, "Behold, I knew them" (48:6-7).

v

Another approach to this subject is proposed by Scandinavian scholars who emphasize the prevalence of mythological patterns of thinking throughout the ancient Near East. Ancient religions of Babylonia, Egypt, and Canaan were based upon the rhythmic cycle of the annual death and regeneration of nature, mythologically represented in the cultic drama of the death and resurrection of the god. In the Babylonian New Year festival, for instance, the cult myth recounted the primordial victory of Marduk over Tiamat, the goddess of watery chaos, and his enthronement as king for another year. In the cult drama this myth was re-enacted or reactualized, at which time the cycle returned to the beginning, to the "first things." It has been argued that a similar festival was celebrated in Israel. The enthronement psalms (Pss. 47, 93, 95-99) are said to reflect an Israelite cultic occasion on which Yahweh's primeval victory at creation was rehearsed and he was reacclaimed king.[24]

[23] As does Rudolf Bultmann, "Ursprung und Sinn der Typologie als hermeneutischer Methode," TLZ, 75 (1950), cols. 206-212.

[24] Cf. Sigmund Mowinckel, *Psalmenstudien*, II (1922).

This ancient mythology is echoed in various passages of the Old Testament. Often the sea is spoken of as a restless power, hostile to Yahweh's sovereignty and held in check by his creative power (e.g., Ps. 104:5-9; Pr. 8:27-29).[25] It is possible, too, that the mythological conversion of the fertile land into a desert has influenced Israel's tradition here and there.[26] But there is no convincing evidence that Yahweh was ever regarded as a dying-rising god and that pagan mythology was appropriated wholesale. Indeed, Israel's historical faith demanded a radical break with the patterns of pagan mythology and their metaphysical presuppositions. For the drive behind the cultic repetition of a mythological drama was the abolition of historical time, and it was precisely this flight from history which was at odds with Israel's faith.[27] What characterized Israelite worship was the remembrance and rehearsal of a real past. And when, under Canaanite or other influence, mythological forms were used, they were brought into the context of history and demythologized.

The historification of mythological motifs is clearly evident in Second Isaiah. In 51:9-11 he cites the old creation myth about the victory over the chaos monster, Rahab, in primeval time (cf. Isa. 27:1; Ps. 74:13).

> Awake, awake, put on strength,
>   O arm of Yahweh;
> Awake, as in the days of old (*yᵉmê qédem*),
>   the generations of long ago (*dōrôt 'ōlāmîm*)!
> Was it not thou that didst cut Rahab in pieces,
>   that didst pierce the dragon?
> Was it not thou that didst dry up Sea,
>   the waters of the great deep (*tᵉhôm rabbâ*);
> that didst make the depths of the sea a way
>   for the redeemed to pass over?

[25] In adition to Gunkel's work, *Schöpfung und Chaos*, see Otto Kaiser, *Die mythische Bedeutung des Meeres in Aegypten, Ugarit und Israel*, BZAW, 78 (1959); also H. G. May, "Some Cosmic Connotations of *Mayim Rabbîm*, 'Many Waters,'" JBL, LXXIV (1955), pp. 9-21.

[26] Cf. Alfred Haldar, *The Notion of the Desert in Sumero-Accadian and West-Semitic Religions* (1950).

[27] Cf. Eliade, *op. cit.;* Brevard S. Childs, *Myth and Reality in the Old Testament*, SBT, 27 (1960).

In a most revolutionary manner, the prophet identifies the mythical time of the conflict with the watery chaos with the historical time of the Exodus, when Yahweh prepared a way (*dérek*) for his people through the Sea of Reeds. Here the prophet has in mind the typological correspondence between the old exodus and the new. Elsewhere, too, he accommodates the chaos mythology to Israel's history. Yahweh makes a way in the sea, a path in the mighty waters (*máyim 'azzîm*, 43:16). He says to the Deep (*ṣûlâ*, probably the watery chaos, *tᵉhôm rabbâ*, cf. 51:10), "Be dry," in order to effect Israel's release through Cyrus (44:27). By his rebuke he dries up Sea (*yām*; see 51:10), and makes the rivers a desert (50:2), showing that his hand is powerful to redeem. Thus Second Isaiah employs mythological motifs in his elaboration of the typology of the old and the new exodus. Although he may have been familiar with the cult myth of the New Year festival, he has given it an eschatological meaning consonant with Israel's historical faith. He does not think of the new exodus as a return to the beginning, a repetition of the events of primeval time, but rather as "the absolutely New" which fulfills and completes the meaning of the old exodus.[28]

In summary, the prophecy of Second Isaiah represents a kind of historical interpretation which is completely different from those views, ancient or modern, whose axis is vertical: the relation between the heavenly and earthly, between eternity and time, between rational, timeless truths and historical illustrations. A faith which takes history with radical seriousness is expressed in a typology that juxtaposes "first things" and the "new things," the beginning and the end. Second Isaiah's eschatological hope is shaped by images drawn from Israel's *Heilsgeschichte*, particularly the crucial event of the Exodus, from which flow consequences reaching into the present and on into the future. The Exodus, then, is a "type" of the new exodus which will fulfill in a more wonderful fashion, with a deeper soteriological meaning, and with world-wide implications, Yah-

---

[28] See Aage Bentzen, "On the Ideas of 'the Old' and 'the New' in Deutero-Isaiah," ST, I, 1-2 (1948), pp. 183-187.

weh's purpose revealed by word and deed in the beginning.

It is not surprising that the New Testament, which has received the legacy of Israel's historical faith and is deeply dependent upon the eschatological good news of Second Isaiah, should also understand the relation between the old and the new in terms of historical typology.[29] There also we hear the good news that God, whose purpose was revealed in the events of Israel's history, has acted decisively in Christ: "the old has passed away, behold, the new has come" (II Cor. 5:17; cf. Rev. 21:5).

---

[29] See Harold Sahlin, "The New Exodus of Salvation According to St. Paul," in *The Root of the Vine*, Anton Fridrichsen, ed. (1953), pp. 18-95.

XIII

The Promises of Grace to David in Isaiah 55:1-5

OTTO EISSFELDT

The relationship between many of the poems of Second Isaiah and certain Psalms has been widely recognized and acknowledged. In the nineteenth and early twentieth centuries, Biblical scholars attributed this relationship to the literary dependence of such Psalms upon Second Isaiah, the Psalms thus being placed at a later date than Second Isaiah. Subsequently, however, things have taken a new turn. Thanks to the work of Hermann Gunkel on the Psalms,[1] begun as early as 1903, and the *Psalmenstudien* of Sigmund Mowinckel,[2] which appeared in 1921-24, the majority of the psalms are no longer assigned to the post-Exilic period. Hugo Gressmann's essay on "Die literarische Analyse Deutero-jesajas"[3] also demonstrated the influence of older literary forms, represented in the Psalter, upon Second Isaiah. As a result, by far the majority of scholars now agree that the relationship between many of the poems of Second Isaiah and the literature of the Psalms is to be explained by the influence of the latter upon the prophet of the Exile. This is not to say that the particular psalms handed down to us in the Psalter have exer-

---

[1] See "Hermann Gunkels Bücher und Schriften" by Johannes Hempel, *Eucharisterion, Hermann Gunkel zum 60. Geburtstage,* Teil II (1923), pp. 214-225.

[2] *Âwän und die indiviluellen Klagespsalmen* (1921); II. *Das Thronbesteigungsfest Jahwäs und der Ursprung der Eschatologie* (1922); III. *Kultprophetie und prophetische Psalmen* (1923); IV. *Die technischen Termini in den Psalmenüberschriften* (1923); V. *Segen und Fluch in Israels Kult und Psalmdichtung* (1924); VI. *Die Psalmdichter* (1924).

[3] ZAW, 34 (1914), pp. 254-297.

cised this influence upon Second Isaiah; we are not in a position to demonstrate with certainty that this or that psalm has been the model for this or that poem of Second Isaiah. The psalms preserved for us in the Old Testament represent only a minute portion of the much richer poetic materials once possessed by Israel. Thus, in my opinion, the similarities between certain psalms and the words of Second Isaiah can and are to be accounted for by the fact that both have drawn upon a common source. With this in mind, one should be very cautious about designating particular psalms of our Psalter as prototypes of particular verses of Second Isaiah, e.g., the "enthronement psalms" as models of those poems in Isa. 40-55 reminiscent of them. The question may well be considered, however, whether and to what extent the prophet, while adopting earlier literary forms, has preserved or transformed their contents. Indeed, it is to be hoped that through such inquiry a deeper understanding of the message of Second Isaiah may be achieved. To this end, a comparison might be made between Ps. 89, a song of lamentation and supplication, and the word of encouragement and promise found in Isa. 55:1-5; or more precisely, a comparison of the meaning of the "inviolable promises of grace to David," which stand at the center of both passages.

I

One must assume that Ps. 89 had its origin in a time when a descendant of David still sat upon the throne in Jerusalem.[4] Despite all arguments to the contrary,[5] the psalm displays literary unity: it consists of a hymn to Yahweh, who has promised grace to David and to his house (vss. 2-38), a lamentation over the violation of this promise (vss. 39-47), and a moving supplication for removal of the bitter national distress which had called the promise into question (vss. 48-53). In all three parts—and this

[4] Support for this presupposition cannot be given here; cf. the literature cited in H.-J. Kraus *Psalmen*, I-II (*Biblischer Kommentar, Altes Testament*, XV, 1960), p. 612.

[5] Among those who deny the unity of Ps. 89 are H. Gunkel, *Die Psalmen*, HKAT, II, 2, 4th ed. (1926), and Hans Schmidt, *Die Psalmen*, HAT, Erste Reihe, 15 (1934).

fact suffices to demonstrate the unity of the psalm—reference is made, at times recurrently, to the promise of grace to David, the covenant made with him, the oath sworn to him, etc. (vs. 2, ḥasdê yhwh, "Yahweh's promises of grace," 'ᵃᵉmûnātᵉkā, "thy faithfulness"; vs. 3, ḥésed, "grace," 'ᵃᵉmûnātᵉkā, "thy faithfulness"; vs. 4, bᵉrît, "covenant," nišbá'tî, "I have sworn"; vs. 25, 'ᵃᵉmûnātî wᵉḥasdî, "my faithfulness and my grace"; vs. 29, ḥasdî ûbᵉrîtî, "my grace and my covenant"; vs. 34, ḥasdî, "my grace," 'ᵃᵉmûnātî, "my faithfulness"; vs. 35, bᵉrîtî, "my covenant," môṣá šᵉpātay, "my promise"; vs. 36, nišbá'tî, "I have sworn"; vs. 40, bᵉrît, "covenant"; vs. 50, ḥᵃsādêkā hāri'šōnîm, "thy former promises of grace," nišbá'tā lᵉdawid be'ᵃᵉmûnātᵉkā, "which thou didst swear to David in thy faithfulness"). Likewise the promises of grace bestowed upon David are found among words of encouragement and promise proclaimed by Second Isaiah to Israel —or more precisely, to the Jews who were languishing with him in Babylonian exile:[6]

> ¹Ho, all who thirst, come to the waters,
>   and those who have no money, come!
> Buy bread and eat, yea come, buy without money
>   and without price wine and milk!
> ²Why will you spend money for that which is not bread
>   and your labor for that which does not satisfy?
> Hearken to me, that you may eat what is good
>   and let your soul delight itself in fatness!
> ³Incline your ear and come to me,
>   hear, that your soul may live!
> I am making with you an everlasting covenant,
>   the inviolable promises of grace to David.
> ⁴Behold, I have made him a witness to the peoples,
>   a leader and commander for the peoples.
> ⁵Behold, thou dost call nations that thou dost not know,
>   and those who do not know thee run to thee
> Thanks to Yahweh thy God,
>   and to the Holy One of Israel, who glorifies thee.
>
> (RSV)

---

[6] The unity of the section 55:1-5, denied by P. Volz, Jesaia II (Kommentar zum Alten Testament, IX, 2 [1932]), seems to me to be defensible. J. Begrich, "Studien zu Deuterojesaja," BWANT, Vierte Folge, Heft 15 (1938), pp. 53 f., also rightly rejects the division of the section by Volz into vss. 1-3a and vss. 3b-5.

II

Thus both Ps. 89, a prayer in behalf of a descendant of David on the throne of Jerusalem,[7] and the word of encouragement and promise proclaimed by the Prophet of the Exile speak of the inviolable promises of grace which Yahweh once made to David. And in both cases, the recollection of these promises signifies the arousal of hope and trust. In view of the above-mentioned dependence of Second Isaiah upon earlier psalmody in general and the presumed pre-Exilic origin of Ps. 89, it is entirely conceivable that this psalm was known to our prophet and that it provided the impulse for his reference to the promises given by Yahweh to David. But since the recollection of such a promise clearly played a great role in the period following and was kept alive not only in the story of the promise to David of an everlasting dynasty (II Sam. 7) but also in other forms (Jer. 33:20 f.; II Chr. 6:42),[8] the fact that this promise plays an important role in both passages under consideration is insufficient argument for believing that Ps. 89 actually prompted Second Isaiah to revive it. Of even greater significance is the fact that both our psalm and Second Isaiah support their petitions for Yahweh's saving intervention or the promise thereof with the reference to Yahweh's power—power such as was revealed in his overcoming of the powers of chaos and in his action as Creator (Ps. 89:6-15; Isa. 41:12-31; 51:9-11 and elsewhere). In so doing both Ps. 89 and Isa. 55:1-5 employ many of the same words and expressions, not often found elsewhere: $b^e\hbar îrî$, "my Elect One,"

[7] The "I" ($^a nî$), vs. 48, and the "my" in "my bearing in my bosom" ($\acute{s}^{e^*}\bar{e}t\hbar b^e\hbar \hat{e}q\hat{\imath}$), vs. 51, could be and have been used to show that the spokesman of our psalm is to be understood as the king himself. But the $^{*e} nî$ of vs. 48 is perhaps to be altered to $^{*e} d\acute{o}n\bar{a}y$, "O Lord," just as such an $^{*e} d\acute{o}n\bar{a}y$ is found in vs. 50; and the "my" in "my bearing in my bosom," vs. 51, may be understood in a collective sense: "our bearing in our bosom." This latter meaning is made the more probable by the fact that the singular "my" in "my bearing in my bosom" stands in parallelism with the plural $^{'a}b\bar{a}d\acute{e}k\bar{a}$, "thy servants"—in the sense of "thy worshipers." It is true that some manuscripts here read $^{'}abd\acute{e}k\bar{a}$, "thy servant"—clearly a reference to the king—and some exegetes accept this reading as correct.

[8] From the wealth of literature on this subject, see L. Rost, Die Ueberlieferung von der Thronnachfolge Davids, BWANT, Dritte Folge, Heft 6 (1926); Rost, "Sinaibund und Davidsbund," TLZ, 72 (1947), cols. 129-134; G. von Rad, "Das judäische Königsritual," TLZ, 72 (1947), cols. 211-216.

Ps. 89:4 and Isa. 42:1; 43:20; 45:4; *mî yaʿarōk lyhwh yidmeh lyhwh,* "Who is like Yahweh, who compares with Yahweh?" Ps. 89:7, and *'el mî tᵉdammᵉyûn 'ēl ûmâ dᵉmût taʿarkû lô,* "With whom will you compare God and what likeness will you put beside him?" Isa. 40:18; *yhwh mî kāmôkā,* "Yahweh, who is like thee?" Ps. 89:9, and *mî kāmônî,* "Who is like me?" Isa. 44:7; *'attâ môšēl bᵉgē'ût hayyām,* "Thou rulest over the pride of the sea," Ps. 89:10, and *hēn bᵉgaʿᵃrātî 'ahᵃrîb yām,* "Lo, by my rebuke I dry up the sea," Isa. 50:2, as well as *hᵃlô' 'at hî' hammahᵃrébet yām,* "Is it not thou who didst dry up the sea?" Isa. 51:10; *'attâ dikki'tā kehālāl rahab,* "Thou didst bore Rahab through like a carcass," Ps. 89:11, and *hᵃlô' 'at hî' hammahṣébet rahab,* "Is it not thou who didst cut Rahab in pieces?" Isa. 51:9; *bizᵉrôaʿ 'wzzᵉkā,* "with thy strong arm," Ps. 89:11, as well as *lᵉkā zᵉrôaʿ 'im gᵉbûrâ,* "Thine is both arm an dstrength," Ps. 89:14, and *zᵉrô'ay 'ammîm yišpōṭû . . . wᵉ'el zᵉrô'î yᵉyahēlûn,* "My arms judge the peoples . . . they hope in my arms," Isa. 51:5, and also *'ûrî 'ûrî libšî 'ōz zᵉrôaʿ yhwh,* "Awake, awake, clothe yourself with strength, arm of Yahweh!" Isa. 51:9; *tēbēl ûmᵉlō'āh 'attâ yᵉsadtām,* "The earth and it fulness, thou hast established them," Ps. 89:12, and *'ap yādî yāsᵉdâ 'éreṣ,* "Yea, my hand has established the earth," Isa. 48:13 (cf. 51:13, 16); *tēbēl ûmᵉlō'āh,* "the earth and its fulness," Ps. 89:12, and *hayyām ûmᵉlō'ô,* "the sea and its fulness," Isa. 42:10; *ṣāpôn wᵉyāmîn 'attâ bᵉrā'tām,* "North and South, thou hast created them," Ps. 89:13, and *yhwh bôrē' qᵉṣôt hā'āreṣ,* "Yahweh, Creator of the ends of the earth," Isa. 40:28 (cf. 40:26; 41:20; 42:5; 43:1, 7, 8, 12, 18); *tārûm yᵉmînékā,* "exalted is thy right hand," Ps. 89:14, and *tᵉmaktîkā bîmîn ṣidqî,* "I support thee with my victorious right hand," Isa. 41:10 (cf. 45:1).

It can be seen that the poems of Second Isaiah are in more than a few instances strikingly reminiscent of Ps. 89; accordingly the possibility that the prophet knew this psalm and that he let it influence him, particularly in his adoption of the motif of the promises of grace to David, deserves the most serious consideration. Nevertheless, all of the above evidence scarcely suffices to demonstrate such dependence. Only one thing is clear: whether or not direct connections exist between the remembrance of the promises of grace to David as expressed in Ps. 89 and their revival in Second Isaiah, the prophet's reference to these promises has an entirely different purpose from that of the author of Ps. 89. A consideration of this difference in purpose can contribute decisively to a better understanding of the proclamation of Second Isaiah in general and in particular to his word of encouragement and promise as found in Isa. 55:1-5.

III

The goal which the poet of Ps. 89 has in mind in his lamentation and petition is clearly the removal of the calamity which has befallen his king and his people. And the petitioner is convinced that the realization of this goal would be furthered and hastened by reminding God of the promises made to David, the founder of the Jerusalem dynasty. The recipient of these promises is Yahweh's "Elect One" ($b^e\underline{h}îrî$, vs. 4), Yahweh's "Servant" ($'abdî$, vs. 4, 21; $'abd\acute{e}k\bar{a}$, vs. 40), and his descendant, who now sits upon the throne, is Yahweh's "Anointed" ($m^e\check{s}î\underline{h}\acute{e}k\bar{a}$, vss. 39, 52). This position of honor held by David and his descendants justifies the hope that Yahweh will take account of them and will feel an obligation to come to their aid. It is utterly unthinkable to our poet that the kingly rule of the Davidic line might be at an end. Rather, he takes it for granted that David's dynasty must continue forever. To be sure, the great calamity which has descended upon king and people puts this certainty to a very severe test. Their distress goes far beyond that which would be comprehensible and endurable: it is no mere affliction, designed to bring king and people back to the rightful way which they have abandoned; nor is it a punishment designed to educate rather then to effect vengeance or destruction. It is rather a catastrophe which threatens the continuance of throne and kingdom, a catastrophe all the more severe since it provides welcome occasion for the enemies to scoff at Yahweh's people and so at Yahweh himself. The psalmist cannot come to an understanding of such terrible calamity—he sees it only as a sign that God cannot or will not keep the promise once made to David. Thus a moving lament over the national distress—a situation which throws doubt upon the promise of God (vss. 39-45) and whose ill effects touch the person of the king himself (vss. 46-47)—and allusions to the frailty of human life and to the scornful triumph of the enemies over the people, a triumph which stands in flat contradiction to the promise made to David and which in the last analysis means dishonor for Yahweh himself, conclude his prayer for the king, who is once more impressively described as Yahweh's Anointed (vss. 50-52).

How different is the word of encouragement and promise of the Prophet of the Exile in Isa. 55:1-5! In his message, the fulfillment of the promise of grace to David lies not in the coming of a descendant of David who will once again sit upon the throne in Jerusalem and, as the highest of earthly kings (Ps. 89:28), rule over a kingdom stretching from the Mediterranean to Mesopotamia (Ps. 89:26). It means rather that the people who now languish in exile will achieve high honor, in that they will find friendly reception and grateful recognition among people hitherto unknown. The language of Isa. 55:1-2 is metaphorical; one cannot determine with certainty what is meant, on the one hand, by the thirst which is to be quenched and hunger which is to be satisfied, or, on the other, by the water, bread, and good rich food which will remedy the want. But so much is certain: vss. 1-2a depict the distress of the exiles, their longing for aid, and their recourse to any means of salvation, however ineffectual. Vss. 2b-3 set over against such futile efforts the reality who alone can help—Yahweh—and call upon the promise of grace which Yahweh formerly made to David. David himself, according to vs. 4, saw the fulfillment of this promise in Yahweh's having appointed him witness for the peoples, that is, proclaimer of the might and greatness of Yahweh as well as prince and ruler of the peoples. With vs. 5 the passage turns to Israel at that time—to the exiles. Authority over other peoples is not envisaged for them. Rather, it is proclaimed that Israel will henceforth call to herself many whom she did not formerly know, and that many who formerly knew nothing of Israel will hasten to her. In this way will Yahweh glorify Israel. With this promise, nothing is meant apart from that which stands elsewhere at the center of the proclamation of Second Isaiah, particularly in the Servant Songs:[9] that Israel, through her vicarious suffering and her silent witness, will convey to all the world the worship of Yahweh, finding grateful recognition on all sides in the fulfillment of this high calling.

IV

In Isa. 55:1-5, as elsewhere in Second Isaiah, there is no reference whatever to that which, for the author of Ps. 89, is the particular content of the promise of God to David: that a Davidic representative should always sit upon the Jerusalem throne and rule over the other nations. This is hardly accidental, for our Exilic prophet does not count the Davidic kingdom among the blessings hoped for in the coming Day of Salvation—though it remains uncertain whether he wanted this to be understood as a complete renunciation or whether he believed it necessary to discard this expectation merely for the time being. In this regard Second Isaiah differs from his predecessors Jeremiah (23:5-6; 33:14-26) and Ezekiel (34; 37:15-28), who expect that on the future Day of Salvation the people will be ruled by David or a Davidic descendant. The prophet also differs from his successors Haggai (2:23) and Zechariah (3:8; 4:6-10; 6:9-15), who see in Zerubbabel the promised Davidic descendant. Thus the honorific title "Yahweh's Anointed," which as we saw was of the greatest importance to the author of Ps. 89, is found nowhere in Isa. 40-55 as the designation for an Israelite figure; it is rather conferred upon a non-Israelite, Cyrus (45:1), and thus withdrawn from the Davidic dynasty. Nor does Second Isaiah apply the word "king" to an Israelite. Except when he uses the term in reference to the kings of other peoples, as in Isa. 41:2; 45:1; 49:7; 23; 52:15, he speaks

[9] It must here be assumed both that the so-called "Servant Songs" stem from the Second Isaiah himself and that the 'Ebed (Servant) in these songs refers to Israel—that is, to the exiles as representatives of the people of Israel. On these questions, see now Otto Kaiser, "Der königliche Knecht; eine traditionsgeschichtlich-exegestische Studie über die Ebed-Jahwe-Lieder bei Deuterojesaja," FRLANT, Neue Folge, Heft 52 (1959), and the literature referred to on pp. 140-145.

only of Yahweh as king: 41:21, "says Yahweh, says the King of Jacob"; 43:15, "I am Yahweh your Holy One, the Creator of Israel, your King"; 52:7, "He who says, 'Thy God is King.'"

Here it would be worth while to compare the titles "Elect One of Yahweh" (*beḥîr*) and "Servant of Yahweh" (*'ebed*) as they appear first in Ps. 89 and later in Isa. 40-55. In the psalm, David is designated both "Elect One of Yahweh" (vs. 4, *beḥîrî*) and "Servant of Yahweh" (*'abdî*, vss. 4, 21; *'abdékā*, vs. 40), whereas in Second Isaiah the two predicates are used exclusively in reference to Israel and Jacob, i.e., to the exiles who represent all Israel.[10] With regard to the first title, we read in Isa. 42:1 the words of Yahweh, "Behold, my Servant whom I support; my Elect One, in whom my soul delights"; also 43:20, "to give drink to my elect people," and 45:4, "for the sake of my Servant Jacob and my Elect One Israel." In the case of the predicate "Servant," it is clear in certain passages that the term refers to Israel and Jacob, inasmuch as Israel or Jacob is specifically designated. These passages are 41:8, "And thou, Israel, my Servant; Jacob, whom I have chosen; seed of Abraham my friend"; 44:1, "And now hear, Jacob, my Servant, and Israel, whom I have chosen"; 44:2, "Fear thou not, my Servant Jacob, and Jeshurun, whom I have chosen"; 44:21, "Remember these things, Jacob, and Israel, for thou art my Servant; I have formed thee for my Servant; thou wilt not be forgotten by me"; 45:4, "for the sake of my Servant Jacob, and of Israel my Elect One"; 48:20, "Say, 'Yahweh has redeemed his Servant Jacob'"; 49:3, "And he said to me, 'My Servant art thou, Israel, in whom I will be glorified.'" But throughout other passages as well—including the "Servant Songs"—the designation "Servant of Yahweh" refers to the people as follows: 41:9, "And I said to thee, 'My Servant art thou; I have chosen thee and have not cast thee off'"; 42:1, "Behold, my Servant, whom I support; my Elect One, in whom my soul delights"; 42:19, "Who is blind but my Servant, and

[10] In Isa. 44:26, where the plural *'abādāw*, "his servants," is probably to be read in place of the singular *'abdô*, "his Servant," the reference is to the prophets as Yahweh's servants. Isa. 49:7, where *'ebed* in the expression *'ebed mōš'lîm*, "servant of the rulers," is probably not used in the customary sense of an honorific predicate, is left out of consideration here. Also left out of account is the expression *'abdê yhwh* in 54:17, since "servants" is here apparently employed in the wider sense of "worshipers, adherents (of Yahweh)."

deaf as my messenger whom I send? Who is blind as the trusted one,[11] and blind as the Servant of Yahweh?"; 43:10, "You are my witnesses," says Yahweh, "and my Servant, whom I have chosen"; 49:5, "And now spoke Yahweh who formed me from my mother's womb to be his Servant"; 49:6, "And he said, 'It is too light a thing that thou art my Servant' "; 50:10, "Who among you fears Yahweh, hearkens to the voice of his Servant?"; 52:13, "Behold, my Servant will prosper; he will be lifted up and exalted and very high"; 53:11, "By his knowledge will the Righteous One, my Servant, make many to be righteous, and he will bear their iniquity." Second Isaiah could certainly have applied the predicates "Yahweh's Elect One" and "Yahweh's Servant" to David, just as he designated him in 55:4 *ēd*, "witness," the plural of which, *ēday*, "my witnesses," is found in 43:10 in parallelism with *abdî*, "my Servant." But significantly Second Isaiah reserves both predicates for the people of Israel, i.e., for their representatives, the exiles. In this way he means to indicate that the endeavor of the exiles—their patient suffering and persistent testimony—constitutes the crown and completion of all that was accomplished by the former bearers of the titles "Yahweh's Elect One" and "Yahweh's Servant," namely, by Moses and David and the prophets.

In yet another way the comparison of Ps. 89 with Isa. 55:1-5 and with the message of the prophet in general provides a deeper understanding of Second Isaiah. The worshiper of Ps. 89 stands helpless and bewildered before the deep suffering which has broken upon his king and his people; only with moving laments can he petition for its removal. Second Isaiah, on the other hand, is able not only to overcome in his own experience the much greater distress which has befallen him and his contemporaries but also to provide his companions in suffering with courage and power to do the same. By making known to them the enduring majesty of their God, Creator of heaven and earth, he enables the exiles to gain new confidence in God and in his readiness to help them, and he gives the people hope by opening their eyes to the blessing which their suffering, accord-

---

[11] The meaning of *mešullām* is uncertain. On this term cf. J. L. Palache, "The 'Ebed-Jahveh Enigma in Pseudo-Isaiah," *Sinai en Paran. Opera Minora* (1959), pp. 69-98 (reprinted from *The 'Ebed-Jahveh Enigma in Pseudo-Isaiah*, [1943]).

ing to God's will, will bring to all the world. The former, Yahweh's capacity and willingness to help, is stated in Isa. 55:1-3; the latter, the task which Israel has to perform for the world and the grateful recognition which awaits her in its fulfillment, in Isa. 55:4-5. Although these verses only intimate rather than clearly express what is meant, there can be no doubt that Israel is here given the same promise which is found elsewhere in Isa. 40-55, particularly in the "Servant Songs," 42:1-9; 49:1-6; 50:4-11 and 52:13-53:12. It is true that the assertion in 55:4-5 is—in part owing to brevity—less emphatic than that found in the verses of 52:13-53:12 which deal with the glorification of the Servant of Yahweh; in like manner, the somewhat unimpassioned description of the exiles' suffering found in 55:1-3 contrasts sharply with the stirring and powerful way in which other sections of chs. 40-55, in particular the relevant verses from 52:13-53:12, describe their tribulation. Yet in both instances the contrasting verses deal with the same subject: the seemingly hopeless distress of the exiles and its coming resolution, which will bring salvation and blessing to all the world and high recognition to Israel.

v

In conclusion, the relationship which exists between Ps. 89 and Isa. 55:1-5—their common reference to Yahweh's covenant with David and to the promises of grace made to him—can be termed only a formal and superficial one. In terms of content, the latter passage is entirely different from the former. In Ps. 89 the content of the promise is interpreted exclusively in the continued existence of the Davidic dynasty—the current threat to which calls the validity of the promise into question. Second Isaiah, however, places the promise before the fate of Israel and its royal house and declares its eternal validity.[12] In so doing, he relates the promise to the mission of Israel in the world, a mis-

---

[12] Cf. Johannes Pedersen, "Additions to the Second Edition" (of *Israel, Its Life and Culture* III-IV [1940]), 1959, p. 794: "The royal feast could only be actual for a few centuries, but it gave the people of Israel a claim for the future through the eschatology, the people taking over the inheritance of the king."

sion which is Israel's destiny and which will bring her honor and recognition. Where Ps. 89 displays a static-rigid conception of the promise of Yahweh, Second Isaiah interprets it in a dynamic-activistic sense: he prevents its becoming involved in the collapse of the Davidic dynasty and thus insures its permanent validity.

XIV

The Samaritan Schism in Legend and History

H. H. ROWLEY

It has long been recognized that the Samaritans receive less than due justice in the pages of the Old Testament. The account of the fall of Samaria in II Kg. 17 gives the reader the impression that the whole of the population of the northern kingdom was carried into captivity,[1] that they were replaced by people brought from various foreign cities,[2] that these colonists subsequently received instruction in the Israelite religion by a single priest who was brought back for the purpose and who dwelt in Bethel,[3] but that they carried on their native idolatries beside this religion.[4] There are inner inconsistencies in the story, suggesting that a later hand has added to it.[5] For instance, in one verse we read that the newcomers feared Yahweh alongside their own gods,[6] while in the following verse we are told that they did not fear Yahweh.[7] The complete unfairness of this story to the Samaritans is often pointed out; nevertheless, it is not seldom referred to as giving a reliable account of the origin of the Samaritan community[8] and an explanation of the relations

[1] II Kg. 17:6; cf. vs. 18.
[2] II Kg. 17:24.
[3] II Kg. 17:28.
[4] II Kg. 17:29 ff.
[5] Cf., e.g., Benzinger, *Könige*, KHC (1899), p. 175; C. F. Burney, *Notes on the Books of Kings* (1903), p. 333; Montgomery-Gehman, *Kings*, ICC (1951), p. 471.
[6] II Kg. 17:33.
[7] II Kg. 17:34.
[8] So, among others, C. W. Wilson, in Hastings' DB, IV (1902), p. 376a; R. A. S. Macalister, in Hastings' D.B. (one vol.) (1909), p. 821a; A. Parrot, in Westphal's

that developed between Jerusalem and Samaria. On the other hand, some scholars have conjectured that it reflects, rather than explains, the relations that developed.[9]

Sargon records that he deported 27,290 people from the northern kingdom after the fall of Samaria.[10] It has been estimated that this represented at the most one-twentieth of the population of the kingdom.[11] The great bulk of the population, therefore, continued to be Israelite. There is no reason to doubt that the Assyrian transferred some people from other districts of his empire to take the place of those deported; but there is much evidence in the Old Testament itself to show that the vilification of the Samaritan population in the passage referred to is without justification. This is the more remarkable since an anti-Samaritan bias has been imposed upon so much of the Old Testament.

Few will gainsay that the Book of Deuteronomy was compiled after the fall of Samaria.[12] It is still the most widely held view that this book was prepared at some time in the seventh century B.C., and to the present writer it seems most probable that it was compiled early in the reign of Manasseh as the program of a new reform of religion that should take account of the lessons of Hezekiah's abortive effort to centralize religion. The long reign of Manasseh and the unimpaired sway of Assyria throughout the reign of Ashurbanipal postponed all opportunity for reform until those who had prepared Deuteronomy were dead, and the program lay unknown somewhere in the Temple until it was discovered in the reign of Josiah.[13] The links of Deuteronomy with the northern traditions as embodied in the E

Dictionnaire encyclopédique de la Bible (1932), II, p. 619a; H. Haag's Bibel-lexikon (1951), p. 1460; Steinmueller-Sullivan, Catholic Biblical Encyclopedia, O.T. (1956), p. 950; O. Plöger, in Brunotte-Weber, Evangelisches Kirchenlexikon, III (1959), p. 781.

[9] So, e.g., W. E. Barnes, Kings, Cambridge Bible (1908), p. 90.

[10] Cf. ANET (2nd ed., 1955), p. 285a, or D. Winton Thomas, Documents from Old Testament Times (1958), p. 59.

[11] Cf. H. G. May, BA, VI (1943), p. 58.

[12] A few scholars, including A. C. Welch, T. Oestreicher, and E. Robertson, have argued for earlier dates but have found little following.

[13] II Kg. 22:8.

document of the Pentateuch have been noted by many scholars,[14] and several have thought that the unnamed central sanctuary of this book was not, in the minds of the compilers, Jerusalem but the older northern sanctuary of Shechem.[15] If this is indeed so, it would seem that in the circles from which Deuteronomy emanated the Samaritans were not regarded as alien idolaters any more than the people of the south.

This is not to suggest that religious conditions in northern Israel were satisfactory after the fall of Samaria any more than they had been earlier, or any more than they continued to be in the southern kingdom. It is but to say that there is no evidence that they were seriously worsened by deportations. The account of the reign of Manasseh which stands in II Kings presents no rosy picture of the purity of religion in the south, and foreign religious practices were certainly as current in Judah as they were in the north.[16]

The book of Deuteronomy belongs to the Samaritan Pentateuch no less than to the Jewish, and it is therefore certain that the Samaritans found no anti-Samaritan bias in this work. There are certain well-known differences between the Samaritan text and the Hebrew,[17] and it is possible that deliberate anti-Samaritan alterations may have been made;[18] but the sacredness and importance of the Shechem area are clearly acknowledged,[19] while there is no word that points unmistakably to the sacredness of Jerusalem. There is therefore nothing to suggest that the compilers of Deuteronomy regarded the Samaritan community in the unfavorable light of II Kg. 17, though there would

[14] Cf., e.g., Oesterley-Robinson, *Introduction to the Old Testament* (1934), p. 50; L. Gautier, *Introduction à l'Ancien Testament* (3rd ed., 1939), I, p. 139; J. Hempel, *Die althebräische Literatur* (1930), pp. 126, 139.

[15] W. F. Albright thinks the nucleus of the material of Deuteronomy came from Shechem (*From the Stone Age to Christianity* [2nd ed., 1946], p. 241); cf. also B. Luther in E. Meyer, *Die Israeliten und ihre Nachbarstämme* (1906), pp. 542 ff.; G. A. Danell, *Studies in the Name Israel* (1946), p. 55 f.

[16] II Kg. 21:1-18.

[17] Cf. E. König, in Hastings' DB, Extra Vol. (1904), pp. 69 f.

[18] The most notable of these is Dt. 27:4, where the Samaritan text has Gerizim for the Hebrew Ebal. Little motive for a deliberate alteration is apparent, however, and the Hebrew is probably the superior reading (cf. König, *op. cit.*, p. 70b).

[19] Dt. 11:29, 27:12. The latter passage is generally held not to have belonged to the original form of Deuteronomy.

be every reason so to regard that community if II Kg. 17 were a true picture. For Deuteronomy is inflexibly opposed to every form of idolatry, and equally opposed to all Canaanite influence because of its religious menace. It could scarcely be supposed that its compilers would be any less averse to the influence of foreign immigrants, likewise alleged to be a religious menace, or that they would contemplate the placing of the one legitimate sanctuary in their midst.

In the days when Deuteronomy was compiled—if the view that it was compiled in the reign of Manasseh is correct—reforming circles could not easily think of the house of David as the guardians of the true Yahwistic tradition, or of the Temple of Solomon as the center of pure worship in harmony with Mosaic tradition. It could well seem to them that reversion to the older northern shrine of Shechem and to the Mosaic tradition which was brought into the land by the people under the leadership of the Ephraimite Joshua—a tradition associated with the Ark, which belonged to the north before it was brought into Jerusalem by David—would provide a better prospect. In addition, it may well have seemed to them that a single sanctuary for the entire land, to be visited by all the Israelite tribes, would be better situated in the center of the land than in Jerusalem.

It was circumstances that determined otherwise. The book of the Law was found in Jerusalem at a time when Judah had a pious and reforming king and the Temple was being cleansed and restored.[20] At such a time it was little wonder that the unnamed central sanctuary of Deuteronomy was identified with the Jerusalem Temple, or that this book became the program of a reform that had already begun. Josiah naturally aspired to be the leader of northern Israel no less than of Judah, and the story that he carried his reform of religion into the north is wholly credible. The reform was the religious side of a bid for freedom. The Assyrian empire was crumbling, and the western states that she had subdued thought the day of liberation had come. The northern tribes no less than Judah must have longed

[20] II Kg. 22:8.

for deliverance. The pitiful years that had preceded the fall of Samaria had left them with no royal line of their own to which they could look for leadership in that hour, and they could hardly do other than welcome the opportunity to make common cause with Judah under the leadership of Josiah, when it promised them freedom from the Assyrian yoke.

In the half-century that followed the reform of Josiah, the Deuteronomic historical work was compiled. One of the marks of this work is its insistence on Jerusalem as the sole legitimate center of worship. To the compilers of this work the unnamed central shrine of Deuteronomy was identified with the Temple, with which it had by now become historically associated through the finding of the book of the Law within its precincts. While we have no record of any challenge to this association from the north at that time, it may well be that there was such a challenge and that this lies behind the anti-Samaritan spirit which marks the Deuteronomic historical work. We know that in a later age there was a dispute between the Samaritan community and the Jews on this question, and there is every presumption that from the start the Samaritan community was aware of all in the book of Deuteronomy that pointed to Shechem and resented the transfer of the central sanctuary to Jerusalem. In the Deuteronomic historical work the northern kingdom is condemned from its inception because its people were diverted from the Jerusalem shrine. If the distorted legend of II Kg. 17 comes in its original form from the hands of the compilers of the Books of Kings, it springs from the same anti-Samaritan bias, though there seems some reason to suppose that it is a post-Exilic addition to the book, reflecting the growing bitterness of later times.[21]

It is significant that Ezekiel does not share this anti-Samaritan feeling and knows nothing of the legend of the substitution of heathen nations for Israelites.[22] In his view Jerusalem was a city of doubtful racial purity. He roundly declares that it was of mixed Amorite and Hittite origin.[23] There is at least as much to be said for this as for the charge of alien origin made against

[21] Cf. Barnes, loc. cit.

[22] Cf. M. Gaster, The Samaritans (1925), p. 14.

[23] Ezek. 16:3, 45. On these verses cf. E. Nielsen, Shechem (1955), pp. 324 ff.

the Samaritans in II Kg. 17. After the Israelite entry into the land, the city of Jerusalem continued to be a Jebusite stronghold until the time of David, when it was conquered and made the capital of the Israelite kingdom.[24] Its people were not annihilated but treated with clemency and generosity, and the Old Testament offers no reason for supposing that they did not continue to inhabit the city alongside the Israelites who came in with David. There was, indeed, a non-Israelite admixture in all the tribes, since the earlier inhabitants were certainly not wiped out but continued to live beside, and to intermarry with, the incoming Israelites. T. H. Robinson has propounded the view that the tribe of Judah was not originally Israelite at all.[25] However that may be, it can scarcely be doubted that Jerusalem continued to be a city of mixed population. Nor did Ezekiel regard the Temple as a place of pure worship. He describes the ornamentation and practices of the Temple in no favorable terms,[26] and it is clear from the book of Jeremiah that after the failure of the Josianic reform idolatrous practices were once more current in the city.[27]

Therefore, when Ezekiel dreamed of the reconstituted Israel and of the new Temple which should be its central shrine,[28] he did not think of Jerusalem as providing the site but depicted it as lying in the center of the whole land.[29] To some it has seemed likely that he was thinking again of Shechem as the site of this Temple.[30] It is therefore hard to suppose that he regarded the Samaritan community as without the pale, a company of alien

---

[24] II Sam. 5:6 ff.

[25] Cf. *Amicitiae Corolla*, Rendel Harris *Festschrift* (1933), pp. 265 ff., and *History of Israel*, I (1932), pp. 169 f.

[26] Ezek. 8:3 ff.

[27] Jer. 7:1 ff.; 26:1 ff.; 44:1 ff.

[28] The present writer has elsewhere reviewed the great variety of recent views on the Book of Ezekiel (BJRL, XXXVI [1953-54], pp. 146 ff.) and offered his reasons for holding the book to represent substantially the work of a sixth-century prophet. For our present purpose it is immaterial whether chs. 40-48 are actually the work of Ezekiel, or of a sixth-century disciple, as some have held.

[29] Cf. Gaster, *op. cit.*, p. 15: "Any one who studies his description of the Temple to be and the place in which it is to be erected in the future, will find that he rejects Jerusalem and selects a central spot in Palestine, which could be nothing else but Sichem or Mount Garizim."

[30] Cf. Cameron Mackay, ET, LV (1943-44), pp. 292 ff.; J. Smith, *The Book of the Prophet Ezekiel* (1931), pp. 66 ff.

idolaters who had no part or lot in the people of God. It has even been suggested that he may himself have been of northern origin.[31]

It is true that Ezekiel stipulates that the Jerusalem priesthood should serve the shrine. The law of Deuteronomy had placed all the tribe of Levi on a common footing and had stipulated that any Levite could go from any part of the land to officiate at the one legitimate sanctuary.[32] By this it is usually held, rightly in the present writer's view, that the compilers of Deuteronomy sought to provide for the displaced priests of the country shrines that would be closed by centralization. But this was the one provision of Deuteronomy that was flatly rejected by the Jerusalem priesthood,[33] and one that, in any case, was not very practicable. The Zadokite priesthood of the Temple was not disposed to share its privileges with others, and retained the exclusive priestly rights in Jerusalem. Ezekiel sought to offer a way through this difficulty and to effect a compromise between the Deuteronomic program and the situation which had been created by Josiah's reform, while that reform had lasted. He proposed a difference of status between the Zadokites of Jerusalem and the Levites from the country shrines,[34] and tried to rationalize this by the theory that the Jerusalem priests had maintained a pure worship, while the country priests had not[35]—a theory that sounds a little hollow when we remember the denunciation, found in the book of Ezekiel, of what had gone on in Jerusalem.[36]

Once more history determined otherwise than the planner had designed. Second Isaiah promised the exiles deliverance at the hands of Cyrus and the opportunity to return to their own land in a way no less wonderful than the deliverance from Egypt,[37] and dreamed of the rebuilding of the Temple, to be

---

[31] Cf. Gaster, *loc. cit.* Smith, *op. cit.*, also held that Ezekiel was a northerner, but he assigned him to the age of Manasseh.

[32] Dt. 18:1 ff.

[33] II Kg. 23:9.

[34] Ezek. 44:11 ff.

[35] Ezek. 44:10, 15.

[36] Ezek. 8:3 ff.

[37] Isa. 40:3 ff.; 43:14 ff.; 44:28.

the center of a community that should include more than Israel.[38] Some of the exiles returned at the beginning of the reign of Cyrus,[39] and it seems likely that a halfhearted beginning was made with the rebuilding of the Temple.[40] But the work was soon stopped as enthusiasm evaporated in the face of the pressing problems that faced the returned exiles. So far from being opposed to this rebuilding, the northern community desired to share in the work, but was rebuffed,[41] and in reporting this approach and rebuff the compiler of the book of Ezra levels the charge of alien origin against the northerners, but in a different form from that found in II Kg. 17. Here it is said that they had been brought into the land by Esarhaddon,[42] and there is no mention of any immigration of foreigners in the previous century. Naturally the rejection of northern co-operation tended to embitter relations between the two communities. We are told that the northerners hampered their southern neighbors, and the blame for the cessation of the work is thrown upon them.[43] For whatever reason, the plan of Ezekiel was forgotten, and Second Isaiah's vision of a restored Temple faded away.

Then, on the death of Cambyses, a new hope filled the community. The Persian empire looked as if it were disintegrating and the dawn of a new day of freedom seemed to have come. The governor of Jerusalem was Zerubbabel, of the line of David, and it must have seemed natural that he should be the leader of a restored Israel. Haggai and Zechariah stirred the people to religious revival and to the rebuilding of the house of God. From every point of view it was only to be expected that it should be the Jerusalem shrine that was to be rebuilt. Zerubbabel soon disappeared from the scene, perhaps because of the re-establishment of Persian power under Darius, but the work of rebuilding the Temple went on. It was questioned, but not by the Samaritans. It was the Persian authorities west of the

[38] Isa. 44:28; 45:22 f.
[39] Ezra 1.
[40] Ezra 3:10.
[41] Ezra 4:1 ff. There is no mention of Samaria here, but the approach is attributed to the people of the land who were the adversaries of Judah and Benjamin.
[42] Ezra 4:2.
[43] Ezra 4:4.

Euphrates who asked for directions from the court as to whether the work should be stopped, but when they found that Cyrus had indeed given permission for the rebuilding it was not interfered with.[44] There is no evidence of that religious hostility between Jews and Samaritans which is reflected in the Deuteronomic historical work—a hostility arising from the substitution of Jerusalem for Shechem in the interpretation of the Book of Deuteronomy. Everything suggests that that hostility had died down.

When hostility was born again, its cause was political rather than religious. In the reign of Artaxerxes I there was an abortive attempt to rebuild the walls of Jerusalem.[45] It was checked by the Persian authorities on an appeal from its agents in the west,[46] and this is now stated to have been inspired by the Samaritans.[47] Here we find in yet another form the legend that the northern community was of mixed racial origin. For now we read that they had been brought into the land by Osnappar, or Ashurbanipal, the successor of Esarhaddon, and their places of origin are different from those given in II Kg. 17.[48] To what extent the people of Samaria really had anything to do with this intervention is hard to determine. In any case it was in no sense the religiously inspired intervention of the Samaritan people. It was essentially the intervention of the Persian authorities in Samaria, who were jealous of the rise of Jerusalem to become once more a city that would rival in importance the city of Samaria.

Later in the same reign Nehemiah obtained the royal permission to rebuild the walls of Jerusalem. He laid his plans with skill and secrecy, so that they should not leak out to the Samaritan authorities, and then executed his plans with such swiftness that there should be no time for a fresh appeal to the court before the work was finished. That there would be Samaritan hostility he was well aware, and it soon showed itself in efforts

[44] Ezra 5 f.
[45] Ezra 4:7-23.
[46] Ezra 4:7-10.
[47] Ezra 4:10.
[48] Ezra 4:9.

to slow down the work so as to allow time for other measures to
be devised, and in plots against the life of Nehemiah that could
find some justification at court if they should be successful. But
all this was political and not religious, and it had nothing whatever to do with the legend of II Kg. 17. Sanballat, the arch-
enemy of Nehemiah and the governor of Samaria, was no ido-
later, but a worshiper of Yahweh who gave his sons names compounded with Yahweh, as we know from the Elephantine
papyri.[49] His daughter married the son of the Jerusalem high
priest,[50] and this provides the clearest indication that there was
no religious hostility between Sanballat and the Jerusalem
priesthood. Still less is there any evidence of hostility between
the people of Samaria and the people of Jerusalem. When
Nehemiah returned from a visit to the court and found the
daughter of his worst enemy married to the son of the Jerusalem high priest, he chased him from the city.[51] He could not
brook the idea that Sanballat, through his daughter, should
exercise an influence in Jerusalem that worked against him.
Similarly, when he found his other enemy, Tobiah, whose name
is once more compounded with Yahweh, allied with the priests
of Jerusalem and assigned a room in the Temple itself, Nehemiah did not rejoice in this evidence of religious sympathy with
the worship of the Temple but threw Tobiah out, lock, stock,
and barrel.[52]

That this political hostility between Nehemiah and Sanballat
tended to poison relations between the two communities is on
every ground probable. Samaritans were not welcome in Jerusalem because they might be the agents of Sanballat. Moreover,
the expulsion of the son of the Jerusalem high priest gave a
religious turn to a political quarrel. When the Samaritans established their temple on Mt. Gerizim we have no means of knowing,[53] and it is profitless to speculate in the absence of reliable
evidence. But if Samaritans, who worshiped the same God as

[49] Cf. ANET (1955) , p. 492 (line 29) , or Thomas, *op. cit.*, p. 264. Their names
were Delaiah and Shelemiah.
[50] Neh. 13:28.
[51] *Ibid.*
[52] Neh. 13:4-9.
[53] Cf. BJRL, XXXVIII (1955-56), p. 190.

the Jews and who cherished the same holy Law, were not welcome in Jerusalem, and if a priest who had associations with the Samaritans was liable to be driven out of the city, it was inevitable that the Samaritan community should increasingly develop its own religious life independently of Jerusalem.

It must not be forgotten, however, that the Elephantine community maintained relations with both the Samaritan and the Jerusalem authorities at the end of the fifth century B.C.[54] The worship of the Elephantine temple was certainly not pure by the standards of the Old Testament, but this reflects no more on the Samaritan worship than on that of Jerusalem. The Jews of Elephantine do not seem to have been aware of any absolute breach between the two communities, or they would hardly have mentioned to the one their approach to the other.[55] Neither do they seem to have supposed that the Jerusalem authorities, any more than the Samaritan authorities, would frown on a temple in Egypt. In fact their appeal seems to have been successful in securing the backing of the Persian authorities in both Jerusalem and Samaria to rebuild their destroyed temple, though we have no means of knowing whether the priests in either city gave it their support.[56]

It is curious that the Samaritans are nowhere mentioned in the Bible in connexion with Ezra, and yet in Samaritan tradition Ezra is associated with the schism more bitterly than is Nehemiah.[57] What seems certain is that, while Nehemiah's hostility to the Samaritans and other non-Jews was political, Ezra was primarily concerned with the religious purity of the Jews. He was charged with putting into effect the book of the Law which he brought with him; and if this was either the Priestly Code or the completed Pentateuch, then it involved a further compromise on the priesthood, a compromise carrying the position beyond that envisaged by Ezekiel to one which was never again changed in theory, though in practice it broke down

[54] Cf. ANET, loc. cit., lines 19, 29, or Winton Thomas, op. cit., p. 263 f.

[55] The approach to the Samaritan authorities is stated in the letter to Jerusalem in the lines indicated in the preceding note.

[56] Cf. ANET (1955), p. 492b, or Winton Thomas, op. cit., p. 266.

[57] Cf. Gaster, op. cit., pp. 28 f.

in the second century B.C. This compromise assigned the priesthood not alone to the Zadokites but also to all who could claim
to belong to the wider category of the Aaronites. The division
between the Jews and the Samaritans, which had developed in
the reign of Artaxerxes I and had taken on a religious flavor
because of the growing segregation of the two communities,
appears to have sharpened and to have become linked more
definitely with religion, though it was in no sense fundamentally
religious in its origin. The two communities continued to drift
ever more and more apart.

By the time of the Chronicler relations must have been very
strained between Jerusalem and Samaria. For in his work the
northern kingdom is ignored from its inception, save where the
story of the kingdom of Judah required it to be mentioned.
Hence the Chronicler does not mention the story of the mixed
population brought into the northern kingdom at the time of
the fall of Samaria, because it lay outside his purview. In the
Book of Ezra he presents the two different forms of the legend
to which reference has been made above and betrays an anti-
Samaritan bias which cannot be mistaken.

We should not overlook two stories which are preserved only
in the work of the Chronicler. In the first he tells us that at the
time of the reform of Hezekiah messengers were sent throughout
the northern tribes to invite the people to come to Jerusalem to
share in the keeping of the Passover.[58] Here it is implied that
Hezekiah did not regard the people of the north as alien idolaters, as might have been expected if they had been brought
into the land from abroad during the time of his reign in
Judah, but as sharers of the same faith as their southern
neighbors. They are addressed as Israelite tribes, and not as
Cuthites and strangers. True, the Chronicler records that the
message was received with scorn by some to whom it went,[59]
but it was members of the Israelite tribes who are said to have
expressed that scorn. Moreover, some are said to have accepted
the invitation.[60]

[58] II Chr. 30:1.
[59] II Chr. 30:10.
[60] II Chr. 30:11.

The second story is of Josiah's reform, in which the Chronicler tells us that for the repair of the Temple the king gathered contributions from Ephraim and Manasseh and of all the remnant of Israel, no less than from Judah and Benjamin.[61] Clearly, therefore, he recognizes that Josiah knew nothing of the idea that the northern people had been brought into the land by Esarhaddon and Ashurbanipal during the time when Manasseh had been on the throne, as might have been expected if there were any truth in the legend to which, as has been said above, the Chronicler gives currency elsewhere.

Nevertheless, even after the Chronicler's time there must have long continued to be some association between the two communities. Montgomery says that "the close relationship in theology and practice of the Samaritans with the later Sadducees, who were of the party of the hierarchy, can best be explained by the supposition of the maintenance of intercourse between the priests of Jerusalem and of Shechem."[62] That the tension between the two communities continued despite any such links is clear from the New Testament, where we learn that the Jews had no dealings with the Samaritans.[63] Yet it is equally clear that the division between the two communities was not that between Jews and pagans. In so far as it was a religious division it primarily concerned the question as to whether Jerusalem or Gerizim was the proper place to worship God. Both communities worshiped the same God and both cherished the same Law.

There is no space here to go into the questions which have been raised by the Dead Sea Scrolls and by the Zadokite Work which seems to have had its origin in the same Qumrân community; yet they must be referred to briefly. There is much to suggest that the Qumrân sect was greatly influenced by the Book of Ezekiel. The 390 years that figure in the opening section of

---

[61] II Chr. 34:9.

[62] Cf. *The Samaritans* (1907), p. 72. Cf. also M. Burrows: "The Jewish Christian 'Pseudo-Clementine' literature connects the Sadducees with a Samaritan named Dositheus, said to have been a disciple of John the Baptist and the predecessor of Simon Magus" (*More Light on the Dead Sea Scrolls* [1958], p. 262). On this see R. North, CBQ, XVII (1955), pp. 184 ff.

[63] Jn. 4:9.

the Zadokite Work[64] have long been recognized[65] to be schematic and to be derived from the Book of Ezekiel,[66] and a number of phrases that figure in the sectarian works seem to have been taken from the same book.[67] The Book of Ezekiel insists on the sole legitimacy of the Zadokite priesthood, and the Qumrân sectaries called their priestly members the "sons of Zadok" and similarly seem to have recognized no other priesthood as legitimate. It has been said above that the Book of Ezekiel betrays no anti-Samaritan bias, and it is possible that the Qumrân sectaries were without such a bias. The Samaritans boasted a priesthood that was traced from Zadok,[68] whereas from the days of Antiochus Epiphanes the Jerusalem sanctuary could no longer claim a priesthood which traced its line back to him. On calendar questions the Samaritan community was not at one with the Jerusalem authorities,[69] and it is possible that their calendar was similar to that favored by the Qumrân sect.[70] There is not sufficient evidence to suggest that the sectaries of Qumrân were directly connected with the Samaritans,[71] and certainly none to indicate that they had any interest in the Temple on Mt. Gerizim, which was destroyed in 128 B.C., that is, either shortly before the founding of the Qumrân center or

[64] Zad. Work I:5 f.; cf. C. Rabin, *The Zadokite Documents* (2nd ed., 1958), pp. 2 f.

[65] Cf. R. H. Charles, *Apocrypha and Pseudepigrapha*, II (1913), p. 800; R. Leszynsky, *Revue des études juives*, LXII (1911), p. 193. So also M. Burrows, *The Dead Sea Scrolls* (1955), pp. 195 f.; Rabin, *loc. cit.*

[66] Ezek. 4:5. E. König holds that the 390 years and the 40 years of Ezek. 4:5 f. were also schematic and were intended to add up to the 430 years of Ex. 12:40 (in Hastings' DB, Extra Vol. (1904), p. 70b.)

[67] E.g., "those who built the wall and daubed it with plaster," Zad. Work, VIII: 12; XIX:24 f. (cf. Rabin, *op. cit.*, pp. 35, 80), is probably drawn from Ezek. 13:10 f., 14 f.; 22:28, as already noted by Leszynsky (*op. cit.*, pp. 191 f.).

[68] Cf. J. Bowman, *Transactions of the Glasgow University Oriental Society*, XVI (1957), p. 6.

[69] Cf. J. Bowman, PEQ, XCI (1959), pp. 23 ff.

[70] Cf. *ibid.*; Burrows, *The Dead Sea Scrolls*, p. 287.

[71] Cf. J. Bowman, VT, VII (1957), pp. 184 ff.; Burrows, *More Light on the Dead Sea Scrolls*, pp. 261 f. K. Kohler thought the Messiah of the Zadokite Work was the High Priest in the Samaritan line of the house of Zadok (AJT, XV [1911], p. 407), while P. Kahle has suggested that the non-Masoretic endings of certain forms in the Scrolls were to be interpreted in the light of Samaritan pronunciation (*Die hebräische Handschriften aus der Höhle* [1951], pp. 41 f.).

very soon thereafter. Nevertheless, all the links between the very strict and conservative sectaries of Qumrân and the Samaritan community in practice and idea are of some importance as evidence against the legend that the Samaritans were of mixed racial origin and faith, and that they were unworthy to have any association with the Jews because of their idolatries.

It is time the Samaritan legend disappeared from any factual account of the origin of the Samaritan schism. There is more reason to question the racial purity of the people of Jerusalem than those of Samaria. The legend comes before us in three different forms, all of which appear to be post-Exilic. There is no evidence that it was known in the pre-Exilic period to which it refers, and in particular it does not seem to have been known to the compilers of Deuteronomy, to Hezekiah, or to Josiah or their advisers. It was apparently unknown to Ezekiel. Moreover, there is nothing in the character of Samaritan religion to give the slightest countenance to it.

Additional note. To share in honoring Professor Muilenburg is itself an honor, as well as a very real privilege. His great reputation as one of the most inspiring teachers of our time in the field of Old Testament studies is easily understood by all who know him, for his charm of personality matches his profound learning. In the ten years since I first met him, my regard for him has continually grown, and I count him one of my warmest friends.

XV

Prophecy and the Prophets at Qumrân

MILLAR BURROWS

The Qumrân Commentary on Habakkuk tells of a "teacher of righteousness, to whom God made known all the mysteries of the words of his servants the prophets," including even matters which the prophets themselves had not understood (col. vii, lines 1-5). The most ardent disciple of James Muilenburg would hardly claim that he understands *all* the mysteries of the words of the prophets, to say nothing of knowing more than they did of the things whereof they spoke; but all who know him and his work will agree that he is both a righteous teacher and a teacher of righteousness, and that he has a rare gift of exposition, especially with reference to the prophetic literature. It seems appropriate, therefore, to dedicate to him these brief remarks on the use of the books of the prophets in the Qumrân community. My pleasure in so doing is enhanced by our long and close friendship, going back to the days when we were both students together under Charles C. Torrey.

The community of Qumrân was established and flourished at a time when prophecy was regarded as belonging to the past and the future. After the death of Judas Maccabeus the distress in Israel was "such as had not been since the time that prophets ceased to appear among them" (I Macc. 9:27). But a revival of prophecy was expected. When Judas recovered and cleansed the Temple, the stones of the polluted altar were stored "in a convenient place on the Temple hill until there should come a prophet to tell what to do with them" (4:46). So too when

Simon made himself master of the country, "the Jews and their priests decided that Simon should be their leader and high priest for ever, until a trustworthy prophet should arise" (14:41). The Qumrân community itself was to be governed according to its prescribed rules "until the coming of a prophet and the Messiahs of Aaron and Israel" (1 QS ix:10 f.).

Josephus, it is true, did not feel that prophecy was dead; but what he meant by prophecy was merely the gift of predicting the future. John Hyrcanus, he says, was a prophet as well as ruler and high priest (*Ant.* XIII.x.7). Indeed, Josephus claims that he himself is able to foretell coming events, having not only dreams and the ability to interpret them but even occasionally inspiration in a state of ecstasy (*Wars* III.viii:3, 9). Divine guidance in dreams and visions is, of course, recognized by the New Testament also (Mt. 1:20; 2:12 f., 19, 22; 27:19; Acts 9:10; 10:3, 17, 19; 11:5; 12:9; 16:9 f.; 18:9; 26:19), but it is not confused with the gift of prophecy.

Josephus tells several stories about men who foretold the future, and the leading part in them is played by Essenes (*Ant.* XIII.xi.2; VX.x.5; XVII.xiii.3; *Wars* II.vii.3). But, whether or not the Essenes of Josephus were the same as the men of Qumrân, we hear nothing of prophets at Qumrân in the Dead Sea Scrolls. The War Scroll speaks of the "ordering of the battles" as made known by "thy anointed ones, seers of testimonies" (1 QM x.7 f.), recalling the parallelism of "my anointed ones" and "my prophets" in Ps. 105:15; but the reference is at best obscure, and the fact that the Biblical prophets are called "the holy anointed ones" in the Damascus Document (vi.1) favors the supposition that the War Scroll too refers to them. It has been suggested that the community's founder or leader, the teacher of righteousness, believed himself to be the anointed prophet who speaks in Isa. 61; but the only basis for this inference is the fact that the language of that chapter is echoed in one of the thanksgiving psalms (1 QH xviii. 14 ff.).

Nowhere is the contrast between the Qumrân group and the early Christian Church more striking than at this point. The first Christians, instead of living the rigidly regimented life of a monastic community, and preparing the way of the Lord in the wilderness by the study of the law (1 QS viii.14), rejoiced already in the outpouring of the Spirit promised by Joel (Acts 2:16 ff.). Several prophets in the Church are referred to by name in the book of Acts: Agabus (11:28; 21:10), Judas and Silas (15:32), not to mention the daughters of Philip (21:9). Paul commended prophecy as a more desirable spiritual gift than speaking with tongues (I Cor. 14:5).

Both the Christians and the Qumrân covenanters, like other Jews of their time, interpreted the reference to a prophet like Moses in Dt. 18:15 ff. as an eschatological promise. The widespread Jewish expectation that Elijah would return in the last days (Mal. 4:5) was presumably shared by the Qumrân sect, as it certainly was by the early Church (Mk. 9:13; Mt. 11:14; 17:10-13), though there seems to be nothing in the texts published thus far to document this assumption. The Christians apparently distinguished Elijah, whom they identified with John the Baptist, from the prophet of Deuteronomy, whom they identified with Jesus (Jn. 1:21, 25; Acts 3:23 f.; 7:37). The Qumrân "Testimonia" quote Dt. 18:18 f. along with 5:28 f.; 33:8-11, and Num. 24:15-17; but there is no indication that this promise was regarded as already fulfilled by their teacher of righteousness. Possibly the expected "interpreter of the law," who is associated with the "branch of David" in the "Florilegium," had some connection with the prophet like Moses; and if the teacher of righteousness was to have any eschatological role at all it may have been that of the Deuteronomic prophet; but as yet these are merely matters of conjecture. What is clear is that there were no prophets in the community which produced the Dead Sea Scrolls.

The spirit of Old Testament prophecy, in fact, is not much in evidence in the Qumrân literature. The men of Qumrân were as convinced as the prophets had been that theirs was an evil generation which was under judgment; but they did not boldly mingle with their compatriots, denouncing rulers and people to their faces, as the prophets had done. John the Baptist was more truly a successor of the prophets than was the Qumrân teacher of righteousness or any of his disciples. A precedent for the attitude of the sect may perhaps be seen in Isaiah's decision to bind up the testimony, seal the Torah among his disciples, and wait for the Lord who was hiding his face from the house of Jacob (Isa. 8:16 f.). It would be interesting to know what a Qumrân commentator would say about this passage, but the fragments of commentaries on Isaiah that have been published do not cover these verses. At any rate, the age of prophecy had gone by. The spirit of the times, both within and without the community of Qumrân, was that of apocalyptic waiting and legalistic observance of the commandments in preparation for the coming struggle and deliverance. The whole situation— political, social, and spiritual—had changed from one of national pride and prosperity, economic and political corruption, and spiritual complacency to one of national humiliation, foreign domination, disillusionment and fear. It was the kind of situation that always favors a resort to apocalyptic dreams. Under such conditions, a new outpouring from on high was needed to replace an earnest but artificial and misguided use of the prophets with the living spirit of prophecy. For that matter, in the Christian Church also, even after Pentecost, there was more prediction than truly prophetic proclamation of the will of God.

Instead of prophecy, the Qumrân covenanters relied on an inspired interpretation of what was written in the Scriptures. The teacher of righteousness himself, as noted above, was endowed with wisdom to understand the words of the prophets (1 Q pHab vii.1-5; cp. ii.8 f.). The closest parallel to this in the New Testament is the statement that the risen Christ "opened" the Scriptures to his disciples on the road to Emmaus (Lk. 24:32). But in addition to the teacher's interpretation, the "masters" of the order were committed to a continuous and intensive study of Torah (1 QS vi.6-8); and the object of this study was "to do according to all that has been revealed from time to time, and as the prophets revealed by his Holy Spirit" (viii.15 f.; cp. ix:3). The opinions rendered by the members of the group in their formal meetings (vi.8-10, 21-3; vii.21) were no doubt concerned largely with matters of specific application and "investigation together concerning cases" (vi.24); but they may have involved also questions of exegesis, because the decisions were supposed to be in accord with the Torah, if not derived from it. That the study of the Scriptures included the prophets as well as the law is attested by the community's numerous manuscripts of the prophetic books, the frequent quotations and allusions in its own literature, and above all the extraordinary commentaries on the books of the prophets.

The method and content of the sect's interpretation of the prophets can be seen most clearly in these commentaries. Not all of them are concerned with the books of the prophets, but most of them are, and the few that deal with other books (Genesis and Psalms) treat them as books of prophecy. Commentaries on Isaiah, Hosea, Micah, Nahum, Habakkuk, and Zephaniah are represented among the manuscript fragments and scrolls. Most of them, unfortunately, are so fragmentary that very little in the way of specific interpretation can safely be inferred from them.

The expository method of the Qumrân commentaries is unique in ancient Jewish literature. In the rabbinic writings and the New Testament isolated sentences and phrases of Scripture, gathered here and there and taken out of context to support statements that have been made, are often cited with an introductory formula, "as it is written" or the like. Such formulas are sometimes used in the Dead Sea Scrolls also with incidental quotations (e.g., 1 QS viii.14 and the citation of Am. 9:11 in the "Florilegium"). The commentaries, however, follow an entirely different procedure which is all their own. Even in the rabbinic Midrashim, which follow the order of the text in their exposition, so many different interpretations are mentioned, so many authorities are adduced, and so many other Biblical passages are cited along the way, that the text which is supposedly being expounded seems hardly more than a string on which all the elements of the far-ranging discussion are loosely strung. In sharp contrast to this procedure, the Qumrân commentaries are terse to the point of obscurity; they are dogmatic and quite oblivious to the possibility of any different interpretation, or indeed to the plain, obvious meaning of the text. After quoting a sentence or part of a sentence, the interpreter states briefly, with complete assurance, what he takes it to mean. Whether the men who wrote these commentaries (if there were several different commentators) all felt that wisdom to explain all the words of the prophets had been given to them, we cannot say; in any case, the serene confidence with which they wrote seems to imply this.

The content of their interpretation is almost as distinctive as its manner of presentation, though not quite so entirely without parallels or precedents. The application of prophetic statements to events and characters of world history in or near the lifetime of the commentator and his readers—the Kittim, the lion of wrath, and even Demetrius and Antiochus by name—is not essentially different in its hermeneutical presuppositions from the interpretation of Jer. 25:11 f. and 29:10 given in Dan. 9. In both Daniel and the Qumrân literature, of course, world history is of interest only as the framework for God's dealing with his elect.

The internal history of the Jewish nation in general or the community of Qumrân in particular is most frequently supposed to be the subject of which the prophets spoke. Here the similarity to the use of prophecy in the New Testament is most impressive. As the evangelists assume that the prophets were constantly talking about Jesus, even to the extreme of supposing, for example, that the son called out of Egypt (Hos. 11:1) was the infant Jesus (Mt. 2:11), so no conceivable connection between the prophetic word and the community's teacher of righteousness seemed too far fetched to be seized upon by the Qumrân commentators. Like the early Christians, they felt that what had happened to them was so obviously the climax of the whole divine plan that it must be what the prophets had had in mind. The most tenuous verbal association seemed, therefore, a sufficient basis for confident exegesis. Not only the teacher himself but his followers and his adversaries also were seen mirrored in many words of the prophets. The followers are referred to by such names as the "elect," the "poor," or the "doers of the law." The "wicked priest," the "prophet of the lie," and the "lion of wrath" are perhaps the most conspicuous of the sect's enemies. There are also, of course, similarly designated figures of the future, including the "branch of David" and the "interpreter of the law," as well as the coming prophet mentioned with the "Messiahs of Aaron and Israel" in the Manual of Discipline.

As a consequence of this approach to the Scriptures, the exegesis of the Qumrân covenanters, if it can really be called exegesis, was atomistic. There was no effort to discover a connected development of thought, or indeed to find any necessary connection at all between one sentence and another. One can almost see the commentator scrutinizing the sacred text and asking himself as he came to each phrase or clause, "What does this refer to?" As he pondered each expression in turn, it would recall some item in the community's history or its hopes, and he would write down without further reflection, *pišrô 'al,* or *pišrô 'ašer* with the explanation that had come to him. The result would be, and was, that there was no chronological order in the historical allusions or logical order in the eschatological references. Each item was put down as it was suggested by the text. Past, present, and future were mingled together in such random fashion that only those acquainted with the whole history and the whole eschatological program of the group could fit the details into their places in the picture.

It must be admitted that some excuse for this procedure was given by the lack of order and sequence in the prophetic writings themselves. The compilers and editors of the oracles of the prophets did not try to arrange them in chronological order and could not have done so if it had ever occurred to them to make the attempt. A modern commentator, with his knowledge of the historical background, finds in the Book of Isaiah, for instance, passages apparently referring to the invasion of Judah by Sennacherib in 701 B.C., followed by predictions of a future time of peace, an account of the prophet's inaugural vision in about 740 B.C. several chapters later, and then prophecies connected with the Syro-Ephraimitic conspiracy of 735. Scattered in between are passages of quite uncertain date and authenticity. It is not surprising that the men of Qumrân, like the first Christians, were able to make sense of the prophets only by taking each sentence by itself.

The commingling of past and future, the fulfilled and the unfulfilled, is also no doubt largely the result of the strong feeling that the end of the age was at hand. The Qumrân community, again like the early Church, was convinced that it was within sight of the great continental divide of history. For the Qumrân commentators, however, the realization of the divine plan had not proceeded as far as it had for the writers of the New Testament. Much of what the prophets had foretold was still reserved for the future, but that future was not far distant, even though "the last period" had been extended "over and above all that the prophets said" (1 Q pHab vii.6-14). The Christians too, of course, still waited for the fulfillment of much that had been promised, but the great climactic events which marked the turn of the ages had already taken place. Both the forerunner and the Messiah himself had appeared, and the decisive work of salvation had been accomplished. What the Church still awaited was not "the coming of a prophet and the Messiahs of Aaron and Israel" (1 QS ix.10 f.) but the triumphant return of the Savior who had lived, died, and risen from the dead, and was now seated at the right hand of God, pouring forth the gift of the Spirit (Acts 2:33). Consequently for the Qumrân sect there was relatively more unfulfilled promise in the prophets than there was for the Christian Church. All the more remarkable is it that they found so much of what had already happened to have been foretold by the prophets.

It would be interesting to know, if there were any way to find out, how far the community's pictures of past and future were derived in the first place from the study of the Scriptures and how far they were taken from other sources or created independently within the sect. Some items can be traced to their origins, and further research may disclose the sources of others. The "branch of David," in whom the commentaries on Gen. 49 and Isa. 10 f., together with the "Florilegium," are particularly interested, is obviously from the Old Testament, as is the prophetic forerunner or companion of the Messiah. The priestly Messiah is not so directly derived from Scripture, but there are precedents and parallels in other Jewish sources. The "interpreter of the law" is more obscure, and his relation to the prophet, the Messiah of Aaron, and the teacher of righteousness is far from clear. The publication of additional texts may shed more light on these problems.

The same question arises in connection with the events of the eschatological program. No systematic, consecutive statement of such a program can be expected in the commentaries or in other texts from Qumrân, and it is unlikely that there was much more unanimity on this subject within the community than there was in Judaism at large. That any member of the group ever worked out a list of coming events in the order of their expected occurrence is improbable. Nothing like Paul's concise statements in II Th. 2:1-8 and I Cor. 15:22-8 is to be found in the Qumrân texts, perhaps because they were not written for Greeks. The nearest thing we have to an explicit program of eschatological events is the War Scroll. Possibly the descriptions of the New Jerusalem and other texts preserved only in fragments or not yet published had more material of this nature.

In any case, it is quite evident that many but not all of the elements in the community's hope came from the Old Testament. The conception of the new covenant, one of the outstanding points of both resemblance and difference between the New Testament and the Dead Sea Scrolls, was of course taken from Jer. 31:31 ff. The general idea of the elect remnant was inherited from the prophetic literature. The designation of the Romans as Kittim was no doubt suggested by the use of that name in the Old Testament, and the whole conception of the eschatological war was a common Jewish inheritance from the prophets, especially Ezekiel, combined of course with Ps. 2 and other passages. All these and other ideas from the prophetic books and other parts of the Old Testament were stirred up together with conceptions from Iranian and perhaps still other sources and were seasoned no doubt with original notions contributed by members of the community itself. The resulting mixture then provided an apperceptive mass for interpreting the prophets verse by verse.

Whatever we may think of the way in which the books of the prophets were used, we can at least be grateful for the fact that the intense interest of the community in the prophets led them to the production and preservation of many copies of the prophetic writings. The text was sometimes handled in a decidedly cavalier fashion in the commentaries, words being freely altered to support the meaning divined or desired by the interpreter.

The commentaries are therefore less reliable as aids for textual criticism than are the manuscripts of the prophetic books, though these too may not be entirely innocent of tendentious readings. Commentaries and copies alike, however, evince a very lively interest in the study of the prophets. Highly as the law was exalted at Qumrân, it does not appear that the prophetic canon was in any way subordinated to the Pentateuch. It was all alike God's Torah, "as he commanded through Moses and through all his servants the prophets" (1 QS i.3; cp. viii. 15 f.).

A Bibliography of James Muilenburg's Writings

R. LANSING HICKS

BOOKS AND MONOGRAPHS

"The Embassy of Everaard van Weede, Lord of Dykvelt, to England in 1687," Lincoln, Nebraska, 1920 (Published as Vol. XX, Nos. 3, 4, of Nebraska *University Studies*.)
Specimens of Biblical Literature. New York: Thomas Y. Crowell, 1923.
The Literary Relations of the Epistle of Barnabas and the Teaching of the Twelve Apostles. Marburg, 1929. (Ph.D. thesis, Yale University, 1926.)
The Way of Israel. New York: Harper, 1961.

CONTRIBUTIONS TO BOOKS

"The Return to Old Testament Theology," in *Christianity and the Contemporary Scene.* Edited by R. C. Miller and H. H. Shires. New York: Morehouse-Gorham, 1943, pp. 30-44.
"The Faith of Ancient Israel," in *The Vitality of the Christian Tradition.* Edited by G. F. Thomas. New York: Harper, 1945, pp. 1-35.
"Survey of the Literature on Tell en-Naṣbeh," "The Literary Sources Bearing on the Question of Identification," and "The History of Mizpah of Benjamin," in *Tell en-Naṣbeh,* Vol. I. Edited by C. C. McCown. The Palestine Institute of the Pacific School of Religion, Berkeley, California, and the American Schools of Oriental Research, New Haven, Connecticut, 1947, pp. 13-49.

"The Interpretation of the Bible," in *Biblical Authority for Today*. Edited by A. Richardson and W. Schweitzer. Philadelphia: Westminster, 1951, pp. 198-218.

"Ethics of the Prophet," in *Moral Principles of Action: Man's Ethical Imperative*. Edited by Ruth Anshen. New York: Harper, 1952, pp. 527-542.

"The History of the Religion of Israel," in *The Interpreter's Bible*, Vol. I. Edited by G. A. Buttrick. Nashville: Abingdon-Cokesbury, 1952, pp. 292-348.

"The Poetry of the Old Testament," in *An Introduction to the Revised Standard Version of the Old Testament*. Edited by L. A. Weigle. New York: Thomas Nelson, 1952, pp. 62-70.

"Introduction and Exegesis to Isaiah, Chapters 40-66," in *The Interpreter's Bible*, Vol. V. Edited by G. A. Buttrick. Nashville: Abingdon-Cokesbury, 1956, pp. 381-773.

"The King Came Riding," in *Sermons from an Ecumenical Pulpit*. Edited by M. F. Daskam. Boston: Starr King, 1956, pp. 119-128.

"Adam and Second Adam," in *A Handbook of Christian Theology*. Edited by M. Halverson and A. A. Cohen. New York: Meridian, 1958, pp. 11-13.

Also announced for publication: article on "Isaiah" (book and prophet) in the new edition of the *Encyclopedia Americana*; articles on "Isaiah," "Jeremiah," "Poetry," and other subjects in the revised edition of *Hastings' Dictionary of the Bible* (one-vol. edition); articles on "Ataroth," "Gilgal," "Holiness," "Jeremiah," "Mizpah," "Obadiah," and numerous other subjects in the forthcoming *Interpreter's Dictionary of the Bible*; and articles on "Hebrew Prophecy" and "Ezekiel" in the new edition of *Peake's Commentary on the Bible*.

ARTICLES IN PERIODICALS

1924 "Teaching the Bible from the Literary Angle," in *Christian Education*, December.

1929 "Luther and Zwingli Quartercentenary," in *The Congregationalist*, December 26, pp. 854-856.

1931 "The German High Church Movement and Its Outstanding Leader—Friedrich Heiler," in *Crozer Quarterly*, VIII, pp. 162-176.

1932   "Literary Form in the Fourth Gospel," JBL, LI, pp. 40-53.

1933   "The Literary Approach—The Old Testament as Hebrew Literature," in JNABI, I, Part II, pp. 14-22.

1934   "Finding the Real Gospels" (a review article on C. C. Torrey's *The Four Gospels*), in *The Congregationalist*, February 22, pp. 130-131.
"The Legacy of Israel and Our Heritage in a Time of Crisis" (presidential address), in JNABI, II, pp. 1-12.
"The Old Testament in the Church School," in *The Christian Register*, September 6, pp. 525-527.

1940   "The Literary Character of Isaiah 34," in JBL, LIX, pp. 339-365.
"What Is Essential in the Christian Religion?" in RL, IX, pp. 352-362.

1942   "Imago Dei," in RR, VI, pp. 392-406.

1944   "Psalm 47," in JBL, LXIII, pp. 235-256.

1945   "The Old Testament and the Christian Minister," in USQR, I, No. 1, pp. 10-18.

1946   "An Evaluation of the Methods and Assumptions of the Historical Study of the Bible," in mimeographed material circulated in November, 1946, by the Study Department of the World Council of Churches.

1952   "The Importance of Archaeology for the Minister," in USQR, VII, No. 3, pp. 15-19.
"The Literary Values of the Revised Standard Version," in *Religious Education*, XLVII, pp. 260-264.

1953   "A Study in Hebrew Rhetoric," in *Suppl.* VT, I (Congress Volume: Copenhagen), pp. 97-111.

1954   "Fragments of Another Qumran Isaiah Scroll," in BASOR, 135, pp. 28-32.
"A Hyksos Scarab Jar Handle from Bethel," in BASOR, 136, pp. 20-21.
"A Qoheleth Scroll from Qumran," in BASOR, 135, pp. 20-28.

1955   "The Beginning of the Gospels and the Qumran Manual of Discipline," in USQR, X, No. 2, pp. 23-29.
"Mizpah of Benjamin," in ST, VIII, pp. 25-42.
"The Site of Ancient Gilgal," in BASOR, 140, pp. 11-27.

1956   "The Birth of Benjamin," in JBL, LXXV, pp. 194-201.
"The Dead Sea Scrolls—A Symposium," in *The New Republic*, April 6, pp. 24-25.

"The Significance of the Scrolls," in USQR, XI, No. 3, pp. 3-12.

"The Theology of the Dead Sea Scrolls," in *Andover-Newton Theological School Bulletin*, XLIX, No. 1, pp. 3-14.

1957 "Is There a Biblical Theology?" in USQR, XII, No. 4, pp. 29-37.

1958 "Preface to Hermeneutics," in JBL, LXXVII, pp. 18-26.

1959 "The Form and Structure of the Covenantal Formulations," in VT, IX, pp. 347-365.

1960 "The Biblical Understanding of What God Requires," in *The Alumni Bulletin* of Bangor Theological Seminary, XXXV, No. 2, pp. 6-11.

"Father and Son," in *Theology and Life* (Lancaster Theological Seminary), III, pp. 177-187.

"Modern Issues in Biblical Studies: The Gains of Form Criticism in Old Testament Studies," in ET, LXXI, pp. 229-233.

"Old Testament Scholarship: Fifty Years in Retrospect," in JBR, XVIII, pp. 173-181.

"The Story of Israel: A Review Article," in *The Alumni Bulletin* of Bangor Theological Seminary, XXXV, No. 3, pp. 14-15.

1961 "The Linguistic and Rhetorical Usages of the Particle *ki* in the Old Testament," in HUCA, XXXII, pp. 135-160.

"The Biblical View of Time," in HTR, XIV, No. 4, pp. 225-252.

BOOK REVIEWS

1935 W. O. E. Oesterley and T. H. Robinson, *Introduction to the Books of the Old Testament* (JNABI, III, p. 54).

1938 J. Baillie and H. Martin, editors, *Revelation* (JBR, VI, pp. 214-216).

G. A. Cooke, *The Book of Ezekiel*, 2 vols. (CC, February 2, p. 145).

M. Crook and others, *The Bible and Its Literary Associations* (JBR, VI, pp. 98-99).

A. Lods, *The Prophets and the Rise of Judaism* (JBR, VI, pp. 50-51).

W. O. E. Oesterley, *A Fresh Approach to the Psalms* (RR, II, p. 486).

1939 M. Buttenwieser, *The Psalms* (RR, IV, pp. 55-60).

E. G. Kraeling, *The Book of the Ways of God* (JBR, VII, pp. 92-93; RR, IV, pp. 342, 347).

W. O. E. Oesterley, *Sacrifices in Ancient Israel* (RR, III, pp. 184-189).

1940 W. A. Wordsworth, *En-Roeh* (JBR, VIII, pp. 116-117).

1941 W. F. Albright, *From the Stone Age to Christianity* (JBR, IX, pp. 41-43).

J. J. Stamm, *Erlösen und Vergeben im Alten Testament* (JBL, LX, pp. 430-433).

1942 B. Heller, *The Odyssey of a Faith* (CC, November 4, pp. 1353-1354).

D. Jacobsen, *The Social Background of the Old Testament* (CC, December 2, p. 1492).

J. Morgenstern, *Amos Studies* (JBL, LXI, pp. 294-299).

R. H. Pfeiffer, *Introduction to the Old Testament* (JBR, X, pp. 39-41).

1943 G. E. Phillips, *The Old Testament in the World Church* (RL, XII, pp. 314-315).

H. W. Robinson, *Redemption and Revelation* (JBR, XI, pp. 176-178).

1944 W. A. Irwin, *The Problem of Ezekiel* (JBR, XII, pp. 203-205).

W. J. Pythian-Adams, *The People and the Presence* (JBR, XII, pp. 254-255).

1945 S. A. Cartledge, *A Conservative Introduction to the Old Testament* (JBL, LXIV, p. 273).

J. D. Davis, *The Westminster Dictionary of the Bible,* revised by H. S. Gehman (RL, XIV, pp. 607-608).

R. B. Y. Scott, *The Relevance of the Prophets* (JBR, XIII, pp. 51-52).

R. E. Wolfe, *Meet Amos and Hosea* (CC, May 2, pp. 552-553).

1946 J. Finegan, *Light from the Ancient Past* (USQR, I, No. 4, pp. 33-34).

H. Fredriksson, *Jahwe als Krieger* (RR, XI, pp. 50-56).

N. Glueck, *The River Jordan* (RL, XVI, pp. 154-155).

1947 G. A. Danell, *Studies in the Name Israel in the Old Testament* (JBL, LXVI, pp. 234-237).
H. H. Rowley, *The Rediscovery of the Old Testament* (JBL, LXVI, pp. 225-226).

1948 M. Burrows, *An Outline of Biblical Theology* (*Theology Today*, IV, pp. 421-422).
J. Coppens, *La Connaissance du Bien et du Mal et le Péché du Paradis* (JBL, LXVII, pp. 396-399).

1949 E. A. Leslie, *The Psalms* (RL, XIX, pp. 143-145).

1950 W. A. L. Elmslie, *How Came Our Faith?* (JBR, XVIII, p. 69).
A. R. Johnson, *The Vitality of the Individual in the Thought of Ancient Israel* (JBL, LXIX, pp. 404-405).
G. Knight, *From Jesus to Paul* (*Theology Today*, VI, pp. 565-567).
R. H. Pfeiffer, *A History of New Testament Times, with an Introduction to the Apocrypha* (*Interpretation*, IV, pp. 93-95).

1951 A. Haldar, *The Notion of the Desert in Sumero-Accadian and West-Semitic Religions* (JBL, LXX, pp. 340-341).
T. J. Meek, *Hebrew Origins*, rev. ed. (USQR, VI, No. 2, p. 47).
H. H. Rowley, editor, *Studies in Old Testament Prophecy* (USQR, VI, No. 2, p. 46).

1952 W. Eichrodt, *Man in the Old Testament* (USQR, VII, No. 3, p. 56).
J. Lindblom, *The Servant-Songs in Deutero-Isaiah* (JBL, LXXI, pp. 259-261).
J. B. Pritchard, editor, *Ancient Near Eastern Texts relating to the Old Testament* (USQR, VIII, No. 2, pp. 55-56).
J. C. C. Van Dorssen, *De Derivata van de Stam '-m-n in het Hebreewsch van het Oude Testament* (JBL, LXXI, pp. 127-129).

1953 *The Revised Standard Version of the Old Testament* (USQR, VIII, No. 2, pp. 40-43).

1955 J. Klausner, *The Messianic Idea in Israel* (USQR, XI, No. 1, pp. 63-65).
J. B. Pritchard, *The Ancient Near East in Pictures Relating to the Old Testament* (USQR, X, No. 3, pp. 58-59).

1956 M. Burrows, *The Dead Sea Scrolls* (JBL, LXXV, pp. 146-148).
R. C. Dentan, editor, *The Idea of History in the Ancient Near East* (USQR, XI, No. 3, pp. 53-54).
B. D. Napier, *From Faith to Faith* (CC, January 4, p. 15).
M. Noth, *Geschichte Israels*, 2nd ed. (*Bibliotheca Orientalis*, XIII, pp. 43-44).
E. Würthwein, *Der Text des Alten Testaments* (*Bibliotheca Orientalis*, XIII, p. 48).

1957 K. Barth, *Church Dogmatics*, Vol. I, *The Doctrine of the Word of God* (USQR, XII, No. 3, pp. 83-86).
J. Bright, *Early Israel in Recent History Writing* (*Interpretation*, XI, pp. 461-462).
G. Davies, A. Richardson, and C. Wallis, editors, *The Twentieth Century Bible Commentary* (JBR, XXV, pp. 60-61).
S. Mowinckel, *He That Cometh* (CC, August 7, 942-943; JBL, LXXVI, pp. 243-246).
G. Östborn, *Yahweh and Baal* (RR, XXI, pp. 177-180).
H. Ringgren, *The Messiah in the Old Testament* (CC, August 14, p. 967).
B. J. Van der Merwe, *Pentateuchtradisies in die Prediking van Deuterojesaja* (JBL, LXXVI, pp. 77-78).
G. E. Wright, *Biblical Archaeology* (USQR, XIII, No. 1, pp. 53-55).

1958 S. H. Blank, *Prophetic Faith in Isaiah* (JBR, XXVI, p. 329).
M. Burrows, *More Light on the Dead Sea Scrolls* (*Saturday Review*, June 7, pp. 21-33).
O. Eissfeldt, *Einleitung in das Alte Testament*, 2nd. ed. (JBL, LXXVII, pp. 258-259).
T. H. Gaster, *The Dead Sea Scriptures in English Translation* (RR, XXII, pp. 73-76).
L. Köhler, *Der Hebräische Mensch* (*Bibliotheca Orientalis*, XV, p. 121).
V. de Leeuw, *De Ebed Jahweh-Profetieen* (JBL, LXXVII, pp. 261-263).
A. Van Selms, *De Rol der Lofprijzingen. Een der Dode Zee-Rollen vertaald en toegelicht* (JBL, LXXVII, pp. 266-268).
D. Howlett, *The Essenes and Christianity;* R. E. Murphy,

The Dead Sea Scrolls and the Bible; K. Stendahl, editor, *The Scrolls and the New Testament* (USQR, XIII, No. 3, pp. 57-59).

1959 M. Burrows, *More Light on the Dead Sea Scrolls* (JBL, LXXVIII, pp. 362-365).

P. J. Cools and others, *De Wereld van de Bijbel* (JSS, IV, pp. 272-274).

F. M. Cross, *The Ancient Library of Qumran and Modern Biblical Studies* (USQR, XIV, No. 3, pp. 54-56).

H. Gese, *Der Verfassungsentwurf des Ezechiel, Kap. 40-8* (JSS, IV, pp. 74-76).

S. H. Hooke, editor, *Myth, Ritual, and Kingship* (USQR, XIV, No. 2, pp. 67-69).

L. Köhler, *Old Testament Theology* (USQR, XIV, No. 2, pp. 66-67).

S. Mowinckel, *He That Cometh* (USQR, XIV, No. 4, pp. 70-71).

M. Noth, *Gesammelte Studien zum Alten Testament* (*Bibliotheca Orientalis*, XVI, p. 242).

J. Van Der Ploeg, *The Excavations at Qumran* (USQR, XIV, No. 3, pp. 53-54).

1960 J. M. Allegro, *The Treasure of the Copper Scroll* (*Saturday Review*, August 6, p. 20).

J. Bright, *A History of Israel* (USQR, XV, No. 4, pp. 327-329).

B. S. Childs, *Myth and Reality in the Old Testament* (JBL, LXXIX, pp. 379-380).

J. Doresse, *The Secret Books of the Egyptian Gnostics* (*Saturday Review*, August 6, p. 20).

C. Rabin and Y. Yadin, *Aspects of the Dead Sea Scrolls* (JSS, V, pp. 92-98).

SERMONS, MEDITATIONS, BIBLIOGRAPHIES, AND REPORTS

1946 "A Survey of Recent Theological Literature: The Old Testament," in USQR, II, No. 1, pp. 23-25.

1949 "A Confession of Jeremiah," in USQR, IV, No. 2, pp. 15-18.

"Report on the Activities of the American Schools of Oriental Research," in JBL, LXVIII, pp. xxxiii-xxxv.

1950   "A Bibliography for Ministers—II" (annotated), in USQR, V, No. 3, pp. 21-27.
        "A Meditation on Divine Fatherhood," in USQR, VI, No. 1, pp. 3-5.
        "Report on the Activities of the American Schools of Oriental Research," in JBL, LXIX, pp. xxxix-xli.
1951   "Report on the Activities of the American Schools of Oriental Research," in JBL, LXX, pp. xxix-xxxi.
1954   "A Letter from Palestine," in USQR, IX, No. 2, pp. 22-25.
        "Report of the Director of the School in Jerusalem," in BASOR, 136, pp. 4-7.
1959   "A Bibliography for Ministers: Old Testament" (with G. Landes, annotated), in USQR, XIV, No. 2, pp. 41-51.
        "Faith Comes by Preaching," in USQR, XV, No. 1, pp. 13-18.
1960   "Psalm 96: A Chapel Meditation," in *The Union Voice* (Union Theological Seminary in Manila), XVI, No. 2, pp. 4-5.

THE REVISED STANDARD VERSION
OF THE OLD TESTAMENT

Dr. Muilenburg became a member of the Standard Bible Committee in May, 1945, and rendered active and significant service through twenty extended sessions of the Committee until the completion of the Old Testament revision in June, 1951. To him was assigned the work of making the first drafts of Isaiah, chs. 1-30, and of Obadiah, as well as a special commission to review the first draft of Isaiah, chs. 40-53. Also he did editorial work, with Dean Luther Weigle and Executive Secretary Fleming James, on the final drafts of Deuteronomy and the Psalms.

Because of his keen perception of literary style and his careful analyses of the forms of Biblical literature, Dr. Muilenburg brought to the Committee expert knowledge of the strophic structure of Old Testament poetry. He undertook special studies in this field for the Committee, and most of his recommendations were adopted.

The chairman of the Committee, Dean Weigle, has characterized Dr. Muilenburg as "a man whose judgment and competence commanded the respect of all his colleagues" and as "a good team worker—a man who can engage in debate with his fellows in a genuine spirit of cooperation in the desire to find the truth and the best way of expressing it."